Readings in Family Therapy Supervision:
Selected Articles from the AAMFT Supervision Bulletin

American Association for Marriage and Family Therapy
Washington, DC

Published by
American Association for Marriage and Family Therapy
1133 15th Street, NW, Suite 300
Washington, DC 20005-2710
(202) 452-0109
www.aamft.org

Table of Contents

Chapter Four: Supervision Structure, Assessment, and Technique 75

Chapter Five: Supervision Modalities— Live, Videotape, Etc. 103

Chapter Six: Problems and Special Issues in Supervision 127

Chapter Seven: Ethical and Legal Issues 155

Chapter Eight: Contextual Variables 179

Chapter Nine: Supervision-of-Supervision 223

Introduction

Staff at the AAMFT office regularly receive telephone and e-mail requests for copies of articles from old *Supervision Bulletins*. "Why not re-publish them all as a set?" several members asked. With that possibility in mind we looked at all the old issues, 12 years worth. We noted that a few articles were about administrative or internal matters and were out of date. Other articles were about clinical supervision and were still quite useful. So, we went through and selected the latter articles for this book of readings.

We have done a minimal amount of editing of the original articles, and only in cases where it was necessary to clarify, avoid confusion or establish a context for the information being presented. Due to the minimal edits, you will run across a few references that are dated. (For example, the Commission on Supervision was renamed the Supervision Committee, and later became the Standards Committee.) We have included the dates the articles were originally published to help you place each article in context. We omitted authors' contact information and affiliations, as many of them have changed since the original publication date. We suggest that you use the AAMFT networking directory (on-line at www.aamft.org) if you need to locate one of the authors.

We considered publishing the articles chronologically as they first appeared, but decided it would be more helpful to group them into chapters. Roughly, they are grouped according to elements of the supervision learning objectives as defined by the AAMFT. You will observe that some articles address more than one objective, and we acknowledge that arguments could be made for a different placement. In any case, we hope that this collection of articles will prove useful to you as you continue to study marriage and family therapy supervision.

Acknowledgments

The AAMFT *Supervision Bulletin* was created in June 1988 by the (then) AAMFT Commission on Supervision to share ideas, information, and questions about supervision issues and concerns. Commissioner Milo Benningfield was the founding editor. Commissioner Anthony Heath took over editorial duties late that year, and continued in the position for two years. In the early years the *Supervision Bulletin* content was primarily about standards and internal announcements. In 1991, an AAMFT Bylaws change meant that the Commission on Supervision was re-named the Supervision Committee. That same year, Committee member Cheryl Storm became the *Supervision Bulletin* editor.

The early and mid 1990's saw a shift in the *Supervision Bulletin* content, to less administrative announcements and more clinically and theory focused articles. Lynelle Yingling took over the reigns of the *Supervision Bulletin* in 1995, and continued that shift. By the time Dorothy Becvar began a two-year stint as editor in 1996, the Supervision Committee had become the Standards Committee. Commitment to the *Supervision Bulletin* as a professional development vehicle remained strong.

In 2000, AAMFT staff assumed responsibility for editing the *Supervision Bulletin*. It continues to be a unique publication, the only periodical devoted exclusively to marriage and family therapy supervision. While remaining true to its original purpose, it has grown into a primary and widely referenced resource for AAMFT Approved Supervisors and supervisors-in-training.

We thank all the AAMFT members and Approved Supervisors who have served on the Standards Committee and its earlier iterations, the Commission on Supervision and the Supervision Committee. They were called upon, and many answered the call, to write for the *Supervision Bulletin*. We owe a special debt of gratitude to those who volunteered their time as editors of the *Supervision Bulletin*. Milo, Tony, Cheryl, Lynelle and Dorothy, your commitment to the community of supervisors will never be forgotten. Finally, thank you to the authors of the articles we have included here. We are pleased and honored to present your work in this new format.

Karen Gautney, M.S.
AAMFT Deputy Executive Director

Chapter 1

Models and Philosophies of Supervision

Solution-Focused Ideas Guide Supervision: An Interview with Eve Lipchik

Interview conducted by Cheryl Storm, AAMFT Supervision Bulletin editor, with Eve Lipchik, M.S.W.

Published in the AAMFT Supervision Bulletin, Vol. VIII, No. 1, Spring 1995.

Storm: *How do solution-focused ideas guide your supervision?*

Lipchik: For the most part, I make the same assumptions about supervision as I do about clients regarding inherent resources, past positive experiences, and uniqueness. In discussing cases with them I will ask very similar questions as I do of clients: What do you think is working for you in this case? What has worked in the past for you when you felt confused? Whose goal is more important at this time, yours or the client's? I also try to understand supervisees' learning styles so I can use them to facilitate our collaboration. An idea that has become very important for me in solution-focused work in the past few years is the emotional climate or context in which therapeutic conversations take place. I believe that clients have to feel respected and comfortable in order to benefit from the collaborative experience and it is the role of the therapist to establish and maintain that climate. Techniques by themselves are not enough. The same goes for the supervisory experience. Supervisees have to feel safe in their relationship with supervisors in order to profit from it. I try to be respectful and understanding at all times of their points of view and their actions. For example, in a situation where a supervisee is giving too many suggestions to a client or may be trying to influence the client in some way, I might talk about "working too hard" rather than being critical. This allows for a much less threatening conversation about options. I also do a lot of experiential exercises with supervisees to help them develop the respectful, curious stance and to maintain the boundaries between themselves and clients that are necessary to do that. At the same time, I cannot assume the nonexpert position on supervisees' views as much as I can with clients because I feel a supervisor has to be guided by some theoretical principles and practice techniques. How these are utilized by supervisees in their collaboration with clients requires some judgment which immediately places the supervisor in the position of expert.

Storm: *Several authors have written about using solution-focused ideas in supervision. They differ regarding how they address "supervisee growth areas." How do your deal with supervisee growth areas you notice?*

Lipchik: There is a difference between personal growth through therapy and growth through supervision. The former is based on the make-up, experience, and needs of a unique individual; the latter goes beyond that to include a specific body of knowledge and how to apply this for the benefit of others. So I think of it as both: first, bringing out the supervisee's strengths and using them, and, second, reinforcing and teaching certain concepts. More specifically, the way I think of the process is to have supervisees identify learning goals and steps toward achieving them. Part of the process is their ability to evaluate how they are moving toward those goals and what they need to keep doing. As their supervisor, I also feel it is my responsibility to point out areas of growth they may not be aware of. They don't have to respond to it, but if I don't offer my perspective, I am limiting opportunities.

I find the most effective form of supervision to be videotape. The rule for watching videos together is that the supervisee, group of supervisees, or I will ask to stop the tape at places where we see something that we think is either very good, or something that we want to question and talk more about. When I stop the tape at areas that I want to highlight I might ask: What were you thinking at this point? What do you think is going on between you and the client here? What do you think the client might be thinking at this time? How many different ideas can you come up with? How does what is going on here fit with the client's goals? How do you think your question (or statement) is helping the client find his or her own answers?

Storm: *One of the logical extensions of solution-focused ideas for supervision is to have supervisees bring a case that they feel is going well rather than a stuck case. Do you practice this?*

Lipchik: No. My experience has been that supervisees want to discuss what is not working, rather than what is working. It is my practice to underscore positives whenever I can anyway, so they already know what I think they are doing right. I have ongoing conversations with supervisees about how their needs are being met, and the most common request I get is to point out more things that they should work on.

Storm: *Some supervisors have noticed that by emphasizing supervisee successes in therapy, supervisees may assume a "Pollyanna" quality in their supervisors. Have you noticed that?*

Lipchik: Yes, sometimes the process of focusing on positives too much can give that impression. After all, when you commit to a program of supervision you expect that there are things you don't know yet and you want the supervisor to help you change them. If the supervisor keeps focusing only on success, supervisees may actually end up feeling shortchanged. It is very important to tell people what they are doing right, but you should also guide them toward areas of continuing growth.

Storm: *Can they get an inflated sense of their competence if positives are overemphasized?*

Lipchik: Yes, that's possible. And that would be a terrible shame. If supervisees get the impression that there is a point where one can know everything there is to know they will be deprived of future growth. Supervision should be a model for self-evaluation for that purpose. But, again, we really shouldn't generalize. Each supervisee is unique, just as each client is.

What is important is that supervisors think about how each of their supervisees learn best. Some people are motivated by praise and others need a little anxiety.

Storm: *Can focusing on "successes" limit the development of supervisees by not pushing them to develop new areas?*

Lipchik: Yes, it can, if carried to an extreme. Some people think of solution-focused therapy in extremes like that...you are only supposed to talk solution talk and no problem talk. Well, that's a theoretical guideline, but if one were to get too rigid about applying this idea it might be more harmful than helpful. That's how I think about it in supervision, too.

Storm: *When supervision is often regarded as an intensive process over time, how does the idea of being brief fit with supervision?*

Lipchik: You know, I have actually had many people who call to inquire about training in brief therapy for their staff or providers, express surprise that it is not brief. I have a hard time convincing them that it takes just as long as any other respectable therapeutic modality. I explain that brief therapy is about a type of conversation between people that opens up new options for them based on who they already are and what they already know. The fact that it is usually brief is a side effect, not the main purpose. Supervision or training of therapists in general has to be an intensive process that takes a longer period of time because it is a process of skill finding and skill building. A person might find a solution to a personal problem in one hour or less, and be the judge of whether that suffices or not. In professional education, people who are designated "experts" because of their standing in the profession make decisions about how long a course of study should be and how satisfactory achievement is to be judged. These standards are based on what has worked in the past for the profession in general, not on individual talents or needs. So being brief in therapy has nothing to do with the supervisory process of people who want to work briefly.

Experiencing Metaframeworks: Learning to be Systemic

Ralph S. Cohen, Ph.D. and Betty MacKune-Karrer, M.A.

Published in the AAMFT Supervision Bulletin, Vol. 9, No. 2, Fall 1996.

Models of Therapy and Supervision

The field of family therapy has evolved to encompass many systemically-based models, each with its own vocabulary, emphases, and techniques. There are several models of teaching and supervising "systemically," ranging from teaching a particular model (e.g., Structural or Bowenian) to presenting a potpourri of various "schools" of family therapy. With the former approach, students are exposed to a narrow view of working systemically. With the latter approach, students often must struggle to see the interrelationships among the models. As students are supervised by trainers who come from various schools of therapy, they often find themselves trying to stay afloat in a conceptual "soup," resulting in confusion and a lack of direction in working with families.

As the field has matured, there has been a greater calling to integrate models of family therapy into a comprehensive approach. Earlier attempts at integration have sought to combine different models (e.g., Colapinto, 1984; Slipp, 1984; Stanton, 1981). A major problem with these "integrative" approaches is that they often represent a combining of models to extend the breadth of often disparate approaches and fail in developing a truly comprehensive and holistic approach. Latter attempts have developed meta-models which transcend idiosyncratic approaches to therapy (e.g., Breunlin, Schwartz & MacKune-Karrer, 1992; Pinsof, 1995).

The *Metaframeworks* model of family therapy (Breunlin, Schwartz, & MacKune-Karrer, 1992) emphasizes the integration of the multilevel contexts of human systems into a comprehensive model for assessing and treating individuals, couples, and families as well as for training and supervising therapists. This meta-model consists of four building blocks: systems theory, presuppositions regarding the nature of human systems, six conceptual domains which are interwoven by a common vocabulary, and a "blueprint" for conducting therapy based on the assumptions of the model.

Presuppositions of the *Metaframeworks* model include the notion of the recursive relationships within and among individuals, families, communities, and societies; a constructivistic stance of "perspectivism" (i.e., that a person's view of reality is interlocked with one's perspective, which sets the initial conditions for any observation); a view of the mind based on the concept of "multiplicity" (i.e., that our internal worlds are based on a "self," which serves as an internal leader and mediator for various "parts" which are complete and distinct psychological entities interacting with one another in a systemic fashion); Bateson's notion of "negative explanation" and theory of constraints (i.e., that people behave in the way they do because they are prevented or constrained from doing or thinking something else); and a shift from viewing human interaction in terms of hierarchy, power, and control to an emphasis on leadership, balance, and harmony.

The six conceptual domains include: the mind (i.e., "internal family system"), development, organization, sequences, gender, and culture. Assessment and treatment principles form the blueprint for therapy, which includes observing and developing hypotheses among the six domains, developing interventions to remove constraints embedded within the various domains by restoring balance and harmony to polarized aspects of the system through reestablishment of internal and external leadership, and responding to feedback from the client system in response to the therapist's interventions. Interventions may be borrowed from various established schools of family therapy as they relate to addressing identified constraints in the system to be released. A fundamental assumption of the model is that by identifying and removing constraints, individuals and families can draw on their own internal resources and leadership to complete their functional and developmental tasks.

The Metaframeworks model provides a set of parameters by which students can understand how each school of family therapy reflects the systems paradigm and by which students can compare and contrast the various treatment models. Schools of family therapy can be compared conceptually by their relative emphasis on one or more *Metaframeworks* domains. This means of comparison provides a context by which trainees may understand and organize a vast array of information and may make interventions in an accountable manner.

The *Metaframeworks* Approach to Training and Supervision

The training and supervision model was developed by the faculty of an MFT postdegree program at the Institute for Juvenile Research in Chicago and has been adopted by a master's program in MFT at Central Connecticut State University and several other programs throughout the country. The faculty from the two programs listed above are collaborating on developing experiential training methods to teach marriage and family therapy trainees to organize, quickly and effectively, the vast array of data presented by families in therapy and to develop a comprehensive treatment "blueprint" based on the *Metaframeworks* model. Teaching and supervisory methods consist of didactic and experiential training integrated with clinical practice, and eventually will include computer simulations and case analyses of their own work using an interactive CD-ROM program which is currently being developed.

The training paradigm exposes students initially to both the *Metaframeworks* model as well as the other major schools of family therapy through didactic and experiential teaching methods. Trainees also learn to identify systemic aspects of their own internal and interpersonal dynamics through various exercises based on the Metaframeworks concepts. The *Metaframeworks* model is reinforced in all coursework in both programs and students learn to "translate" the language of other models into the language of the meta-model.

In the supervisory context, a developmental approach is taken to move trainees through the processes of discovery, skill development, proficiency, and amplification. As new trainees begin to work with clinical cases, they are expected to identify the domains in operation as a major component of their assessment and to begin to develop and test hypotheses about the constraints in the system that maintain symptoms and prevent the accomplishment of developmental tasks. Supervisors model the presuppositions by assisting trainees to identify and work with their own constraints among the six domains in the clinical context, and assume that supervisees will be able to access internal and external resources as constraints are lifted. Supervisors work with trainees to identify data to test hypotheses and assist them in developing interview skills which will elicit feedback regarding their hypotheses. Advanced students in the postdegree program participate in a live supervision team approach that reinforces this process. Supervisory functions at this stage are to observe the therapist in action and to explore the trainee's choices of interventions. The supervisor also provides input and feedback regarding the trainee's therapeutic technique and style. Students are expected to be able to articulate their choices of interventions based on their hypotheses and clinical feedback. As the trainee becomes more advanced and develops more technical competence, a shift is made to focusing on the trainee's personal constraints in working with a client base representing diverse sociocultural backgrounds and a broad range of clinical symptoms.

Trainees have demonstrated a very quick grasp of this model and have demonstrated an ability to apply the model in clinical situations early in their clinical work. The developmental approach taken in supervision is isomorphic to the process of discovery, skill development, proficiency, and amplification that are the hopeful outcomes of both therapy and training. Students report a high satisfaction with the model, and they ease into the clinical setting with a high degree of confidence in their understanding of what to observe and do in family therapy.

Future Directions in Training and Evaluation

Currently, work is being done to develop self-directed learning paradigms for the model through the use of interactive CD-ROM computer technology. Beginning students will be able to work through an analysis of simulated therapy sessions and track their responses to the session based on the *Metaframeworks* model. Advanced students in supervision will be able to transfer their videotaped sessions onto a recordable CD-ROM disk to be able to perform detailed metaframework analyses of their own work, which can then be used in a focused manner in supervision.

This technology also will allow for outcome data to be generated and collected on various indices of learning in the perceptual, conceptual, and executive skill areas (Tomm & Wright, 1979). The ability to track students' response styles at different stages of training will provide much insight into the developmental processes of students in learning to "be" systemic.

Editor's Note: The CD-ROM mentioned in this article is now available. To order, contract Ralph Cohen at cohenr@ccsu.edu or (860) 832-2122.

References

Breunlin, D.C., Schwartz, R. C., & MacKune-Karrer, B. (1992). *Metaframeworks.* San Francisco: Jossey-Bass.

Colapinto, J. (1984). "On model integration and model integrity." *Journal of Strategic & Systemic Therapies,* vol. 4, p. 38–42.

Pinsof W.M. (1995). *Integrative problem-centered therapy.* New York: Basic Books.

Slipp, S. (1984). *Object relations: A dynamic bridge between individual and family treatment.* New York: Jason Aronson.

Stanton, D. (1981). An integrated structural/strategic approach to family therapy. *Journal of Marital and Family Therapy,* vol. 7, p. 427–439.

"Supervision" as a Collaborative Learning Community

Harlene Anderson, Ph.D.

Published in the AAMFT Supervision Bulletin, Fall 2000.

At the heart of my philosophy and practice of supervision [1] as a collaborative learning community are three Cs—connect, collaborate and construct: Supervisees and supervisors developing relationships that invite jointly creating knowledge (Anderson, 1998; Anderson, 1997; Anderson & Goolishian, 1990; Anderson & Swim, 1997). By knowledge I mean that which is new and unique to each participant. This view is based in the premise that knowledge is not imparted by another or a knower who bestows on a not-knower. Rather, knowledge is fluid and communal, yet personalized. When we share our knowledge with one another, we cannot know what each brings to the sharing; determine how each will interact with the shared knowledge; nor predict what each will create with it. Whatever the outcome, it will be something different than either started with, something socially constructed.

I place my philosophy and practice under a postmodern umbrella (Anderson, 1997). Briefly, by postmodern I refer to an ideological critique of the tradition of meta-narratives that represent universal overarching truths and the inherent risks in this certainty tradition. Postmodernism includes itself in this critique and owns the same risks. A notion of postmodernism is language and knowledge as relational and generative. Central to this notion is dialogue as a dynamic creative conversation with room for all voices, with each person unconditionally present and with a full sense of belonging. Dialogue also entails two-way exchanges and crisscrossing of ideas, thoughts, opinions, and feelings. What is put forth in dialogue is interacted with and interpreted by the other. New meanings, understandings, and knowledge are inherent in dynamic dialogue.

Connecting, Collaborating and Constructing in a Supervisors Seminar

Conceptualizing language and knowledge as generative invite collaborative learning communities that maximize new and individually tailored learning. I will briefly describe and highlight selected aspects of one collaborative learning community- a seminar for supervisors. (See Peters and Armstrong, 1998 for an excellent discussion of collaborative learning communities.)

Participants

Diversity among participants enhances the quality and quantity of learning that is produced. Each person brings differences in terms of age and life stage, personal and professional experience, degree and discipline, theoretical orientation, work and educational setting, learning style and agenda, or any of the diversity "isms." Varieties of voices provide a richness of perspectives and realities. A seminar might include experienced and rookie supervisors supervising in various clinical and educational settings with sundry degrees, each coming for distinct reasons. Often half the participants have completed the "required seminar" and continue in the next seminar because they value the experience.

Relationships and Conversations are Inseparable and Influence Each Other

To invite and maximize collaborative learning I must act and talk consistent with my philosophy. I must live it, being genuinely and naturally collaborative. This includes respecting, inviting and valuing each voice, being flexible and responsive, and creatively doing what the occasion calls for on the spot. Foremost, this includes trusting the other and our process.

I want to create and facilitate learning relationships and processes where participants can identify, access, elaborate, and produce their own unique competencies, cultivating their seeds of newness in their personal and professional lives outside our organized context. I want to talk and act to invite and encourage participants to take responsibility for and to be the architects of their learning. I also want each participant to experience our task and relationship differently from the familiar hierarchical and dualistic teacher-student relationships and learning processes they may have experienced.

Being collaborative does not mean that I deny or ignore my wealth of ideas and experiences, but that I too must be a learner, believing that I can learn as much as the participants. Importantly, collaborative teaching and learning challenge participants and me to reconstruct how we think about teaching and learning.

Nor as critics and skeptics of postmodernism often believe does the perspective discount previous knowledge and experience. Participants find that this is not the case. The difference is the intention with which that knowledge and experience is used.

Towards these ends collaborative learning begins with the first conversation I have with each participant whether in person or by telephone. I show a keen interest in learning about the person and preview my expectations and agenda for the seminar, being forthright about my prejudice for learning and knowledge from a postmodern perspective are also important.

Inviting Collaboration by Doing

Collaborative relationships and processes spontaneously emerge out of the experience itself, learning by doing rather than through lecturing about or instructing participants on how to be collaborative. At the first seminar I say that I have many ideas and experiences to share but that I need their help in selecting what to share. I do not want to unilaterally select. To learn about them and allow them to learn about each other, I invite participants to form small conversational clusters. I might pose beginning questions such as: What are your expectations of supervision and of me? What is your learning agenda? How do you learn? What do you think is important for us (I tend to use collective language) to know about you and your everyday contexts that would help us best meet your learning needs? I do not expect answers; the questions serve as starters. Clusters might respond to all questions, address only one, or talk about something different. I ask each to record the generated material on a large tablet, a small pragmatic action that enhances engagement and conveys my serious interest in their voices.

The clusters reconvene and share the highlights of their conversations. I post their tablet sheets on the wall. We might ask questions to make sure that we understand their thoughts or participants might clarify with each other. Through this process, and at each meeting thereafter, participants add to our agenda and prioritize agenda items and ways to address them.

Selecting and Addressing Content

Collaborative learning occurs within a broad context of expectations, including credentialing and licensing bodies, professional associations, work settings and the discourse of top-down knowledge. I keep in mind that multiple investors hold distinct assumptions about the learning purpose and how learning will be accomplished. I also realize that my role bestows power and authority on me as a teacher and supervisor, placing me in hierarchical position. I hold the personal freedom, however, to choose how to exercise that power and authority. What I am most interested in is how can I position myself within these contexts and assumptions to best offer what I have to offer, and for the learner to summon control over his or her own learning.

I give participants seminar syllabi that include a variety of topics required by external institutions and those deemed important by me. Participants have a voice regarding agenda and forum. One may volunteer, or I might invite someone to share a supervision experience related to a content area and to choose the way to address the experience and content. For instance, she may seek a consultation, or request another participant interview her, followed by a general discussion, a reflecting process in which the participants listen "as if" they were a part of the cast of characters in the supervisory dilemma (Anderson, 1997; Anderson & Rambo, 1987). Participants may bring their supervisees to a session. The supervisor and supervisee direct us in how we might be helpful to them- whether performing their supervision as usual with us as reflectors, or being interviewed by another participant. They might simply want a fresh perspective or they might have a specific question. If there is no preference we might offer suggestions and they tailor a choice to suit their needs.

A primary vehicle for content is dialogue, sometimes occurring in relation to a reading, videotape, experiential exercise, consultation, or shared information by facilitator or participants. Content is seldom entirely covered in a discrete time frame or as a discrete entity. Instead, a variety of content weaves throughout each session and throughout the seminar in various ways. The content agenda is always so full that participants do working lunches, clustering around content topics. As one participant put it, "Agenda building is a great tool... to state what is important, puzzling, exciting... so that everyone's needs are stated, even though there may be too many items to address!"

Reflecting Promotes Self- and Other Dialogue

An important part of learning is reflecting with oneself and others, putting silent thoughts into spoken or written words. I incorporate reflections in a variety of ways. Throughout each session I openly reflect on our process and relate it to my postmodern bias and their learning. I have designed various experiential and consultation exercises with reflecting components.

I give participants a reflection sheet at the end of each session, asking them to share their after thoughts at the next session. Reflections might focus on their experience of the last session, how they used their learning, new thoughts or questions, new agenda items, or recommendations for my role as facilitator. Participants say the reflection sheets are a valuable learning tool. Writing the reflections provides a way to keep the seminar process alive and a forum for self-dialogue. The reflection process furthers several interrelated purposes. It consistently builds in continuous self, other, seminar, and teacher evaluation. It encourages learners to be active and purposeful in their learning and in determining its direction. It encourages reflection as part of everyday practice among supervisor and supervisee, and among therapist and client.

I silently read their reflections at the beginning of each session and incorporate what I learn. Importantly, the reflection process helps me continually learn the participants' changing needs. Their reflections provide an opportunity for me to improve my teaching/facilitating and adjust my style to best serve their individual and combined needs— to accommodate to what each group, occasion, circumstance, and relationship calls for at any one time.

What We Have Learned About Collaborative Learning

Although collaborative learning is often mistaken as unstructured learning, participants find it is simply another kind of structure. Participants overwhelmingly report that the learning process is more important than the content. Participants consistently report amazement at the richness and meaningfulness of the process. They comment on the generativity of the conversations, the emergence of new learning, and the surprising changes in their thoughts and practices. They express gratefulness for the opportunity, although at first unfamiliar and challenging, to be thoughtful active learners. They appreciate and develop the richness of possibilities as they move from a need for certainty and closure to a sense of being comfortable with uncertainty and the yet-to-come. In one participant's words, giving "a new sense of self-confidence." As a learner in group supervision put it, "The atmosphere beckoned to me, 'Take a chance'."

Participants report that the new learning is useful in their everyday work. They learn to appreciate what their supervisees bring to the table—listening and hearing it differently. As one participant said, "respect for the supervisor-supervisee relationship as well as for each of their positions—that no one position is of greater importance than another." One said she valued learning to talk about supervisees and clients with "critical thinking and compassion" rather than with a pejorative and judgmental attitude. Another said, "I am constantly amazed at how my supervisees change, as they are willing to learn more about their clients' lives, their struggles, their histories. Their negativity usually reduces in proportion to their openness. I amaze myself when I am willing to be more open-minded as well." And another reported, "My supervisees have reported that my non-hierarchical and collaborative model of supervision is refreshing compared to previous supervision in which the supervisee felt intimidated and judged." These experiences with supervision as a collaborative learning community reported by supervision seminar participants and their supervisees are consistent with other accounts of supervision from a postmodern perspective (Caldwell, Becvar, Bertolino & Diamond, 1997; Anderson, London & Punsky, 2000).

Also noteworthy is that participants express pride of ownership in the seminar and accountability for their learning. They also describe a new sense of responsibility to each other, congruent with McNamee and Gergen's (1999) notion of relational responsibility. That is, as one positions oneself differently with another—as I position myself differently with learners—we boldly experience that no one holds sole responsibility. When responsibility is shared—as participants connect, collaborate, and construct with each other— the learning relationship and process are more mutually gratifying and rewarding.

---

[1] I prefer to use "consulting with" or "having a conversation about" in my daily practice, rather than the words "supervision" or "therapy".

References

Anderson, H. (1998). Collaborative learning communities. In McNamee, S. & Gergen, K.J. (Eds.), *Relational responsibility: Sources for sustainable dialogue.* (pp. 65–70). Thousand Oaks, CA: Sage.

Anderson, H. (1997). *Conversation, language, and possibilities: A postmodern approach to therapy.* New York: Basic Books.

Anderson, H. & Goolishian, H. (1990). Supervision as collaborative conversation: Questions and reflections. In H. Brandau (Ed.), *Von der Supervision zur Systemischen Vision,* (pp. 69–78). Salzburg: Otto Muler Verlag.

Anderson, H., London, S. & Punsky, N. (2000). Postmodern Supervision in Two Countries. Presentation at the Texas Association for Marriage and Family Therapy annual conference, Jan. 27–30, 2000, Houston, TX.

Anderson, H. & Rambo, A. (1987). An experiment in systemic family therapy training: A trainer and trainee perspective. *Journal of Strategic and Systemic Therapies.* 7, 54–70.

Anderson, H. & Swim, S. (1995). Supervision as collaborative conversation: Connecting the voices of supervisor and supervisee. *Journal of Systemic Therapies.* 14 (2), 1–13.

Caldwell, K., Becvar, D.S., Bertolino, R. & Diamond, D. (1997). A postmodern analysis of a course on clinical supervision. *Contemporary Family Therapy.* 19 (2), 269–287.

Peters, J.M. & Armstrong, J.L. (1998). Collaborative learning: People laboring together to construct knowledge. In *New Directions for Adult and Continuing Education* (pp. 75–85). No 79, Fall 1998. New York: Jossey-Bass.

Postmodern Questions

Postmodernism and Supervision

Kenneth Stewart, Ph.D.

Published in the AAMFT Supervision Bulletin, Vol. VII, No. 3, Fall 1994.

If therapists want supervision, what would they get from a "postmodern" supervisor? Postmodernism—as it applies to the practice of supervision—suggests that no one story, theory, or set of techniques constitutes the way to do therapy. There are no final solutions to the dilemmas faced by therapists or families. The appeal of postmodernism as it applies to our work is its critique of the political, philosophical, and psychological assumptions of therapy. Nothing is taken for granted or accorded an apriori status. Supervisors or therapists cannot simply use such metaphors as "differentiation," "boundaries," or even "system" as easily as they did in modern times. A postmodern critique of these taken-for-granted terms would warn us against thinking that we have captured the essence of any phenomena under observation. Supervision from a postmodern perspective invites the supervisee to pay attention to the ways in which therapeutic realities are created through language that is ever-shifting in meaning. No one story tells the whole story. Instead, there are bits and fragments of local knowledge that are pieced together to pragmatically make do. Philosopher Richard Rorty says that "truth" is the compliment we pay to a few ideas that work. And what works now may not work tomorrow, so we had best be on the lookout for temptations to think we've finally "got it."

Postmodernism is less interested in grand schemes that pull it all together and solve problems once and for all than it is in the effects of various ways of thinking and acting. Ideas about living, about therapy, and about supervision have their real effects. We need to deconstruct these real effects so that various constructions don't weigh us down. We encourage supervisees to use a lot of ideas gained from years of experience by others, but we also encourage them to travel lightly—to not let any one set of ideas or practices define the therapeutic moment.

Is Postmodernism the New Truth?

Ronald Richardson, D.Min.

Published in the AAMFT Supervision Bulletin, Vol. VIII, No. 1, Spring 1995.

My question is, how can anyone working from a postmodernist or constructivist position require anything of anyone? Doesn't this "truth" apply to the construct of postmodernism itself? Or is postmodernism the "truth" that is somehow above all other ways of constructing reality, and thus a "real truth"? And if this is true, doesn't that then deny the truth of postmodernism? I found it particularly striking that Stewart, who eschews little interest "in grand schemes that pull it all together" in fact seems to be offering us such a grand scheme that purports to do this. Postmodernism seems to be the theory that is above all other theories, rather than simply one more interesting way of thinking about reality. Please help me with this. If I were a postmodernist, what would be the basis of making my way of thinking about reality a requirement for others to think in the same way?

Changing the Line: An Interview With Edwin Friedman

Interview conducted by Cheryl Storm, AAMFT Supervision Bulletin editor, with Edwin Friedman, M.A.

Published in the AAMFT Supervision Bulletin, Vol. IV, No. 3, October 1991.

Storm: *You have been heavily influenced by Bowen's ideas. How has his work shaped your supervision?*

Friedman: Any philosophy of supervision is related to the goals of therapy, and the relationship of supervisor and supervisee obviously should be isomorphic to the relationship of therapist and client. Bowen taught us three interrelated goals for therapy: (1) teaching people to conceptualize emotional phenomena in terms of a multigenerational, emotional system rather than categories of psychodynamics or personality, (2) promoting in people more capacity for self-regulation of their reactivity (anxiety) to others, and (3) helping them work on their own differentiation, which includes the first two but is basically the capacity to be separate while remaining connected. That, in turn, has a lot to do with helping people define their personal goals and beliefs as well as working to know where they end and others in their life begin. The Bowen-oriented supervisor tries to keep the therapist focused on these goals of therapy through both teaching and working on maintaining a differentiated relationship with the supervisee. With both therapy and supervision, the major concern is the emotional being of the client, not his or her technique. In fact, the major therapeutic intervention of a Bowen-trained therapist may be asking a question.

Storm: *Then, is the role of supervisor and therapist the same?*

Friedman: Essentially, yes, but not because the supervisor is doing therapy, rather because the therapist is doing supervision. The title of an early Bowen paper was "From Couch to Coach." He was coming in at a tangent to the usual dichotomy between insight therapy, with its emphasis on transference and the behaviorist school, with its concern for phenomenology. Bowen thought the transference issues were critical, but instead of working to interpret them, which made emotion leap towards the therapist, he wanted to keep the emotional processes within the family so that the therapist could be more objective about them. He also believed that to the extent the therapist got homogenized into the family's own emotional process, it would inhibit rather than facilitate change. He thus developed a style of therapy which in effect turned the family member he was coaching into the therapist—that is, the agent of change. Change occurred not because some family members actively tried to change others, but because of the differentiated quality of their presence.

Storm: *How then does the Bowen-oriented supervisor function?*

Friedman: Speaking for myself, I supervise members of the helping professions either individually or in small groups. I mix all the professions together (therapists, physicians, clergy, educators). I tell them they can bring in three kinds of cases: a client family, their work system, or issues from their own family of origin. (The latter, by the way, is mistakenly assumed to be the "all" of Bowen therapy by those who focus on technique.) As I tried to describe in my book, *Generation to Generation,* I believe all members of the helping professions are involved in these three systems simultaneously and that it is the confluence of their emotional processes within that larger emotional system that is the source of our stress. According to Bowen theory, however, all three can be understood within the same perspective, so that increased knowledge of one's functioning in any one usually brings about more differentiated functioning in the other two. Supervisees attend clinical sessions biweekly or monthly and then everyone is brought together for a theory morning, usually every other month. The focus throughout is on teaching a way of thinking and promoting differentiation of self rather than on learning specific techniques for particular symptoms.

Storm: *But isn't that mixing personal therapy with clinical practice?*

Friedman: My urge is to answer that question naively, "What's wrong with that?" I, of course, realize that "mixing systems," as I like to call it, is generally frowned upon by many who consider "dual relationships" unethical or unhealthy. But that very way of thinking comes out of a different model. If the goal is always to promote differentiation (which requires the supervisor and the therapist being supervised to constantly work to maintain his or her own) then the context is irrelevant Every relationship is grist for the mill. I actually see "dual relationships" as challenging opportunities for promoting self-differentiation. I remember an early supervision session in which Murray described how he was working with a neighbor and how that was really putting him to the test of his own theories. Of course, 20 years experience as a clergyman has also influenced me greatly, since ministers, priests, and rabbis are constantly counseling people whom they work with administratively, and who are often in effect their boss. All clergy, no matter what we are doing at any given time, are constantly in the midst of one humongous, complex hunk of dual relationships. It is the context of our being, and that is why differentiation is the path to salvation.

Storm: *Why bother with clinical cases at all? If the goal of supervision is to help supervisees work on their own differentiation, why not just have everyone work on issues in their family of origin?*

Friedman: There's something to that. In some supervision groups there have been individuals who worked almost exclusively on family of origin issues rather than clinical situations. And sometimes I have wondered if such individuals weren't more interested in "therapy" than in professional training, but almost always, despite the fact that their primary focus was on personal issues, their "handling of cases" greatly improved. There seems to be immediate carry over to any person's functioning in any other system when they succeed in being able to deal less anxiously with fundamental issues in their own extended family. Bowen found that to be true years ago with the psychiatric residents, and I have found the same to be true with members of the clergy. I don't want to give the impression, however, that "technique" is totally irrelevant; discussing cases in context affords opportunities for becoming familiar with the specific emotional context of therapy. I am filled with ideas for how to deal with resistance and transference, but I am always primarily concerned with maintaining as differentiated a relationship with my supervisees as I would have them maintain with their clients. It is not a matter of emulation, however, but of creating the kind of climate that promotes a more mature (less anxiously reactive) approach to life. As I tried to describe in my essay on Bowen therapy (Friedman, 1991), it is almost as though the verb *to be* were transitive (could take an object), and one, by one's presence, could be (that is, have an effect upon) someone else. Put another way, from this perspective the effectiveness of most techniques depends primarily on the degree of differentiation in the therapist (or supervisor) employing it, but not on the situation or the therapist's gender or background. It is also the critical factor in being able to distinguish empathy from anxiety.

Storm: *But aren't you concerned about the legal liability of supervision that does not always directly focus on cases?*

Friedman: As I see it, the focus on liability in the helping professions is an indication of how much they are caught up in society's anxiety, the power of victims, and the consequent failure of healers to understand and nourish their own strengths. I believe, for example, that you can gauge the degree of anxiety in any mental health care institution, and the lack of differentiation in its leadership, from the extent to which people focus on issues such as confidentiality and malpractice. When I began, I could not get malpractice insurance immediately. When I mentioned my concern to Bowen he said simply, "Malpractice is most likely to occur when the professional gives too much promise." "Of course," I thought, "malpractice is largely a breach of promise suit. Not everyone sues who finds the pains they are experiencing are due to a forgotten scalpel. Some are happy to find it was only a scalpel; they are just glad to get it out." The larger issue, of course, is what Bowen was trying to teach me of staying focused on my own functioning, rather than being buffeted about by anxious forces, of modifying the surrounding emotional system and the consequent functioning of others with that focus. You can't do it entirely, but the degree to which one is reactive or well-differentiated can make the difference. This is equally true in therapy or supervision. This is also why I urge all those I supervise to watch Peter Falk's detective character, Columbo. You rarely get sued for being too stupid, only for being too smart.

References

Friedman, B. (1991). Bowen theory and therapy. In A. Gurman & D. Kniskern (Eds.), *The handbook of family therapy.* New York: Brunner/Mazel.

Friedman, E. (1985). *Generation to generation.* New York: Guilford Press.

Drawing the Line? An Issue for All Supervisors

Published in the AAMFT Supervision Bulletin, Vol. IV, No. 3, October 1991.

According to the AAMFT definition, supervision is not therapy. Our ethical code requires us to avoid dual relationships. In fact, the code specifically prohibits supervisors from providing therapy to their supervisees. Yet many supervisors believe therapists' own family of origin relationships influence the therapy process. If you were supervising a therapist and it became obvious his own relationship with his father was impeding his provision of therapy, at what point, if any, would you draw the line and refer him to someone else for therapy? If half of your supervision time was focused on his relationship with his father? If four supervision sessions were? If a pattern developed and every case was presented as indicative of his family of origin issues? If no cases were presented? If he presented therapy received prior to his training as a marriage and family therapist as supervision?

The Supervision Committee is wrestling with these questions as we try to determine when supervision crosses over into therapy. Please help us in this struggle by telling us where you draw the line.

- Cheryl Storm, AAMFT Supervision Bulletin editor

Letter to the Editor

Published in the AAMFT Supervision Bulletin, Vol. V, No.2, June 1992.

Dear Editor:

We read with interest your editorial statement in the October issue. The statement invoked AAMFT's definition of supervision as distinct from therapy and yet posed a series of questions illustrating the indistinct boundaries between supervision and therapy. While we applaud the Supervision Committee's (SC) invitation to join them in "wrestling with these questions," we must step out of the ring and implore the field of family therapy to reconsider the bout. In our view, you are wrestling with the wrong questions.

The question, "When does supervision cross over and become therapy?" implies that it is logical and/or heuristic to separate these two processes. Supervision as distinct from therapy implies that skills and techniques can be taught to therapists separate from and independent of the internalized structures relevant to the process of therapy that trainees bring to their training. It cordons off, for special attention, work trainees must complete on their family-of-origin with little connection to particular struggles with particular client issues. It suggests a conceptualization of the process of therapy and the training of therapists, bereft of a theory of human relationships. So long as therapists and supervisors continue to think that it is possible to separate what therapists do from what is inside therapists they are not looking squarely at the *practice* of psychotherapy.

What of those few trainees with extremely dysfunctional structures, uncovered in the process of supervision? Requiring that trainees enter psychotherapy is a closed system move that implies a hierarchical organization with a fixed view of pathology. At Kantor Family Institute (KFI) such decisions are reached consensually by trainees, supervisors and possibly other faculty members. KFI supervisors do take responsibility to (1) identify problematic structures that may emerge in trainees' therapy with clients, (2) work with trainees on these problematic structures within the constraints of a group supervision format and, (3) in extreme cases, suggest trainees do more work on a problematic structure before they go on to the next level of training or graduate. What trainees choose to do with our suggestions is their decision. They may choose individual therapy, additional group supervision, a spiritual retreat, a winter cruise or "40 days in the desert." Our response to the SC's questions about problematic cases is not specifying when supervision should become therapy or when trainees should be referred for therapy. It is in identifying dysfunctional or problematic structures so that trainees are free to make choices to address (or not address) what we have helped them uncover. Our job as supervisors is to help trainees understand and integrate their internal structures such that, as practicing therapists, they are as open and interpersonally flexible as is possible for them.

We suspect that the driving force behind the SC's questions is supervisors' concerns with a very small number of trainees who are not at all suited to practice psychotherapy. Supervisors do encounter trainees with extremely dysfunctional structures and must take responsibility to guide them in the redirection of their career. Such judgments are always difficult interpersonally, politically complicated and extremely painful for everyone involved. But such infrequent, albeit intense experiences should not drive an entire profession's best thinking about the nature of its primary endeavors—supervision and psychotherapy.

Structural-Analytic Theory

Structural-Analytic Theory explains the nature of human relationships with a special emphasis on the complexities of the psychotherapeutic relationship. Human beings, by their very nature, internalize experiences from their world into what we are calling structures. These internalized structures represent all that individuals have construed as relevant or important to them over the course of their life. Similarities can be noted among individuals' internalized structures because most of us spend the vast majority of our early years in a family system of some sort. What is crucial to the understanding of the psychotherapeutic relationship, however, is not that all of us have families of origin. Rather, it is the precise nature of therapists' internalized structures relevant to the therapy process that demands attention in supervision. The term "family of origin" is too broad, too imprecise, merely offering a buckshot approach to the understanding of the therapist portion of the therapy process.

When two individuals form a relationship, in or outside of a psychotherapy office, it can be understood as the interplay of two different sets of internalized structures that act on one another and are affected by the interaction. These "forming structures" constitute the relationship. It makes no sense to try to understand the relationship as something apart from what each individual brings to the encounter or to ignore how each is influenced/affected by the en-

counter. We cannot separate what an individual does from what an individual is.

What distinguishes therapeutic relationships from all others, is not that therapists leave themselves out of the relationships, but is precisely what they bring to the relationships. In our terms, this special set of internalized structures brought to hear in the profession of psychotherapy (as well as elsewhere) is called the Boundary Profile. Knowledge therapists have about their internalized structures, their awareness of their world view, preferences, styles, and critical identity images provides them with the tools necessary in forming therapeutic connections with their clients. Therapists' ability to "use themselves," or in our words, their degree of Boundary Profile awareness, determines the course and the success/failure of psychotherapy.

The Training Model

Where does skill and technique training fit in? The first year of training at KFI is devoted to imitating the techniques of the several models of family therapy: Structural, Strategic, Systemic, Experiential, Intergenerational. Trainees are required to enact a paradoxical intervention, sculpt a dysfunctional family, reorder a cross-generational coalition, construct a genogram. They are asked to "put on hold" any discomfort or confusion they may experience. They are learning the skills and techniques for "doing therapy." According to our theory, the skills and techniques will become embedded into internalized structures trainees bring with them. Trainees learn to express the tenants of each model with varying degrees of clarity, but what they actually do in therapy sessions is informed primarily by their internalized structures and only secondarily by the techniques they were taught. Then there is a consolidation of the various family systems models, and a focus on Boundary Profile issues, including the discomforts experienced earlier. Next, trainees have the opportunity to more fully develop their own model of therapy in the live supervision setting.

Model Building

The technique is not the method; the method is not the practice. What we at KFI have taken on as our mission is to build a theory which explains the *practice* of psychotherapy. Therapists develop a model to inform their work. It is not simply a set of skills and techniques. As we stated above, therapists cannot enact another therapist's model. They can adapt what they have learned from imitation into their own internalized therapy practice structures. They can modify, magnify and even mutate their structures as they develop their own model. They will, hopefully, become extremely well informed about the internalized structures that come into play in their work. They will know "where to look" when they feel "stuck" with a client system. Their model of the practice of therapy will be shaped by their Boundary Profile, their theoretical method and the client systems with which they interact.

Our purpose in this letter is to stimulate new thinking about the processes of supervision and therapy, and thereby continue the dialogue about these crucial issues. As a first step, we suggest that the therapy/supervision dichotomy be abandoned and replaced by theories of therapy and supervision that are richly informed by theories of human relationships.

From the Kantor Family Institute Faculty,
David Kantor, Ph.D.
Emily Mitchell, M. A.
Jane Traupmann Pillemer, Ph.D.
Alan Slobodnik, M.S.W.

Collaboration in Supervision: Flattening the Supervision Relationship

Marshall Fine, Ed.D.

Published in the AAMFT Supervision Bulletin, Vol. VI, No. 2, Summer 1993.

As I became aware of and open to increasing alternatives in my personal and professional lives, I began to appreciate the limitations of the therapy theories I held and imposed on clients and therapists. Through social constructionism I found the words that fit my shifting experiences, ultimately leading me in the direction of an oxymoron—collaborative supervision.

My supervisory practices typically reflect personal and professional premises regarding therapy. A strategic indoctrination had led me to privilege elegance in theory-driven hypotheses. The therapist's hypotheses had to be refined and well supported in client-based "evidence" to restrain me from favoring my constructions. As I drifted toward a co-constructive orientation, I became more personal and interested in the supervision relationship itself. Tomm (1993) has noted similar shifts. However, unlike Tomm, my concern about the formal evaluative power I am granted "over" student therapists in a degree-granting program, and my personal interpretation of the current AAMFT *Code of Ethics,* have prevented me from wandering into the realm of therapy with the supervisees.

Collaboration in supervision is not a process of asking questions and solving difficulties. Rather, it is being-in-the-issue with the therapist. It is joining in a search for ideas where questions are lost in the joint formation of new thoughts. Process is in the direction of joint venture-co-construction.

In order to participate in a joint venture and open space for conversation, I more freely share, in a tentative and self-questioning way, my experiences and ideas about clients and about the supervisory relationship. My greatest challenge occurs when I am not feeling free to comment on certain aspects of the supervision relationship (e.g., my feeling of constraint or discomfort in offering feedback to a therapist). While voicing my experience often results in some of the most honest and generative supervision relationships I have experienced, the process may meet with times of caution and confusion.

Caution might arise given that my observation may he viewed as directed at a personal characteristic of the therapist, thus suggesting that my hesitation to give critical feedback seems related to what I perceive as the therapist's threatening or defensive posture at such times. Confusion may occur because of my willingness to explore how my observation may be related, in part, to my own issues as they are triggered in relationship with the particular therapist. This type of disclosure invites a candid, personal and less hierarchical discussion—begging questions for both participants, "Who is the supervisor/therapist? A friend, a colleague, an evaluator, a student?" In addition, caution and confusion might rise when participants wonder if and how this "personal conversation" might be documented in the form of a written evaluation of the therapist's performance. Collaboration is an ideal which cannot achieve complete expression in a relationship where one has evaluative power over the other.

I am aware of three practices that I consider in the preceding situation in order to open space for all participants, to provide some clarity and to decrease the possibility that my position of power might suck the air from the voice of the therapist. First, and as indicated above, I consciously open myself to becoming curious regarding the experience and questions of therapists and of myself in relation to my feedback. Second, increasing sensitivity to my relationship with power summons me to talk openly about how power is played out in supervision. For example, I acknowledge my contextual power in relation to therapists (gender being an important consideration) and I talk of my discomfort and struggles with power. I may talk of my past experiences in relation to the power of my teachers and supervisors, and convey my understanding that there are times when therapists might wish to "protect" themselves. Third, and in a similar vein to Turner (1993), I offer the opportunity for myself and therapists to bring in a consultant. This serves as a safeguard in the event that any participant may feel unsafe or concerned that their words or meanings will not be heard.

Because I was tempted by my understanding of social constructionism to take contextual, relational, collaborative and aleatory perspectives, my supervision stance became less instructional and more exploratory. I now encourage open and mutual generation of ideas, where therapy suggestions are tentatively selected and modified based on thoughtful fit with clients, therapists and supervision—not on my position or preference. In retrospect, I have observed that this practice encourages therapists to speak more forcefully about their ideas. I am more frequently challenged on my thinking and principles—leading, on occasion, to feeling quite stretched.

In that I feel stretched more often, "drawing the line" becomes an ongoing personal conversation. Although this issue invites a prolonged and serious discussion, in brief I don't consent to any therapy plan that I consider unprofessional and/or unethical according to the profession's ethical code. In a rare situation, where I believe the welfare of clients would be in jeopardy in relation to the plans of a therapist, I supersede the collaborative relationship and use my position to impose limitations. Limitations along with their rationale can provide the basis for the resumption of a more collaborative search for alternate plans that fit with the position of all supervision participants.

As I review this paper, I am aware of how much I have to account for the concept of power in collaborative supervision. My fantasy is, that, if I am at all "successful" in my supervisory efforts, it has somewhat less to do with the words I use and more to do with the visible struggle therapists' observe me having as I grapple for what I believe is fairness in the collaborative supervision relationship.

References

Tomm, K. (1993). Defining supervision and therapy: A fuzzy boundary? *Supervision Bulletin, VI, 1.*

Turner, J. (1993). Males supervising females: The risk of gender-power blindness. *Supervision Bulletin, VI, 1.*

Self-Supervision? A Goal for All Supervisors

Thomas C. Todd, Ph.D.

Published in the AAMFT Supervision Bulletin, Vol. V, No. 1, February 1992.

Virtually all supervisors profess that they regard self-sufficiency as one of the ultimate goals of their supervision. Remarkably little has been written on this subject, perhaps because the worthy goal of self-sufficiency is too general to be optimally useful. I propose a more focused alternative, that of explicitly helping supervisees learn self-supervision. The following guidelines are offered to aid in this process, independent of the theoretical orientation of the supervisor.

1. Make self-supervision an explicit goal of supervision. When supervisors are clear with supervisees that they will work together to make supervisees self-sufficient, the process changes. Supervisees become more equal partners in the supervisory process and better able to give precise feedback to supervisors.

2. Take inventory of the assets and skills of supervisees. While again most supervisors claim to do this, we do not always make this inventory explicit. We also need to help supervisees conduct their own "search" of assets and skills in order to find the resources necessary to be helpful in a given case. These resources may be the result of previous training or of general life experience.

3. Help supervisees to understand their own learning style. How do they learn best? What do they retain from one supervision session to the next? What supervisory input leads to behavioral change in the therapy being supervised? Helping supervisees answer questions such as these leads to a greater capacity to help themselves.

4. Help supervisees to achieve a coherent therapy approach that is fully congruent with themselves. The ability to self-supervise presupposes an adequate theoretical framework within which to function. Using such a framework, it is easier for supervisees to critique their sessions and look for behaviors that would be considered an "error" within that framework.

5. Encourage well-formed goals and questions for supervision. The less homework and preparation done by supervisees, the more dependence there is on supervisors to structure sessions, ask the right questions, and give sage advice. Conversely, a well-formed question often contains its own answer. Initially, supervisees do not always recognize good questions. Much of the early work of supervision is often helping supervisees to recognize good questions and learn to refine poorly formed goals and questions.

6. Have supervisees self-select clinical material for supervisory review (and preview!). Having made goals and questions explicit, supervisees need to look for clinical material that bears on these issues. Again, once supervisees are able to do this, it is a small step to self-supervision.

7. Help supervisees stay focused. As supervisees discuss cases or review sessions, supervisors should continue to ask how the material presented relates to goals for supervision. The need for this corrective feedback diminishes as supervisees learn to self-monitor.

8. Encourage specificity about feedback for line-tuning. Help supervisees learn from client feedback. Ask supervisees to reflect on the kinds of feedback that indicate an intervention was on target versus indicating further fine tuning was necessary.

9. Encourage supervisees to learn through small increments rather than expecting giant steps and then getting into self-blaming for not making such strides. In his work, Kagan (1975) stressed the importance of helping supervisees examine changes that were within their grasp during the session, rather than having supervisors engage in "Monday morning quarterbacking." Even in self-review this is important. Supervisees will change through small steps and should not condemn themselves for changing too slowly.

10. Be transparent. Avoid the temptation for

"gee whiz!" interventions in supervision. If self-supervision is the ultimate goal, any interventions which seemingly come out of nowhere will not help and may well be counterproductive. If supervisors' thoughts are not obvious, supervisees should feel comfortable in asking questions.

11. Generate alternatives, not answers. If you agree that no question in supervision has a single answer (Todd & Greenberg, 1987), then it does not make sense to provide only one answer, especially for advanced supervisees. Often it is helpful to engage in a brainstorming process of generating alternatives and then help supervisees to examine the process of choosing alternatives that fit best.

12. Promote generalization. Ideally, the goal of supervision is "learning how to learn" (Bateson, 1972). Even if it is necessary to provide specific help for supervisees to handle an immediate situation, it is still important to move beyond this to more general principles which allow supervisees to extend the principles to other situations. Creative combinations of supervisory modalities may be helpful here, such as using live supervision for immediate input and then reviewing a tape of the same session to insure generalization.

13. Contextualize recommendations. It is equally important for supervisors to articulate those differences which make a difference. What changes in context would result in changes in recommendations? Particularly crucial is to have supervisors address important differences between themselves and their supervisees (e.g., gender, age, status) that could have a bearing on the appropriateness of particular interventions.

14. Save time for feedback and reflection on the supervision process. The last five minutes of each session should be reserved for a discussion of what was useful for supervisees and why. This not only provides immediate feedback for supervisors, but also helps supervisees to understand how they learn.

15. Encourage development of other resources beyond supervision. Self-supervision does not have to be a solitary process. It can include the use of peers or less formal resources such as spouses or friends. One major advantage of group supervision or shared supervision is that the supervisee can learn to better use such resources.

The author would like to acknowledge the ideas of Robert Miller; Ph.D. and Jaime Esquivel, M.A., who helped to stimulate the development of these principles.

References

Bateson, G. (1972). *Steps to an ecology of mind.* New York: Ballantine Books.

Kagan, N. *(1975). Interpersonal process recall: A method of influencing human interaction.* Lansing, MI: Michigan State University.

Todd, T. C., & Greenberg, A. (1987). No question has a single answer! Integrating discrepant models in family therapy training. *Contemporary Family Therapy, 9* (1–2).

Positive Self-Monitoring: Positive Images Lead to Positive Actions

Cheryl L. Storm, Ph.D.

Published in the AAMFT Supervision Bulletin, Vol. VIII, No. 1, Spring 1995.

Positive self-monitoring or focusing on what one does well has been found to be highly effective in the learning of new tasks. Kirschenbaum (1984) compared two groups of new bowlers who both received lessons on the components of effective bowling. In one group, videotapes were reviewed with the bowlers for what they were doing well. In the other group, instructors highlighted ways the bowlers could perform differently. The groups that focused on the positives improved more than 100 percent! Other research has confirmed these results—for learning social skills, math and gold. But what do these results have to do with supervision? If we consider supervision to be about learning, then these results are significant for our work. They suggest supervisees may learn more from being helped to identify their successful therapeutic moves rather than focusing on bringing "stuck cases" to supervision. Conducting a microanalysis of the helpful actions of supervisees during therapy sessions may be more successful than reviewing videotapes for alternative responses. Further, supervisors may be more effective if they assist their supervisees to monitor their work on an ongoing basis for what they want to repeat rather than for what they want to avoid. Since positive self-monitoring enhances learning, excellent supervision may be developing this capacity in supervisees.

For supervisors, there are benefits to focusing on competencies rather than "growth areas" in therapists. Supervisors' images of supervisees dramatically change. Supervisees with limited English language skills are also therapists highly skilled in connecting with clients nonverbally. Supervisors uncomfortable with conflict are seen as masters at finding compromises. These positive images of supervisees alter supervisory responses. Cooperrider (1990), reviewing research on the ways that positive images lead to positive action, notes that teachers who have positive images of their students have been found to be more emotionally supportive to these students, offer clearer, more immediate and increased positive feedback regarding students' performances and provide better opportunities for students to perform and learn more challenging material. These positive actions which are beneficial to supervisees can also lead to supervisors feeling more effective in their work. Supervisors, as teachers, may find positive self-monitoring an effective method for themselves as well as for their supervisees.

References

Cooperrider, D. (1990). Positive image, positive action: The affirmative basis of organizing. In S. Srivastva, D. Cooperrider & Associates (Eds.), *Appreciative management and leadership: The power of positive thought and action in organizations.* (pp. 91–125). San Francisco: Jossey Bass.

Tailored Supervision

Debby L. Schwartz-Hirschhorn, M.S.

Published in the AAMFT Supervision Bulletin, Vol. VII, No. 2, Spring 1994.

My grandfather, I understand, was a tailor. I know, from the stories I have heard, that he felt the same suit might fit his customers' needs better at one stage of their lives than at another. Maybe that is why it makes sense to me that some modes of supervision fit supervisees better at some times than at others.

The first mode of supervision that I had was based on applying recognized systemic therapy models (e.g., brief therapy, solution-focused, etc.). In this mode, a supervisor, highly competent in a particular theory of therapy, attempts to inculcate an appreciation of that model in the supervisee. It is the supervisee's job to reflect what has been gleaned from the supervision by applying (correctly) the supervisor's model to the supervisee's clients.

Another mode of supervision entails the supervisor attempting to assist supervisees in developing their own therapy style. In this mode of supervision supervisors allow supervisees to experiment with integrating the various models of therapy that they have been exposed to previously. In addition, if group supervision is used, the refusal of the supervisor to guide supervisees down a particular path creates an atmosphere in which group members feel comfortable turning to one another for ideas. Thus, supervision not only becomes an opportunity to integrate previous experiences, but also, through contact with colleagues, an opportunity to integrate unfamiliar models.

In experiencing these two supervision modes, what is useful to me is that each came at the right time to best help me in my professional development. Initially, I required something tangible to copy. I came from a non-systemic background and was interested in shelving all previous learning for a while to make room for new ideas. A supervisor who did not adhere to a particular model of therapy would have left me confused and frustrated. A supervisor giving concrete directions for adhering to a particular therapy model gave me a clear path on which to move forward.

This kind of supervision requires a balance on the supervisor's part between demanding adherence to a model and recognizing that, for the supervisee, it is not easy to suspend one's former "self" (Gergen, 1991) in order to function in a different way than before. For example, my first supervisor, who combined an Ericksonian and a Mental Research Institute (MRI) model of doing therapy, developed engaging metaphors and expected that they be threaded through future family sessions. He would question closely to see if a family's interaction cycles were tracked, and he would model the types of interventions he thought suitable. Furthermore, if he liked a particular intervention, he believed in "pushing" it, something I had not been comfortable with. While I had to suspend my former "self," I learned how to do therapy without hedging.

My second supervisor was committed to solution-focused therapy. There was much comment, regarding my work, about avoiding "problem talk," not wasting precious minutes getting to the miracle question, and how to join with clients without focusing on problem description, but rather by inquiring about their interests.

In spite of the beneficial aspect of total immersion in a new model, one of the side effects of that mode of supervision is that supervisees may have very little to contribute to discussions. Interaction can center on how to best apply the particular model favored by the supervisor. Since the supervisee is in a one-down position relative to the supervisor as an expert in the use of the model, such discussions can merely become demonstrations that the supervisee is "catching on" to the use and philosophy of a new model. That is not at all bad—quite the opposite. But after the catching has been established, an opportunity to see if the model "fits" for the individual appears to me to be very helpful. When the supervisor prefers that a supervisee construct a personal model of therapy, the supervisee does not need to impress the supervisor with his or her understanding of the model. The understanding necessary in such a situation in effect pits the supervisee against him or herself: How can I use my understanding of theory and practice to support the actions I am taking in the therapy room? Such an environment encourages open discussion and use of previous experience.

By the time I had a third supervisor, I felt like I needed space to try out some of the ideas I had formed in previous supervision. I was very impressed with solution-focused therapy, but wondered about how some aspects of it fit for me. I needed a clarification of the model and the flexibility to apply it somewhat differently. The timing for a supervision style in which a supervisee constructs his or her own model of therapy was perfect for me.

At the outset, my supervisor asked me what my goals were for professional development. I told him that I liked solution-focused therapy but was unsure if I could join and get to the miracle question as quickly as my last supervisor preferred. My new supervisor helped me to remain solution-focused by taking my time to join with families. He also blended in some of the learning I had acquired from my first supervisor by helping me to develop metaphors suited to each client. I felt encouraged for the first time to do therapy on the basis of my "own voice" (Rambo, Heath & Chenail, 1993, p. 132) rather than on the basis of what fit the model I was working with. Practicing therapy on the basis of what feels right is a way of being that seems to me more suited to therapists with some experience behind them than to novice practitioners.

From the foregoing, it would seem that a beginning therapist might be more comfortable and absorb more under the supervision of someone preferring a particular model of therapy, while a more experienced therapist would perhaps flourish best within a spacious style that allows for personal exploration and modification of existing therapeutic models. Supervisors aware of the level of experience of their supervisees can then tailor supervision to fit the stage of their supervisees' professional development.

The author is endebted to Dr. Jim Rudes for his "tailored supervision" and his encouragement.

References

Gergen, K. (1991). *The saturated self: Dilemmas of identity in contemporary life*. New York: Basic Books.

Rambo, A. H., Heath, A., & Chenail, R. J. (1993). *Practicing therapy: Exercises for growing therapists*. New York: W. W. Norton.

Getting Tangled Up in Minute Record Keeping

Leslye King Mize, Ph.D.

Published in Supervision Bulletin, Vol. IV, No. 2, June 1991.

When I was a teenager, one of my passions was to show horses. One particular time I was preparing for a show in which my horse had to do an unusual move. We worked on this move for days and I finally believed he was just being stubborn and not doing it the way he should. I literally forced him to move in a specific way and when he did he fell and rolled on me. I was very lucky not to be hurt too badly, but what I learned was that he knew more about being a horse than I did, or at least his particular kind of horse, and from now on I would honor that in him.

This incident reminds me of an issue we are having in our training program. Ours is a master's degree program approved by the AAMFT Commission on Accreditation. Our students are a selected group; we admit only *25%* of those who apply. Before entering their internships, they have had at least a year of academic training and clinical practice. Then, they are placed in community agencies with Approved Supervisors who willingly volunteer their time and energy to train our students. I believe we have developed an optimum structure because of the multiple resources available to us. Our problem is the time and attention interns and their supervisors must give to minute record keeping. This reminds me again of my struggle with my horse and I can't help but wonder where we are getting our feet tangled up?

Six months ago, I struggled for hours devising a form that quantified all the supervision hours the students needed to report to me to send to AAMFT. I thought I had finally gotten it right, all bases were covered, and students and supervisors knew what we were asking. Yet, there are still questions and I am not sure any form can meet our needs.

However, what I fear is that we are losing sight of what we are really concerned about in training marriage and family therapists (MFTs)—the qualitative process. In quantifying the specifics such as whether the supervision was audio, video, live, or dis-

cussion, are we squeezing the very life out of what we provide, the wisdom of our supervisors and the spontaneity of the supervisory process? We may be actively forcing students to demand steps that they may find themselves rolled over on later. Should we put them in the position of demanding certain experiences from their supervisors just to meet the quantification needs of the report form? Who is in charge here?

I continue to be amazed and awed at the vast experiences our students report to us that they are having at their internship sites. Our students at a veterans administration hospital report remarkable learning experiences that emphasize cross-cultural and gender issues while other students are being trained in specific theoretical models at their sites. Many of our sites are steeped in team work and provide the richness of having various creative minds focusing on one case or family. And, in once-a-month get-togethers with us, students discuss cases and share stories of themselves. This we have found helps them bring their experiences to another level of awareness so that they can value what they are learning as well as learn from each other.

One of the draws of our profession for me has been the multi-disciplined roots of MFT. I have appreciated the kaleidoscopic approach and feel that it is this approach that has been so appealing, not only to the clients we service but also to the students we train. They can use their various life experiences to enrich their training and provide the creativity they need to help others solve tough human dilemmas.

I am not suggesting that we throw away requirements, or open the profession indiscriminately, but I am concerned that in giving students and supervisors such specific requirements, their focus on minutiae may get in the way of their creative process together.

In summary, legislating a specific format for a learning experience cannot be foremost in our minds. Quantification cannot be helpful unless it enjoys a complementary fit with the quality of experience. I am suggesting that we keep this in mind when we are creating guidelines for trainers and not lose sight of the creative leap, as Peggy Papp has so eloquently described. By awarding supervisors the rank of Approved Supervisor, haven't we designated to them that we trust their abilities to train and make decisions according to our standards? Trying not to get tangled up in our own feet and the avoidance of rolling over on ourselves is, I think, a worthy strategy.

References

Papp, Peggy (1984). Creative leap. *Family Therapy Networker.*

Chapter 2

Developing a Personal Philosophy of Supervision

From Philosophy of Therapy to Philosophy of Supervision: Making the Connection Clear

Candyce S. Russell, Ph.D.

Published in the AAMFT Supervision Bulletin, Vol. 10, No. 3, Winter 1998.

Systems thinking is what has made family therapy unique as an approach to human problems and intervention at the level of relationships. Part of thinking systemically is learning to put data into a relationship context, to recognize patterns, sequences, and redundancies, often across system levels. As every family therapist knows, learning to "think systems" is not an easy task. It is learned in fits and starts and takes many years of practice to become second nature. When a therapist takes on the additional role of supervisor, the challenge to think systemically moves to a higher order. The unit of analysis becomes the supervisory system: the therapist, the client system (including other helpers engaged with the family), and the supervisor. It is not surprising, then, that the Approved Supervisor Designation requires demonstration of the sophisticated use of systems theory in Philosophy Statements from supervisors-in-training (SITs) and a coherent connection between ways of organizing data on the level of the family-therapist system and ways of organizing data about the family-therapist-supervisor system.

Specifically, SITs are asked to demonstrate: *Your theoretical orientation by articulating your philosophies of therapy and supervision as well as the connection between them. (AAMFT, 1997, p. 15)*

The key to doing so is consistency and coherence as we move from a focus on the therapeutic system to a focus on the supervisory system.

One tool for helping SITs identify the links between their way of thinking about therapy and their developing philosophy of supervision is to ask them to complete the grid of supervision models from Storm and Todd's sourcebook (1997, p. 86), along with a similar grid for models of therapy. As the SIT identifies the goal of supervision, the nature of the supervisory relationship, supervisory methods, and interventions from each of several models, the parallel between ways of thinking and functioning as therapist and as supervisor will become apparent. This may also be a useful way to generate creative supervisory interventions that are inspired by familiar models of family therapy. When this exercise is used to highlight the connection between the SIT's philosophy of therapy and philosophy of supervision, it is useful to add a column for "concepts" that are central to each model in addition to the columns identified by Storm and Todd.

Figures 1 and 2 (next page) are examples of how this exercise may be completed for Bowen and Structural/Strategic models at the levels of both therapy and supervision.

Increasingly, our field is becoming integrative in its theoretical approach (Lebow, 1997). "Schools" of family therapy are less rigidly adhered to and interventions more and more are being tailored to specific presenting problems and populations. We have also expanded our conceptual lenses to include a consideration of both smaller systems (the individual as a biological, gendered, and psychological entity) and larger systems (communities identified by race, economics, ethnicity, religion, sexual orientation, etc.) as they impact the recipients of the therapeutic and supervisory services we offer. Thus, the personal philosophies of our SITs are increasingly individual and specific to their work context and their personal backgrounds and values. This means that the final Philosophy Statement will be more complex than the grids outlined below would suggest. It also means that the SIT will need help in making clear how disparate parts of their models of therapy and supervision fit together. For instance, both Bowen theory and Structural/Strategic approaches may inform the work of a particular SIT. This SIT will want to specify when elements of each model are brought into his or her thinking, in what sequence, at what junctures, for which popula-

UNIT OF ANALYSIS: Therapeutic System

Goal	Relationship	Concepts	Methods	Interventions
Ability in client to: *Stay calm *Think about self in context of family system *Define a position to significant others *Stay in contact *Avoid triangulation	Coach	Anxiety Differentiation Triangles Overfunctioning/-underfunctioning Cuts off Fusion Multigenerational transmission process	*Works with moat motivated members of the system *Constructing family's genogram *Action: "Moving differently in the system"	*Managing anxiety in the therapist *Diagramming emotional process *Staying detriangled by taking a clear position and staying incontact with both legs of the triangle

UNIT OF ANALYSIS: Supervisory System

Goal	Relationship	Concepts	Methods	Interventions
A differentiated supervisee who is able to: *Stay calm *Think about self in the therapeutic system *Define a position with clients * Stay in contact with relevant parts of the system *Find humor in the shared experiences of being human *De-triangle	Coach	Anxiety Differentiation Triangles Overfunctioning/-underfunctioning Cuts off Fusion Transmission of anxiety across all system levels	**Constructing supervisee's genogram and client's genogram: "Double Genograms" *Bowen therapy experience for the supervisee *Careful study of Bowen theory *Case consultation with supervisor	*Managing anxiety in the supervisory system *Modeling differentiated stance *Sharing own experience with detriangulation attempts *Diagramming emotional process in the therapy system (and isomorphically in the supervisory system)

Fig. 1. Bowen Family Systems theory.

tions and presenting problems, and for what reasons.

For instance, the SIT may believe that he or she is best able to facilitate change when the system is calm, believing, as Bowen theory would suggest, that people are better able to identify their role in patterns when things are calm. Yet, especially with child-focused cases, the SIT may believe that one effective way of reducing parents' anxiety is to attend to their immediate concern (a contractual issue) and make an early structural or strategic intervention that helps the parents feel like they are "doing something" for their child's problem. Then, as things get calmer in the family the therapist may introduce ideas of fusion, triangles, differentiation, and multi-generational transmission patterns as they relate to the family's problem. As supervisor, the SIT is then challenged to

UNIT OF ANALYSIS: Therapeutic System

Goal	Relationship	Concepts	Methods	Interventions
A family system with: *Clear Hierarchy *Clear boundaries	Hierarchial Expert Directive	Hierarchy Boundary Enmeshment Disengagement Detouring	*Conjoint family session	*Joining *Enactment *Reframing *Restructuring directives *Paradoxical injunctions *Unbalancing *Reconfiguration of space

UNIT OF ANALYSIS: Supervisory System

Goal	Relationship	Concepts	Methods	Interventions
An active interventionist able to: *Attend to process and content *Join, separate, challenge and support	Expert/Trainee Hierarchial	Structure *Is the goal of therapy clear? *Clarity of boundaries-- are all the appropriate players in therapy? Sequence, pattern, redundancies in interaction between therapist and client system	*Live supervision with phone-ins and walk-ins and pre-planning sessions *Video Analysis of interactional sequences in therapy sessions *Team consultations	*Directives *Role play *Observing supervisor as therapist * Supervision in stages (expect mistakes) *Ordeals, restraining (use of paradox) *"Pretending" (e.g. "Behave as you would if you were confident in your role")

Fig. 2. Model: Structural/Strategic.

take these ideas to the next higher level and think about how they can be used to inform his or her supervision. The SIT may realize that the principle of lowering anxiety is important in one's philosophy of supervision as well, and that establishing a clear supervisory contract and being available for live supervision helps to lower anxiety in beginning supervisees. The SIT may also believe that being available to offer "directives" to beginning supervisees from behind the mirror is an additional way of reducing anxiety in the supervisee. At later stages of supervisee development, the SIT may spend more time asking questions that help the therapist define his or her own position (differentiation). The SIT may also engage the intermediate supervisee in diagram-

ing "triangles" within the therapeutic system that maybe contributing to an impasse. Thus, the SIT clarifies how both Structural/Strategic and Bowen approaches inform his or her supervision, in what order and for what reasons.

As SITs "flesh out" these grids, they are able to generate new and creative ways of helping their supervisees by drawing upon the inspiration of the theories they are familiar with in therapy. They gain experience in moving from the therapy system as the "unit of analysis" to the supervisory system as the "unit of analysis." They become more experienced in identifying the basic assumptions that underlie their professional practice and how to provide a logical rationale for how concepts from different models fit

UNIT OF ANALYSIS: Therapeutic System

Goal	Relationship	Concepts	Methods	Interventions
Family System with adult leaders able to: *Non-reactively respond to challenges *Define a position *Stay in contact with important parts of the emotional system	Collaborative	-Differentiation -Clarity of-boundaries -Hierarchy -Detouring -Overfunctioning/-underfunctioning -Anxiety -Fusion -Gender roles -Care -Connection -Life cycle stage	Conjoint and individual sessions	*Staying calm *Taking an "I" position *Reframing/normalizing *Directives *Homework *Detriangling *Teaching about emotional systems: *Genograms *Identifying gender roles

UNIT OF ANALYSIS: Supervisory System

Goal	Relationship	Concepts	Methods	Interventions
A differentiated therapist who is: *Active *Able to challenge and support *Able to engage clients in reflection upon their own process *Aware of the impact of gender, economics and minority status on presenting problems	Collaborative	-Differentiation -Role Clarity -Overfunctioning/-underfunctioning -Anxiety -Fusion -Gender roles -Care -Connection -Developmental stage -Hierarchy	*Live supervision *Video replay *Case consultation *Family -of-origin work for the therapist *"Double Genogramming"	*Managing anxiety in the supervisory system *Modeling a differentiated stance *Diagramming emotional process in therapy and supervision systems *Directives *Role play *Supervision in stages

Fig. 3. Personal Integrative Model (Bowen/Structural-Strategic) with feminist overlay.

together in their emerging model. The final step in the grid exercise is to go through the process of identifying the goal, central concepts, relationship style, methods and interventions for the SIT's own model of supervision. (The integrative grids described may look like those in Figure 3.)

By constructing a grid using therapy as the unit of analysis as well as one for supervision as the unit of analysis, the SIT hopefully will be impressed with the similarities between the two levels of analysis and will be challenged to reconcile areas of contradiction.

In addition to being a systems thinker, the SIT in this example is also committed to a feminist perspective and uses that frame to personalize her philosophy further. She prefers a more collaborative relationship with supervisees than either Bowen or Structural/Strategic purists would. Connection is an important value to her, and she uses the concepts of care and connection as she thinks about the goal of differentiation and the kind of relationship she wants to establish with her supervisees. This SIT also has a background in human development and believes that an understanding of context is enhanced when life cycle stages and gender are taken into consideration. Thus, the contract she develops with a middle-aged supervisee who is launching her children and a new career simultaneously may be different from the contract she establishes with a younger supervisee who is more intimately involved in separation from her family of origin. Yet each of these professional values finds a place under the "umbrella" of systems thinking and her belief that human problems are best understood within the context of relationships. She approaches challenges in supervision from the same perspective and includes herself in the analysis of the supervisory system.

As supervisors of supervision, we can help SITs become clear about their personal integration of models of therapy and supervision by encouraging them to construct grids as illustrated. In addition, it is also helpful to talk about our own models of therapy and supervision and how we see the connection between them. For many of us, our models continue to develop as we accumulate additional experience as therapists and supervisors. Including our SITs in our own "revisionist" thinking illustrates an openness to thoughtful integration and nurtures the confidence to question, test, revise, and update philosophies of therapy and supervision. It also provides an occasion to struggle to make clear the connection between the way we conceptualize treatment systems and the way we conceptualize supervisory systems.

References

Lebow, J. (1997). The integrative revolution in couple and family therapy. *Family Process*, 36(1), 1–17.

Storm, C L & Todd, T. C. (1997). *The reasonably systemic supervisor resource guide.* Boston: Allyn & Bacon.

What Is a Systemic Orientation—Really?

Lynelle C. Yingling, Ph.D.

Published in the AAMFT Supervision Bulletin, Vol. 10, No. 2, Fall 1997.

The one distinguishing requirement of marriage and family therapy is the ability to work from a systemic orientation. For example, The 1991 Texas Civil Statutes define marriage and family therapy as follows:

> "Marriage and family therapy" means the rendering of professional therapy services to individuals, families, or married couples, singly or in groups, and involves the professional application of family systems theories and techniques in the delivery of therapy services to those persons. The term includes the evaluation and remediation of cognitive, affective, behavioral, or relational dysfunction within the context of marriage or family systems. (Title 71, Chapter 6 B-I, Art. 451 2c- 1, Sec 2(5))

Since supervisors are the true gatekeepers of any profession regulated by licensure, AAMFT Approved Supervisors must protect this distinguishing requirement in order to preserve the unique identity of our profession.

The October 1993 *AAMFT Approved Supervisor Designation: Standards and Responsibilities* handbook introduces the required learning objectives with a paragraph that includes the following statements: "Approved Supervisors may work from a variety of MFT theoretical approaches and may practice supervision in many ways. However, all Approved Supervisors must work from a systemic orientation" (p. 3). The October 1997 *Approved Supervisor Designation Standards and Responsibilities Handbook* introduction changes slightly in that the statement about systemic orientation is separated from the required learning objectives and is reworded as follows: "Approved Supervisors work from a systemic orientation, using a variety of MFT theoretical approaches in their practice" (p. 1). Though little systemic language is incorporated into the nine required learning objectives, guidelines for completing the written materials describe the process in systemic terms and the first two required evaluation criteria for the Philosophy Statement are specifically systemic:

> 1. Does the SIT think about treatment and supervision in relational terms?

> 2. Does the SIT have an awareness of patterns and sequences of replication at various system levels? (p. 22)

Many of the other criteria, especially those for the Case Study, also are written in systemic terms.

If the legal definition of our practice, and the justification for our separate existence, is using a family systems orientation, what does that really mean? Many MFT texts, such as Becvar and Becvar's *Family Therapy: A Systemic Integration* (1996), provide extensive definitions of a systemic orientation as the foundation to various MFT models. The systemic understanding is applied to supervision in two primary sources: Liddle, Breunlin, and Schwartz's *Handbook of Family Therapy Training and Supervision* (1988) and Todd and Storm's *The Complete Systemic Supervisor* (1997). However, the clearest definitions of a systemic orientation for me come from the following two sources:

1. The Global Assessment of Relational Functioning (GARF) in the DSM-IV appendix, which describes the components of any relational system as (a) organizational structure which provides identification of the system to which members belong, (b) interactional processes which maintain the functioning and continuously adapt that structure, and (c) emotional climate which provides the nurturance for its members to grow and become strong enough to developmentally reorganize the system (explained more fully in Yingling, Miller, McDonald, & Galewaler, 1997).

2. The systemic definition provided by Dr. W. Edwards Deming (1993), the statistician/physicist who revolutionized the field of manufacturing and service organization management with human system quality concepts such as "a network of interdependent components that work together to try to accomplish the aim of the system" (p. 50).

More specifically how do I train supervisors to develop an increasingly systemic orientation? My theory answer is simply that I try to create a relationship context where systemic interventions can be isomorphically experienced. I believe that a healthy functioning relationship will lead to a good output—written verification of that growth-oriented supervision-of-supervision relationship—which isomorphically influences the supervisor–supervisee and supervisee–client and family member-family member relationships.

How do I implement that philosophical statement? From July 1994 to September 1995, as a member of the AAMFT Supervision Committee, I was privileged to do 39 qualitative reviews of Approved Supervisor applications. As an outside reviewer, one thing I learned was to look carefully at the Supervision of Supervision Experience report. The systemic characteristics of that relationship—or lack thereof—could often be traced into the written description of the Philosophy Statement and the Case Study. Specific characteristics I looked for in those reports included a clear description of systemic MFT therapy models adhered to, as well as recognition of how many of these same intervention techniques could be applied to supervision. I also looked for the ability to systemically hypothesize about the supervision relationship in reciprocal response terms, i.e., how does the interaction of supervision goals and techniques promote continuous development of skills in both? The feedback procedure of those qualitative reviews was to make recommendations for change that would bring the papers up to standard. The language of those recommendations had a critical impact on response. My evaluations were first derived from an objective rating sheet, similar to the current criteria rating sheet required of the training supervisor. Then I tried to carefully shape the comments into supportive, provocative questions that would lead toward continued growth—an assumed goal for the applicant.

As a training supervisor for Supervisors-in-Training and an active member of the supervision training system, how do I provide an evaluative process which will help the SIT meet the AAMFT standard? Since I am very closely engaged in this system, assessing the relationship clearly is more challenging. However, I have found several techniques to be useful:

• My initial contracting includes a self-assessment of the SIT's MFT skills, using an objective rating sheet I also use with supervisees. We discuss the strengths and weaknesses of the SIT in understanding and competently using a variety of MFT models. Incidental or formalized reference to desired skill development is used throughout the supervision internship experience. Isomorphically, without direction, the SIT generally uses this same rating sheet with supervisees. I find that a lack of confidence in knowing and using MFT intervention skills in the supervisor frequently blocks effective MFT supervision for the supervisee. As the supervisor's skills increase, so do the supervisee's. The objective rating sheet helps expand opportunities for growth in a nonthreatening way.

• Throughout the supervision internship, I probe for clarification of systemic work as supervision cases are discussed. Often I use the same systemic intervention techniques as used in therapy, such as circular questions, paradoxical/straightforward directives for change, go slow directive, reframe, reenactment, identification of family-of-origin or other contextual influences, metaphor, redirected communication interchanges, rearranged seating, and behavioral skills training. I frequently ask for hypothesizing about the functioning dynamics of the supervision-of-supervision system, especially when there are two SITs working together.

• In order to facilitate experiencing isomorphic transfer of patterns to different systems, I require some live supervision of supervision using a reflecting team supervision model. Experiencing this concept live is always a very powerful intervention strategy for all of us to better understand systems. This experience also provides a good window of opportunity to discuss each participant's responsive pattern in the system dynamics. This self-awareness can lead to more intentional behavior on the part of the SIT when interfacing with supervisees/clients.

• In order to promote and reward more clear systemic conceptualization, I generally encourage SITs to consider sharing their views with other professionals through presentations or writings. The best way to clarify one's thinking is to teach it to others.

• My evaluative role for the required paper work and recommendation is addressed in the contracting stage. SITs are fully aware of my intent to maintain a high standard of performance. This mutual desire for quality is agreed upon in the beginning. Having spent 20 years in academia, this approach seems comfortable to me. However, the evaluative role can be carried out as a collaborative process. Learning from my review experience on the Supervision Committee, I use an objective rating sheet for each component that is shared with SITs in the beginning. Each of the members of the system (myself and both SITs, if there are two) rate the papers and discuss our ratings in order to collaboratively define ways to improve. Referring to specific readings is often especially helpful at this time, although shared readings are used throughout the supervision internship. Deadlines for submission of first drafts of the papers are scheduled before the internship is to be completed. That parallel review process allows us to relate concepts from the philosophy paper to the supervision cases being discussed during the latter part of the internship. Rewrites are done until there is mutual agreement that the papers have attained a sufficient level of quality for submission to AAMFT. We both know that the papers are never really complete, but that we must agree on a stopping point.

Hopefully I will continue to improve my understanding of a systemic orientation and what that really means. As I change and grow, there will be ways to influence others to do the same.

References

AAMFT. (1993). *Approved Supervisor designation: Standards and responsibilities.* Washington, DC: AAMFT.

AAMFT. (1997). *Approved Supervisor designation standards and responsibilities handbook.* Washington, DC: AAMFT.

Becvar. D. S., & Becvar. R. J. (1996). *Family therapy: A systemic integration,* Boston: Allyn & Bacon.

Deming, W. E. (1993). *The new economics for industry, government, education.* Cambridge, MA: Massachusetts Institute of Technology Center for Advanced Engineering Study.

Liddle, H. A., Breunlin, D. C., & Schwartz, R. C. (1988). *Handbook of family therapy training and supervision.* New York: Guilford.

Todd, T. C., & Storm, C. L. (Eds.). (1997). *The complete systemic supervisor.* Boston: Allyn & Bacon.

Texas Civil Statutes, Title 71, Chapter 6 B-1, Art. 4512c-1 Licensed Marriage and Family Therapist Act.

Yingling, L. C., Miller, W. E., McDonald, A. L., & Galewaler, S. T. (1997). *GARF assessment sourcebook.* Bristol, PA: Brunner/Mazel.

Theoretical Consistency: Cut Flowers or Living Plants?

Dan Ratliff, Ph.D.

Published in the AAMFT Supervision Bulletin, Vol.11, No.2, Winter 1998.

Of all the challenges faced by supervisors-in-training (SITs) as they write their Philosophy Statement, the standard requiring theoretical consistency is perhaps the most daunting. Thus, the SIT is required to demonstrate: *Your theoretical consistency, whether from one prominent model or from an integrative perspective. If the latter, demonstrate a logical integration of models. (AAMFT, 1997, p.15.)*

Addressing this standard requires a conceptual clarity that precedes efforts to describe guiding principles of supervision, to cite the supervision literature, or to discuss how the methods facilitate supervision goals. The SITs theoretical perspective is the lens through which she or he makes judgments about what is important and what is irrelevant regarding guiding principles, the literature and methods of supervision. The relationship between theory and practice has been addressed in the supervision literature regarding the role of cognitive development in therapy. The major emphasis is on how the supervisor can tailor the supervision to meet trainee learning needs (Birk & Mahalik, 1996; Holloway & Wampold, 1986; McLennan, 1995; Rigazio-DiGillo & Ivey, 1991).

Cognitive processes also are addressed in developmental theories that give attention to the experienced clinicians' development. Dreyfus and Dreyfus (1986), in their model of expertise, show how education and experience increase skill. As therapists develop, according to this theory, they shift from using abstract, context-free cognitrons to guide clinical experience to using their own personal and clinical experiences (Thomas, 1990). In one of the few empirical investigations of postgraduate counselor development, Skovholt and Ronnestad (1992) describe how therapists move from cognitive processing of conceptual ideas and techniques during academic training toward experienced therapists' authenticity and integration of personally selected ideas and techniques.

This essay draws on these two models of counselor development (Dreyfus & Dreyfus, 1986; Skovholt & Ronnestad, 1992). Clinical examples used to illustrate ideas are all fictional.

I view the relationship between assumptions, theory, and techniques in terms of the metaphors of cut flowers or living plants. A "cut flower" approach focuses only on pragmatics with little attention to theory and underlying assumptions. A "potted plant" approach is one in which there is a superficial grasp of the assumptions, theory, and techniques of a single model with no appreciation of the ways in which context shapes one's understanding and actions. A "transplant" refers to a deeper understanding of a single model with a flexibility to extend the model into unique clinical situations. A "grafted plant" describes an integrated theory in which core concepts are joined with compatible techniques. The final metaphor is that of "home grown," in which the plant emerges from seed, which is composed of the best attributes of several species. The latter approach reflects the ways in which experienced clinicians internalize and integrate information from formal and informal sources.

Cut Flowers: Eclectic Techniques

The "cut flower" approach refers to the gathering of clinical techniques with little regard to theoretical consistency. I use the invective, "eclectic," uttered in my most derisive tone, to describe this approach. The following composite example of a supervision philosophy illustrates this approach:

I am a solution-focused supervisor. I try to look for the things that my trainee is doing well and seek to strengthen them.... During the early phases of supervision I assess where the trainee needs to develop.... In the first session I have my supervisee complete a genogram noting how significant authority figures gave and received criticism.... In live supervision I look for emotional reactions on the part of my trainee to indicate one's "trigger family" walked in the door, a family that triggers unresolved issues in the trainee.

As the supervisor of supervision, I'm wondering, "How is assessment of trainee deficits, and focus on historical emotional process, consistent with solution focused therapy?" The trainee may have been attracted to the strength-based focus, but a different theory is needed to frame the techniques more coherently.

Potted Plant: Inflexible Single Theory

The "potted plant" approach is seen in the single model trainee who has an incomplete and inflexible focus on the guidelines and concepts of one theory which guide both clinical practice and supervision, with insensitivity to contextual factors that warrant some modification in the way that therapy or supervision is conducted. For example, structural family therapy was the orienting theory of an SIT, whose central theoretical axiom was, "If you change one part of the system, the entire system must change." In a case presentation, a therapist with a step-family client in which a thirteen year old daughter ran away from home was described. During the course of treatment the SIT had discouraged the therapist from reading material on step-families, seeing this as inconsistent with the theory. The SIT explained the outcome of therapy as successful. That is, with the running away on the part of the daughter, a systemic change had occurred. One part changed, consequently the entire system must change. The SIT thus overlooked other dimensions of the orienting theory that would apply to the unique situation of step-families. Also overlooked was the theory's preference for maintaining structural stability while promoting change. Such an inflexible, context insensitive approach is characteristic of the novice professional (Dreyfus & Dreyfus, 1986; Thomas, 1990).

Transplant: Competent Use of Single Theory

The "transplant" approach is reminiscent of an established plant which has been rooted in a new context. There is flexibility in applying a single theory to the novel complexities inherent in the clinical context. Thinking remains consistent with the theory, but the practice extends the theory to new situations and applications. This trainee knows the full repertoire of techniques of a theory and is able to invent new techniques for unique situations that are consistent with the theory.

It may be easier to achieve theoretical consis-

tency when writing the Philosophy Statement from a single theory. The task is simply to identify the underlying clinical theory and extend the core concepts and techniques to supervision. The challenge when writing from such a perspective is to make sure one describes a philosophy of supervision rather than a philosophy of therapy. All the examples should be drawn from supervision practice rather than therapy practice.

In my own supervision Philosophy Statement, I identified axioms of therapy that influenced my supervision. For each axiom of therapy I wrote a brief summary (no more than six lines) of the clinical theory and practice, citing relevant therapy literature. I then stated a corollary axiom for supervision, illustrating the compatible supervision techniques with reference to the supervision literature. For example, one axiom of therapy was drawn from solution-focused therapy: Clients can over-focus on what is going wrong and overlook exceptions to the problem. After giving a brief summary of key clinical concepts and citing relevant authorities, I extended the therapy axiom to supervision: Something worthwhile is happening in the trainee's work. I discussed supervision techniques that I found compatible with a solution-focused orientation, citing appropriate references. The references demonstrated my understanding of the supervision literature.

Grafted Plant: Integrative Theory

One form of integrated theory occurs when the SIT identifies common themes that link techniques derived from different sources. Early in the supervision training process, I ask my SITs to compose a "Good Ideas" paper which simply lists supervision techniques that appeal to them with little regard to theoretical consistency. While this is the clearest example of the "cut flowers" approach, as we do supervision of supervision I help them to identify theoretical themes that connect the various techniques. This begins the process of growing an integrative, theoretically consistent supervision philosophy.

When my SITs begin the task of writing the Philosophy Statement, I tell them to sit meditatively with a pad of paper and pencil in front of their bookcase (soft music, deep breathing, repetitive mantra). Without opening any books, I have them note which sources have been influential in their clinical thinking. As they record the source and idea that has been influential, they also make note of a clinical vignette that was influenced by that source. After recording influential ideas and clinical vignettes, they begin looking for common themes across the ideas which define their clinical theory. As they do supervision, I encourage them to identify how their clinical theory influences what they focus on and ignore in their supervision.

RiGazio-DiGilio (1997) gives four examples of integrative approaches to supervision which link different theoretical approaches and extend the implications to supervision. These integrative models are illustrative examples of how others have integrated related theories.

Grown from Seed: Internalized Theory and Practice

For the practicing professional who is five or more years out of graduate school, theoretical consistency tends to be more home grown. While the first two approaches cited above generally are characteristic of the novice, the next two approaches tend to apply to those who are more experienced, although not necessarily proficient. At these levels, the integration of theory and practice is a highly cognitive activity. By contrast, effective clinical practice may dominate the attention of experienced professionals. Their integration of theory and practice is accomplished internally through experience rather than in a cognitive manner.

To explain, as therapists develop expertise, their focus moves from external authority derived from conceptual ideas and techniques to a focus on internalized authority based on personal authenticity and clinical experience (Dreyfus & Dreyfus, 1986; Skovholt & Ronnestad, 1995; Thomas, 1990). Consequently, these SITs may have greater difficulty explaining why they do what they do. Their typical response is, "I've seen lots of clients like that and this is what works."

For these clinicians, theory and research have less influence on their practice than peer consultation, client interaction, and their own personal life. Theories, techniques, and clinical knowledge are acquired more selectively through attending workshops, reading journal articles that catch their interest, or talking with colleagues. Providing supervision is a significant learning influence as their trainees elicit reflections about why they do what they do. Although

they are creating their own theory based on their experience, the challenge is to articulate that theory in a coherent and consistent manner.

Summary

Of the five metaphors used to illustrate the ways in which the relationship between assumptions, theory, and techniques within the supervision philosophy may be understood, three reflect theoretical consistency: "transplant," "grafted plant," and "grown from seed." While "cut flowers" and "potted plants" also may be represented among SITs, they are likely to require guidance in the process of attaining and describing theoretical consistency.

Those SITs with a competent use of a single theory may have the easiest time demonstrating theoretical consistency between clinical theory and supervision theory. On the other hand, the integrative SITs may be challenged to do the additional effort to identify themes derived from different authorities and show how the concepts are related to one another.

Paradoxically, experienced therapists may be the most theoretically consistent, yet have the most difficulty articulating consistency between therapy and supervision models. Their process of internalizing sources of clinical knowledge produces a personal authenticity of thinking and acting. But this selective internalizing process may make it difficult to identify the source of the influence and relate it to the recognized authorities in the field.

References

AAMFT. (1997). *Approved Supervisor Designation: Guidelines and responsibilities handbook.* Washington, DC: Author.

Birk, J., & Mahalik, J. (1996). The influence of trainee conceptual level, trainee anxiety and supervision evaluation on counselor developmental level. *Clinical Supervisor, 14,* 123-137.

Dreylus, H., & Dreyfus, S. (1986). *Mind over machine: The power* of *human intuition and expertise in the era of the computer.* New York: The Free Press.

Holloway, E.L., & Wampold, B. E. (1986). Relationship between conceptual level and counseling-related tasks: A meta-analysis. *Journal of Counseling Psychology, 33,* 310-319.

McLennan, J. (1995). Counselor conceptual level and counseling: A reappraisal. *Journal of Psychology 129,* 651-663.

Rigazio-DiGilio, S. (1997). Integrative supervision: Approaches to tailoring the supervisory process. In T.

Todd & C. Storm (Eds.) *The complete systemic supervisor: context, philosophy, and methods.* Boston: Allyn & Bacon.

Rigazio-DiGilio, S., & Ivey, A. (1991). Developmental counseling and therapy: A framework for individual and family treatment. *Counseling and Human Development, 24,* 1-20.

Skovholt, T., & Ronnestad, M. (1992). *The evolving professional self: Stages and themes in therapist and counselor development.* New York: John Wiley & Sons.

Thomas, E (1990). *Solution focused supervision.* Paper presented at the meeting of the American Association for Marriage and Family Therapy, Washington, DC.

Greasing Your Pen: Showing You Know the Literature

Cheryl Storm, Ph.D.

Published in the AAMFT Supervision Bulletin, Vol. 11, No.1, Summer 1998.

Many supervisors-in-training (SITs), even highly experienced ones, seem to dread the process of writing their philosophy statement. Not only does it seem like a daunting task to articulate one's philosophy, but many SITs unnecessarily freeze when they realize they also must show that they are knowledgeable of the supervision literature and articulate how their supervision philosophy methods relate to the current supervision literature. The purpose of this article is to help these SITs decrease their dread, grease their pens, and complete the task at hand by demonstrating *"that you understand MFT supervision literature by citing recent articles, chapters, and/or books, and how your supervision philosophy and methods of supervision related to the current MFT supervision literature."(AAMFT, 1997, p. 15)*

A Simple Method for Getting Started

If you are an SIT dreading the task (or if you are a supervisor who is supervising an SIT at this phase suggest they) try this exercise. Sit down with a piece of paper and a pen. First, write down the major assumptions you have that guide your supervision. How do supervisees become competent therapists? For example, do you see supervision as a process of learning specific therapy skills, as supervisees identifying how their family of origin patterns are interfacing with their cases, as providing the context where supervisees find their own answers, or perhaps a combination of ideas like these? In what ways are your supervision assumptions similar and in what ways different than those you have for therapy?

Second, describe your beliefs about the supervisory relationship. Are you most like a teacher, a coach, a collaborator, or an interviewer? How do you deal with problems or issues when they occur? Third, explain how you insure that you are a contextually sensitive supervisor who acknowledges such influences as gender, culture, socioeconomic, and race in super-

vision. How do you develop this ability in your supervisees? Fourth, as a result of these ideas, what are your preferred structures, methods of intervention and ways of evaluating supervisees' progress? Finally, how do you deal with the legal and ethical issues of supervision? Add some headings to organize these ideas and you have a basic outline of your philosophy statement.

Piercy and Sprenkle (1997) provide a set of comprehensive questions that address the following areas of supervision: who has influenced SITs, isomorphism, change and components of supervision, developmental stages of supervision, self of the supervisor, gender issues, diversity issues, accountability/assessment, and ethical issues for SITs to use to jog their thoughts and fill out philosophical statements. Russell (1998) describes an exercise that SITs can do to make the conceptual leap from their therapy model to their supervision model, while showing the connection between them. Storm and Todd (1997) have found that having SITs watch a videotape of someone supervising usually helps them quickly discover their underlying assumptions as they agree or disagree with the supervisor's actions. The important thing is to get started and rough out a few initial ideas.

Adding Support from the Literature

Once SITs have the basic ideas of their philosophy statement articulated and have widely read the supervision literature, showing that they are knowledgeable is easier than most SITs think. If they have taken a solid supervision course that was an overview of MFT supervision, the assigned readings for the course may be a place to start. If it has been a while since they have taken a course or their readings centered on a specific model of supervision such as Bowen, they may find books like Liddle (1988) or Todd and Storm (1997), which provide an overview of MFT supervision, a good read. Other books that are overviews of psychotherapy supervision, such as Mead (1990) and Bernard (1992), also may be useful resources. Another way is for SITs to ask themselves:

"What books have had the most impact on my approach to family therapy supervision? What theorists? Why? In what other ways does my supervision theory relate to current MFT and supervision literature?" (Piercy & Sprenkle, 1997, p. 101). Essentially, SITs are answering these questions: Who seems to think most like me about supervision? Where do my ideas about supervision connect with other writers?

SITs frequently lament about accessing supervision literature when they rarely have time to spend in a library. In an effort to make this easier for SITs, we (Storm & Todd, 1997) included in our book accessible resources which include readings and tapes on various supervision topics. However, the lists are only reasonably complete and are somewhat dated. For example, if an SIT is most influenced by recent innovations in supervision in the field, such as narrative therapy ideas and how they are used in supervision, a trip to the library may be required. Also included in our book are a couple of actual philosophy statements and case studies—one is a statement that integrates ideas from several models (Fishbane, 1997) and one is a statement that is more consistently out of one school of thought of supervision (McDowell, 1997). These examples are well referenced and illustrate how supervision literature can be used effectively to support an SIT's philosophy statement without losing the SIT's uniqueness.

Showing a Relationship with the Supervision Literature

When SITs have done a solid job of referencing their ideas by the method proposed above, showing how their supervision philosophy and methods relate to the current supervision literature has already been accomplished. Since most supervisors have a highly individualized philosophy, it is rare to find writers (and practicing supervisors) in the field who have supervision philosophies exactly alike. However, SITs, who liberally cite writers with similar ideas, provide support for their ideas, show they are familiar with the MFT supervision literature, and demonstrate they are practicing supervision within the standards of the field.

Fatal Flaws

There are a few fatal flaws that may occur in referencing philosophy statements. Some SITs cite therapy rather than supervision literature. Since the body of supervision literature is substantial, these SITs are failing to demonstrate knowledge of supervision literature. No matter how well read SITs are as therapists, this is not considered a substitution for being knowledgeable of the MFT supervision literature.

Others fail to mention obvious support that exists in the literature for their ideas. Consider for a moment SITs who have been heavily influenced in their work by solution-focused ideas, but never cite any of the several excellent articles on solution-focused supervision (Frank, 1994, Wetchler, 1990, Selekman & Todd, 1995). Does this leave the impression of individuals knowledgeable of the supervision literature when they fail to cite literature regarding their preferred ideas?

And still others summarize the supervision literature without stating their beliefs about supervision. The philosophy statement is meant to be a highly personal document. "I believe... about supervision. My preferred way of supervising is... I use these methods because..." are common phrases in philosophy statements. The literature is then used to connect the SIT's preferred ideas, methods, and style to the field.

Once SITs have added support from the literature for their ideas, then making sure their case study illustrates their philosophy statement completes the task.

References

AAMFT. (1997). *Approved Supervisor designation: Standards and responsibilities handbook.* Washington, DC: Author.

Bernard, J., & Goodyear, J. (1992) *Fundamentals of clinical supervision.* Needham Heights, MA: Allyn & Bacon.

Fishbane, M. (1998). An example of an integrative supervision philosophy. In C. Storm & T. Todd (Eds.) *The reasonably complete systemic supervisor resource guide* (pp.104–114). Needham Heights, MA: Allyn & Bacon.

Frank, T. (1994). Solution-oriented supervision: The coaxing of expertise. *The Family Journal, 2,* 11–18.

Liddle, H., Breunlin, D., & Schwartz, R. (1988). *Handbook of family therapy training and supervision.* New York: Guilford.

Mead, D. (1990). *Effective supervision: A task-oriented model for the mental health professions.* New York: Brunner/Mazel.

McDowell, T. (1997). An example of consistent supervision philosophy. In C. Storm & T. Todd (Eds.) *The reasonably complete systemic supervisor resource guide.* (pp. 100–103). Needham Heights, MA: Allyn & Bacon.

Russell, C. (1998). From philosophy of therapy to philosophy of supervision: Making the connection clear. *Supervision Bulletin, 10(3)*.

Selekman, M. & Todd, T. (1995). Co-creating a context for change in the supervisory system: The solution-focused supervision model. *Journal of Systemic Therapies, 14,* 21–33.

Storm, C., & Todd, T. (1997). *The reasonably complete systemic supervisor's resource guide.* Needham Heights, MA: Allyn & Bacon.

Wetchler, J. (1990). Solution-focused supervision. *Family Therapy,* 17, 129–138.

Helping our Supervisors-in-Training (SITs) Write Their Supervision Philosophy Statement

Charles Figley, Ph.D.

Published in the AAMFT Supervision Bulletin, Vol. 10, No. 2, Fall 1997.

'I just froze," said Fred (fictitious name), a senior PhD student, rushing to get his application for Approved Supervisor into the mail. He was scheduled to go for a faculty appointment interview. He wanted to say that his application was submitted. He had completed all of his training as a supervisor in training (SIT). He has everything in the envelope, including the application fee of $150.

Only one more task: Write the 3 single-spaced pages about his philosophy of supervision; his approach to supervising family therapy trainees. All he needed to do was write down how he approaches both practice and supervision in family therapy. "I knew what I did and why," he said. "And I know that the trainees I supervised were pleased, as are my clients."

The AAMFT Standards Committee has been aware for some time of the phobia many SITs experience when the time comes to prepare the written statements. Indeed, Storm and Todd (1996) have noted how they continue to be astonished that so many of their colleagues and students "freeze completely when asked to commit their philosophy of supervision in writing." (p. 99). I therefore have been asked to write down a few words about any advice I might have. My goal in this article is simple: To make the task easier.

Over the years I have seen the field of family therapy grow and mature. Today, family therapy supervisors are the key ingredients in the training of family therapists. Unlike other mental health fields, most family therapists are not trained exclusively in accredited programs, although the Commission on Accreditation for Marriage and Family Therapy Education would like to change that picture. More established fields (e.g., psychology, psychiatry, and social work) have much greater percentages of clinical

members from accredited programs. Also, AAMFT has attempted to decentralize the screening process for evaluating the quality of supervisor training. Trainers of supervisors in training (SITs), in contrast to the past, are now responsible for the evaluation of their trainee's readiness to assume the designation. This includes evaluating the trainee's supervision philosophy statement.

Brief Review of the Literature

Liddle (1982) notes that therapists should declare their own values, attitudes and beliefs about therapy at regular intervals to clarify their clinical identity. Storm and Heath (1985) provide a fine initial guide to developing their philosophy through an excellent dialogue between supervisor and SIT.

Piercy and Sprenkle (1986) provide several examples of pedagogical tools to facilitate the development of the trainee's own evolving theory of therapy they practice. The Triad Interview is an exercise in which two fellow students interview the third student in the group about using a series of questions. The answers help clarify the students philosophy or theory of family therapy. They ask such questions as:

How does change occur? What are your basic goals in therapy and how do you propose to achieve these goals? How important are the following in your own evolving theory: skill building, affect, assessment, administrative control, therapist-client relationship and enrichment? (p.8-9)

They also discuss the Theoretical Tenet Continuum:

This exercise involves designating complimentary theoretical tenets to opposite walls of the room, and then ask each student to decide on the place he/she would stand on an imaginary line between these two theoretical tenets (p.9).

Other techniques include the supervision worksheets, the personal theory paper and videotape presentation, in addition to other methods such as dyad discussions, simulation papers, position papers, reaction papers, and others. Storm and Todd (1997) devote an entire chapter, "Supervisory Challenge 7, Creating Your Own Philosophy," in which they note that it is important for applicants to remember that they:

• Already have the knowledge; it is just a matter of articulating it in three single spaced pages.

• Sometimes just a few words of encouragement is all that is needed.

• Would be wise to attend to the questions they pose in their article (1997, p. 99).

They offer more than forty questions divided among the following categories:

• *Influence* (e.g. What modes of therapy have most influenced your supervision approach? What models of supervision have most influenced your approach?)

• *Isomorphism* (e.g. In what ways is your model of therapy similar to your model of supervision? In what ways is it different?)

• *Change and Components of Supervision* (e.g. What do you attempt to do in the supervision you provide? What does this tell you about your theory of supervision?)

• *Developmental Stages of Supervision* (e.g. What developmental stages do you conceptualize in the supervision process?)

• *Self of Supervisor* (e.g., How have your personal values, beliefs, life experiences and theoretical assumptions had an effect on your philosophy and practice of supervision?)

• *Gender Issues* (e.g., How has the feminist critique of MFT informed your approach to supervision?)

• *Diversity Issues* (e.g., How does your evolving supervision theory incorporate issues of culture, ethnicity, class, sexual orientation, disability, and other aspects of diversity?)

Although an excellent example of a philosophy statement also is provided, it appears to be longer than the three page limit. The structure and content seems to be very useful, however.

The FSU outline for Writing the Supervision Philosophy Statement

We have developed a format for our students that may be useful to others, We expanded and re-ordered the AAMFT Guidelines into a structure for writing

the supervision philosophy statement. Thus, SITs are urged to use the seven subheadings and complete the following instructions for each:

1.) Brief Description of Your Philosophy: [insert the best name for it here]

State in one single paragraph a summary of your theoretical orientation reflected in your philosophies of therapy and supervision and the connections between these philosophies. Cite here first your basic assumptions about clients and supervisees. Then identify 3-10 basic axioms, propositions, assertions, principles, or characteristics of your therapy philosophy that are identical to your philosophy of supervision.

2.) Knowledge of Current MFT Supervision Literature

Demonstrate how knowledgeable you are regarding current MFT Supervision literature in explaining your supervision philosophy and methods of supervision. Cite here recent articles. chapters, and/or books that have influenced or supported your approach.

3.) Systemic Orientation

Note how you think about treatment and supervision in relational terms. Relational in terms of patterns, sequence and context for example. And how are you aware of patterns and sequences of replication at various systems levels? Levels in terms of interconnection and interrelationships of individual and family clients, therapist, supervisor and the context of training, for example.

4.) Theoretical Identity

Note how your theory or philosophy of supervision is consistent with either the root theory or collection of theories, in the case of your adapting an integrative perspective.

5.) Contextual Sensitivity

Note how your supervision philosophy is sensitive to development, culture, family-of-origin, gender and the disabilities and other challenges that may create distance and misunderstanding between you and your supervisees.

6.) Personal Influences

Note the ways, if any, that personal values, beliefs, life experiences and theoretical assumptions influence your philosophy and practice of supervision.

7.) Description of Methods

Note the specific methods you employ as a supervisor that are applications of your philosophy/theory and provide support that these methods facilitate achievement of supervision goals.

Final Thoughts

The wisdom of Doug Sprenkle, Fred Piercy, Howard Liddle, Cheryl Storm, Tony Heath, Tom Todd and all of the early contributors to the supervision literature suggests, among other things: Start early developing one's practice theory or philosophy. We need to encourage our trainees to immediately begin to think about and work on their practice theory long before it is required for their Approved Supervisor Designation application. The Piercy-Sprenkle methods of theory development have great merit and should be tried, along with the outline for the Philosophy Statement. Thinking theory and practicing throughout the training program is a good way to avoiding the dreaded Philosophy Statement Phobia.

References

Liddle, H. (1982). Family therapy training: Current issues and future trends. *International Journal of Family Therapy*. 4, 87-97.

Piercy, F. P. & Sprenkle, D. H. (1986). Family therapy theory building: An integrative training approach. *Journal of Psychotherapy and the Family*, 1, (4), 5-14.

Mead, D. E. (1990). Appendix: Professional History, Preparation for Supervision. In D. E. Meads (Ed.), *Effective supervision: A task oriented model for the mental health professions*. New York: Brunner/Mazel.

Storm, C. L., & Heath, A. (1985). Models of supervision: Using therapy theory as a guide. *The clinical supervisor*, 3, 87-96.

Storm, C. L. & Todd, T. C. (1997). Supervisor challenge 7: Creating your own philosophy. In T. C. Todd & C. L. Storm (Eds.), *The reasonably complete systemic supervisor resource guide*, 99–130. Boston: Allyn & Bacon.

The Standard of Care for Supervision: Finding Our Way through the Fog

Cheryl Storm, Ph.D.

Published in the AAMFT Supervision Bulletin, Fall 2000

What is the acceptable ratio of supervision to therapy? How many therapists should a supervisor supervise? What supervisory responses are enough and what may be too much when a supervisee has not fulfilled professional responsibilities? These questions all address the standard of care for supervision. Essentially, what would a reasonable, prudent supervisor do in this situation? The standard of care for supervision can be radically different when one considers it at the national level versus the local level. In my opinion, it is critical for supervisors to be able to answer this question because in the event that a problem arises, it is one of the major standards upon which supervisors are judged.

Clients, supervisees, supervisors, supervisees' employers, consumers, lawmakers, the profession of MFT, related professionals, and a variety of other stakeholders have a perspective about how a reasonable, prudent supervisor will supervise. For example, lawmakers define acceptable supervision in regulatory laws. Managed care companies define what they will believe is acceptable care and tie payment to this standard, and consumers have expectations about ways supervisors are looking out for them when they receive services from therapists who are in the process of becoming qualified clinicians. Supervisors seem increasingly accountable for their supervision to multiple stakeholders who seem highly invested in having quality supervision occur, but do not always agree about what constitutes quality. Overall, the standard of care for supervision seems more important than ever before, while being increasingly elusive to many supervisors. At times, some supervisors may even feel like they are supervising in a fog.

The Fog: Confusion in the Standard of Care for Supervision

After reviewing the literature and the standards for MFT supervision, my colleagues and I concluded that there are significant gaps between what is written as the standard for supervision and what constitutes the common practice of supervision (Storm, Todd, Sprenkle, & Morgan, in press). Gaps we found included: differences in what supervisors believe they are responsible for and what they will be held accountable for, the frequency in which multiple relationships occur in supervision even though the ethical code requires supervisors to avoid them, ideas about what the best methods of supervision are, and so on.

Tom Todd, Doug Sprenkle, Michael Morgan, and myself shared our ideas for dealing with the confusion during our institute at the 1999 annual conference. For example, due to the surprising lack of research support for the effectiveness of supervision, we confessed that we are more modest with supervisees, consumers, and the community at large about our effectiveness and are more realistic about what supervision can and can not accomplish. We noted that this particularly applies to our claims regarding the effectiveness of supervision, the protection of consumers, the success of our own and our supervisees [1] preferred therapy approaches, and the degree to which we actually serve as gatekeepers for the profession. We shared how helpful it has been to clearly define what responsibilities we are personally and professionally agreeing to assume when we take on the role of supervisor, and how we spell this out in a written, formal contract that is periodically reviewed. Because the public and legal view is that supervisors are overseeing supervisees' entire caseloads, we shared how we insist that supervision is frequent and extensive enough so we can responsibly oversee supervisees' caseloads. These were just a few of the ideas we presented. We have discussed the gaps we found and have suggested best practices for addressing them in an effort to refine the standard of care for supervision in a recent article (Storm, Todd, Sprenkle, & Morgan, in press).

Supervisors Respond and Cut a Path in the Fog

When we asked 1999 conference attendees for ideas about resolving the discrepancies, the group of advanced supervisors made several suggestions for addressing the confusion. They recommended:

• *Clarify, clarify, clarify.* Supervisors reaffirmed AAMFT as the chosen leader to clarify and set standards for supervision. They further proposed that AAMFT increase efforts to define the standard of care. Supervisors noted that our success in regulating marriage and family therapists has resulted in a miss mash of regulations regarding supervisor qualifications and supervision requirements that should be changed to meet a national standard.

• *Decrease isolation and increase connection among supervisors.* Support mechanisms should be developed for supervisors to use as they wrestle with determining the standard of care. Noting national, regional, and local differences that always exist in standard of care issues, supervisors suggested supervision tracts at divisional conferences and local forums for Approved Supervisors to interact with one another.

• *Conversation needed.* More dialogue was seen as critical between supervisors in training programs and training site supervisors, between supervisors and researchers, between postgraduate supervisors and those setting standards, and supervisors of various settings. Technology such as web sites, list serves, and so on was seen as an effective way to address this issue.

• *Creation of a community of supervisors.* Overall, supervisors wanted a community where supervisors support, problem-solve, keep each other abreast of changes, and hone their supervisory abilities.

Technology: Adding to the Density of the Fog

The use of technology in supervision seems to be adding to the confusion regarding the standard of care for supervision, but has not yet adequately been addressed by the supervision community (Long & Storm, in press). It requires us to do some thoughtful standard setting and clarification in a new and complex arena. For example, Steve Spinella, a therapist who works in Taiwan, recently asked if supervision could occur on-line. He first noted advantages of having access to a supervisor who could assist him with some very difficult cases in a timely manner without having to travel great distances. He further raised the difficulty in determining how much supervision had occurred even if on-line supervision was acceptable. If he sends an e-mail with his concerns and the supervisor responds with questions and ideas, would the credit for supervision be lines typed, time to read the material, or some newly created measuring unit? Supervision is currently defined as a personal encounter between supervisor/supervisee. Could the "face to face" be between a supervisor and a supervisee both in their own offices who are watching each other via their computers?

Supervisors are already wrestling with the effects of technology and confidentiality. They are assisting supervisees to distinguish when a cell phone can be appropriately used, such as in emergencies, and when it cannot be used to contact clients and supervisors. Similarly, distinguishing when is it appropriate to use e-mail to contact supervisors and clients, and what information can be included requires good ethical judgment on the part of supervisors and supervisees. Although some steps can be taken to make cases anonymous, this process raises serious questions about whether the supervision that is needed is actually occurring. Do the real supervisory issues emerge when cases are disguised? Do supervisees receive the assistance they need and do consumers receive the protection they deserve? Technology may very well add to the increasing accountability of supervisors due to the fast pace of information transfer. If supervision is delivered on-line, how responsive will supervisors be expected to be and to what degree will clinicians be expected to keep their supervisees informed about their work? What will the various stakeholders expect of supervisors in emergency situations? Will supervisors always be on call?

Finding Our Way Through the Fog

As supervisors, it seems to me that it is in our best interests to be proactive and vocal in our local communities and nationally with each other and with the other stakeholders to clarify and expand the standard of care for supervision. It seems to me that it is supervisors, like you and me, who know intimately the constraints and opportunities of everyday supervisory practice that should set the standard for the reasonable and prudent supervisor. Otherwise, we leave it up to the other stakeholders who may have little understanding of what is possible and realistically doable. Please join me in finding my way through the fog.

[1] A special thank you to the supervisors who attended the Advanced Supervision Institute (at AAMFT's 57th Annual Conference in Chicago) and so generously offered their suggestions to Tom Todd, Douglas Sprenkle, Michael Morgan, and myself.

References

Long, J., & Storm, C. (in press). Educational standards, supervision, and training issues in supervision. In C. Cole, A. Cole, and V. Frusha (Eds.) *Marriage and family therapy in the new millennium.*

Storm, C., Todd, T., Sprenkle, D., & Morgan, M. (in press). Gaps between mft supervision assumptions and common practice: Suggested best practices. *Journal of Marital and Family Therapy.*

(How) Am I Competent to Supervise?

Frank Thomas, Ph.D., Adam Coffey, M.S., Shari Scott, M.S., and Kristi Shappee

Published in the AAMFT Supervision Bulletin, Fall 2000.

Family therapy is fascinated with supervision. The literature is replete with articles focused on the theory, research, and practice of training and supervising MFTs. We are continuing this tradition, but we hope the direction we are taking is less familiar and opens new inquiries for us and for family therapy. As members of the Research on Training and Supervision (ROTS) Project at Texas Woman's University, we share a common interest in exploring facets of supervision that have not yet been exhausted, and our interests have both diverged and converged over the course of the project. Currently, we are investigating the following areas:

- context (influence of public and religious training contexts),
- culture (international trainee supervisory experiences),
- virtuoso supervision (i.e., what makes a "master supervisor" [as nominated by trainees] masterful),
- the market (factors that influence choice of supervisors in the open market, utilizing the Internet for surveying temporary licensed mental health professionals),
- the development of therapist expertise,
- the experiences of trainees across theoretical orientations, and,
- perspectives of personal competence.

We are very open to connecting with others in the field and are interested in combining efforts when our curiosities overlap. [1]

Views of Competency

One research question seemed to pull all of us together as we began our investigations: What do we know about how supervisors view themselves? Our curiosity led us to impressions of competence and expertise as well as ideas around the forming of relationships: How do supervisors view their competence to supervise? What do they feel qualifies them to supervise? And (when they have choices), what goes into forming supervisory relationships? We sampled 44 professionals who supervise family therapists, nearly all of whom are AAMFT Approved Supervisors. [2] Fifty-seven percent (25 of the 44) e-mailed responses to our preliminary questions so far, and we were able to analyze 20 responses for this article. Thirteen males and 7 females representing 3 countries replied, including 3 ethnic minority respondents. Considering the hectic lives these professionals lead, we think the high return rate and their enthusiasm around these questions indicates an important need for further inquiry. We thought it would be interesting for MFT supervisors to read and reflect on some preliminary themes from our respondents.

We will only cover two areas of this venture in this article. Item #1 was: What qualifies a person to supervise family therapy? Then we asked for a response to Item #2: (Assuming you believe you are competent to supervise family therapists, please respond to this) "I am qualified to supervise family therapists because..." The responses were analyzed for recurring themes (Huberman & Miles, 1998). The following themes stimulated our conversations and views of our own supervisory competencies and relationships, so we thought you would be stimulated by them as well.

Item #1: What Qualifies a Person to Supervise Family Therapy?

Value-Saturated Interaction. These supervisors believe every MFT supervisor should hold to certain patterns of interaction around values and process. They hold the autonomy of the supervisee in high regard, stating that supervision should first and foremost benefit the supervisee's development. By holding both not-knowing (Anderson & Goolishian, 1991) and what we have come to call "not-cloning" positions, interaction should promote the agentive formation of the supervisee. They feel one must have the ability to maintain a process of supervision that includes both teaching and relating to mutual interests in order to promote this trainee progression. Some excerpts might help illustrate this theme:

S7: I believe that one is ready to supervise family therapy when one... is able to allow [a] supervisee to be a competent clinician as him/herself and not as a carbon copy or clone of the supervisor... I bring to the supervisory situation a willingness and receptiveness to support supervisees to be themselves and to grow as clinicians whether or not I approve of how they conduct therapy... today's maverick/heretic can be tomorrow's standard.

S8: He/she must have an appreciation for someone else's skill and point of view and use those to help the supervisee to grow professionally and develop his/her own style.

Meeting Personal and Professional Standards. These supervisors say that simply achieving AAMFT Approved Supervisor status is not enough. Having extensive clinical experience as well as strong family therapy educational backgrounds are necessary qualifications to these supervisors.

S5: [A supervisor must have] experience in doing family therapy [to qualify]. It takes knowing how to do it to help someone else learn how to do it.

S7: Being qualified [by satisfying specific requirements] does not... competency, effectiveness or readiness make... I'm not comfortable with the current practice of a new Ph.D. leaving school with a degree and a[n] [Approved] Supervisor's designation in the same hand.

Think Like an MFT. Many said that one must be theoretically sophisticated to qualify as an MFT supervisor, clearly fitting with the tradition known as systemic therapy.

S8: An MFT supervisor should really know and understand systemic practice and work according to those principles.

S14: I am not crazy about the idea of a person from another profession training me to be something they [sic] are not, i.e., a psychologist supervising family therapy. If we truly believe that we are a distinct discipline with our own literature base and set of rules and regulations as a discipline [ethics], then how can I expect someone from a different profession to train me in the basics of a profession to which the trainer does not belong? What is basic to qualifying persons to supervise family therapy is that they are part of the profession.

Item #2: I am Qualified to Supervise Family Therapists Because...

The second item elicited similar responses, but there were some noteworthy differences. In addition to the first three themes above, the following emerged as central ideas:

The Value of the Relationship. Relationship values are central to the personal qualifications of these supervisors. Respect, collaboration, and validation were key themes that were not general supervisory themes from Item #1.

S13: I am supportive and respectful of [supervisees]. I get a much bigger kick out of seeing my students progress professionally than I do out of receiving personal accolades.

S17: Despite my many imperfections, trainees experience me as committed to them as people and students, and even the targets of my sharp tongue can eventually acknowledge my support for their work.

Supervisor Skill Development and Personal Growth. Their continuing growth is vital to their personal qualifications, even though they do not hold ongoing development as a standard for all qualifying supervisors in the field.

S2: I am willing to learn from my supervisees, clients, [and] new situations... I recognize that I don't know everything and believe myself [to be] a life-long student and learner.

S3: Carl Whitaker once said it takes 10 years to become a therapist. I believe the same is true of becoming a supervisor. Of course, it does not mean we cannot supervise before that time, it is just that we do not become "one with the practice" until some time has passed.

S15: [After all these years,] I still think that I am a beginner.

New Questions... and Application

Four of our team of 7 supervise, and the process of articulating our personal thoughts as well as developing conversations around competency have led us in two distinct directions. First, we feel that any response a supervisor writes will be incomplete without other sources of information; that is, we are pursuing supervisee views of supervision to develop a richer perspective of ourselves. How I am competent to supervise depends on interaction with and the perspectives of supervisees. Without these perspectives, our view is always incomplete.[3] Second, we see the need to include the voices of clients in our views of competence. If effective supervision develops competent clinicians, should not others influenced by our services inform the process?

We propose you write your own responses to these items: What qualifies a person to supervise family therapy? and, I am qualified to supervise family therapists because... Reviewing your personal standards may result in re-forming the values, theory, and practice of your supervision, and we welcome all responses to this exercise as we continue our own personal and professional examinations.

Postscript

Most of our colleagues in this research were passionate about their responses, including comments such as these:

S2: [These are] very tough questions and forces one to search one's soul and review and remind [one]self about what is important and what is not. I think this set of questions should be asked of supervisors at least once a year... I don't think that's asking a lot, considering the responsibility we all have.

S4: This has been a really good exercise in reflecting on what I do and how I do it.

S9: As you can tell, I am still trying to figure out this business. [This] manage[d] to make me think.

S15: I have been thinking [about these questions] the whole week... I thank you for sending the questions. It was an honor.

We hope you find new passions to examine your supervisory identity and practice.

---

[1] Feel free to contact us at FThomas@twu.edu.
[2] Because we invited supervisors internationally, not all hold this credential. Confidentiality was promised to all respondents.
[3] See Ratliff, Wampler, & Morris (2000) as well as Metcalf, Thomas, Miller, Hubble, & Duncan (1996) and Laszloffy (2000) for studies in this area.

References

Anderson, H. & Goolishian, H. (1991). "Not knowing": A critical element of a Collaborative Language Systems therapy. In D. Sollee (Ed.), Constructing the future: AAMFT 1991 Annual Conference, Dallas, Texas. Washington, DC: AAMFT.

Huberman, A. M., & Miles, M. B. (1998). Data management and analysis methods. In N. K. Denzin, & Y. S. Lincoln (Eds.), *Collecting and interpreting qualitative materials* (pp. 179–210). Thousand Oaks, CA: Sage.

Laszloffy, T.A. (2000). The implications of client satisfaction feedback for beginning family therapists: Back to the basics. *Journal of Marital and Family Therapy*, 26, 391–397.

Metcalf, L., Thomas, F.N., Miller, S.D., Hubble, M.A., & Duncan, B. (1996). Client and therapist perceptions of solution focused brief therapy: A qualitative analysis. In S.D. Miller, M.A. Hubble, & Duncan, B. (Eds.), *Handbook of solution-focused brief therapy: Foundations, applications, and research* (pp. 335–349). San Francisco: Jossey-Bass.

Ratliff, D.A., Wampler, K.S., & Morris, G.H.B. (2000). Lack of consensus in supervision. *Journal of Marital and Family Therapy*, 26, 373–384.

Shifting From Supervision to Superaudition

Bradford P. Keeney, Ph.D. and Wendel A. Ray, M.S.W.

Published in the AAMFT Supervision Bulletin, Vol. V, No. 2, June 1992.

Scholars have critiqued the hegemony of *vision* in Western culture (Ong, 1977; Tyler, 1987). Their argument is that sight is given an unfair, privileged status over sound (and other sensory modalities) in a wide variety of contexts. For instance, in court when you say you saw it, it's the "evidence of an eye-witness," whereas if you say you heard it, it's "mere hearsay." In therapy, we easily recognize the meaning and relevance of *supervision*, but are puzzled when the sensory metaphor shifts to "superaudition." In this article we explore the possibilities offered to therapy when we introduce the notion of *superaudited* (or *superheard*) clinical work.

Supervised clinical work reaches its fullest expression with an observer supervising behind a one-way mirror. Superaudition, on the other hand, would deconstruct the primary emphasis on the seen, perhaps by closing a curtain on the mirror. Observers would be placed in the dark, either in the clinical room or an adjacent place. In this absence of vision, blinded observers become doubly reliant upon their hearing. In this situation, supervisors are set up to superaudit (or superhear).

Superaudition would emphasize the technology of sound, placing more emphasis on sensitive microphones and audio mixing rather than cameras and lenses. The production of audiotapes would challenge the supremacy of videotapes. Qualities of the spoken word, such as tonality, timbre, loudness, pitch, cadence, frequency, rhythm, resonance, and melody would be addressed. Superauditors of a session could phone in therapeutic suggestions to change the resonance of a spoken word, direct a therapist to speak more softly, or instruct a client in how to change pitch.

A whole host of unique therapeutic strategies could be derived from an emphasis on the heard. Imagine a superauditor entering a session with the following suggestions: "I hear the lyrics of what you're saying, but I can't hear the music. Why don't you repeat what you just said by singing it to them? Just sing whatever melody comes out."

Any emphasis upon the heard may also directly address the rhythms of therapy. Percussion instruments could be used to accompany and underscore client therapist talk. Consider this intervention: "I think what you said was in 4/4 time. Let me grab my brushes and cymbal and accompany you this time...Now, say it again, and I'll provide the rhythm— one, two, one, two, three, four..."

A voice synthesizer would provide further intervention possibilities. A child's voice could be heard as an older adult, or a parent's voice could be transformed into that of an infant. The therapist's voice could change age or sex, or even become a chorus; it could be changed into the sound of another creature or instrument. Clearly, new advantages arise when the seen is made less clear and the heard's status is amplified in therapy. Supervisors are invited to experiment with suspending their habits of critical vision and have an experience in a session where the heard is given a more privileged status. Putting on shades to block the light sometimes helps one hear the beat.

References

Ong, W. J. (1977). *Interfaces of the world: Studies in the evolution of consciousness and culture.* Ithaca: Cornell University Press.

Tyler, S. A. (1987). *The unspeakable: Discourse, dialogue, and rhetoric in the post-modern world.* Madison: University of Wisconsin Press.

Supervisor and Supervisee: The Picture Takers

Cheryl H. Litzke, M.F.T.

Published in the AAMFT Supervision Bulletin, Vol. VII, No. 3, Fall 1994.

Cameras are used to view and to capture for future reference. The "camera" I use has a wide-angle lens which is both the starting and foundational point for conceptualizing systemically. It also has a zoom lens which can be used for assessment at the individual level of the system. The genogram is the three-dimensional photograph of the family. I use it as a standard tool for looking at the family multigenerationally. The wide-angle lens helps me take in the larger ecosystem of societal systems as well as prevailing socioeconomic, cultural and political phenomena. At this point, my thinking and practice have evolved to include some kind of retroflexive attachment that would take into account the "picture taker," i.e., the treating professional, as well as the "subject of focus," i.e., the family. If all observations are "observer-dependent" (Anderson & Rambo, 1988) how can the "picture-taker" not be a part of the ecological system where treatment is to occur?

Chapter 3

Supervisor-Therapist-Client Relationships

Supervisors as Social Engineers: Creating Family Therapy–Friendly Organizations: An Interview with Salvador Minuchin

Interview conducted by Cheryl Storm, AAMFT Supervision Bulletin editor, with Salvador Minuchin, M.D.

Published in the AAMFT Supervision Bulletin, Vol. VI, No. 3, Fall 1993.

Storm: *What are the assumptions underlying your supervision?*

Minuchin: My emphasis is on learning the style and personality of the therapist. Therapists are the unique instrument that is brought to therapy. However, they always have a partial view. Every encounter, whether supervision or therapy, is a limited encounter. Therapists are always limited by their own history, personality, etc. I believe that, like families, therapists are idiosyncratic. Supervision for therapist A is very different than if is for therapist X. In group supervision, supervisee Y knows that I would not tell supervisee X the same thing. It would not be useful. The supervisor enters into the supervision process to expand the therapist's style by creating a larger repertoire of interventions. Each therapist will finish their work with me in a different way. Therapists should be richer by being less limited than when they came.

Storm: *There has been a recent trend in supervision of flattening the hierarchy between supervisor and therapist with an emphasis on collaboration. This is in contrast to the idea of a supervisor as an expert. In your opinion, must a supervisor be an expert?*

Minuchin: If not, why should supervisors be paid? People hire therapists, not friends. Likewise, therapists hire supervisors, not friends. By definition therapists and supervisors are experts. They are being paid for their expertise and use of themselves in a particular way. The field is divided at this point in the way we see the therapist and thus the supervisor. These notions seem to stem from constructivist ideas. The claiming of the lack of expertise is absurd. Constructivists use their "expertness" in a particular way. They define themselves as experts in organizing, manipulating, and expanding stories. Therapists, like supervisors, whether willingly or unwillingly, wittingly or unwittingly, are an influence. These influences are idiosyncratic. Families and therapists will be different with a different therapist and supervisor. Therapists who do not know this will be blind to their influence. If I know the directions of my influence, my influence will be respectful. If I do not know this, my influence will be generic, inefficient, and perhaps disrespectful.

Storm: *Recently you wrote that families are shaped by the realities of age, disease, ethnic identity, class, race, gender, and economics. Some would argue that an expert stance does not account for these realities. Supervisors and therapists would have to be an expert in all areas.*

Minuchin: I see it completely differently. As I've grown and become more of an expert with working with different groups, I have become more effective. Today, I am an expert on law, the judicial system, the child welfare system—how they demand certain responses from families. People do not live within their heads. The social political context organizes the ways that families live.

Storm: *Some supervisors would argue that the role of the therapist is to empower families to deal with these systems.*

Minuchin: This is naive. These supervisors don't understand the social context. They are ignorant of society's control of families and the powerful effect of welfare institutions. Maybe it isn't naive but a middle-class view.

Storm: *Another trend in supervision is to look at therapists' strengths rather than emphasizing teaching a model, skills, or specific interventions. This seems counter to your style of supervision.*

Or is this a misreading of your work?

Minuchin: I work with the expansion of people. I do focus on strengths, but also on the absences, the edges, the narrowness. People learn in a variety of ways. Some through words and listening, some through acting, some by experiencing. My supervision takes therapists as individuals. It is as complex as therapy. My supervision can be supportive, loving, and seductive. Or it can be stressful. There is no one particular way of supervising. I don't believe one must be positive. I use positive and negative emotions in supervision. I work to create contexts through enactments to create alternative experiences in therapy. My supervision is to create alternative experiences for therapists.

Storm: *When you are working with a therapist whose clients are involved with professionals from several agencies, then do you create a context for the therapist, other professional and family to interact in a new way? To have a new experience? Am I following you?*

Minuchin: No, then I become a social engineer. It becomes essential to understand the politics of the organization. For example, I currently supervise a therapist working in a school setting. As I watched his first presentation, I saw him as helping the parents become more controlling of an adolescent. I began to talk with him about how his school was helping him contain the adolescent. Although he is very bright, he is constrained by his position in the field. His job organized his thinking about his case. Supervision then becomes looking at his context and freeing him from the constraints of his context. As a supervisor, I must enter into the world organizational politics. I am also supervising a director of a psychiatric hospital. To help the therapist change to work with families I must first help the hospital change the way they do intakes. We then realized that we had to change the way the hospital was constructed to arrange for space to interview families. We must create new social structures that are family therapy friendly.

Storm: *So you would encourage supervisors to be willing to get involved in organizational politics and not shy away from them?*

Minuchin: Absolutely. If agencies and institutions remain individually oriented, training family therapists is disfavor to the field. If we do not change the mental health delivery system, we have failed.

Storm: *How can supervisors create change in agencies?*

Minuchin: Supervisors should work with agency hierarchies in a way that they can effect change. If you are working with therapists that are low in the hierarchy, you are creating an unhappy context for them. We must not work at the level of individuals but must find the champions of family therapy within the system and change the larger context. Overall, we need to change the mindset of the larger system by working with individuals to create family-friendly institutional contexts.

Storm: *If an agency is not open to becoming more family therapy friendly but a therapist is, would you be willing to still supervise her?*

Minuchin: I would say to the therapist that she cannot work in this agency and be a family therapist. In our work we will be too limited by the agency.

A Matter of Balance: Challenging and Supporting Supervisees

Peter Goldenthal, Ph.D.

Published in the AAMFT Supervision Bulletin, Vol. VII, No. 2, Spring 1994.

Supervision, regardless of theoretical orientation, involves balancing competing demands regarding the supervision process. All supervisors place importance on their particular theoretical orientation in supervision. For example, in supervising family therapists, I tend to focus on contextual therapy concepts such as loyalty, constructive and destructive entitlement and multidirected partiality. All supervisors naturally have their own sets of constructs and frameworks to offer to their supervisees.

But when it comes to the process of supervision, we have much more in common than might be suggested by widely varying theoretical orientations. Many of these common ingredients in supervision involve achieving a delicate balance between competing pressures. Most supervisors agree that supervision requires balancing: (1) the needs of supervisees and clients; (2) supervisory responsibilities to supervisees and clients; (3) support for supervisees while challenging them, as appropriate; (4) a focus on clients with a focus on supervisees' professional growth; (5) discussions of immediate clinical and practical decisions regarding cases and more general clinical issues; and (6) the emphasis on technique and case management issues with discussions, directed readings, etc. designed to help supervisees develop their own coherent theoretical rationale.

One final matter of balance involves juggling supervisory assessments of what experiences will benefit supervisees with facilitating conversations regarding supervisees experience of supervision (i.e., what is working well and what is not). One of the issues that has concerned me the most has been the difficulty of achieving a balance between challenge and support, and of finding a way to gauge this balance in terms of supervisees' experiences. Minuchin (1993) believes that supervisors are being paid for their expertise perhaps implying a rejection of egalitarian, non-hierarchical or "democratic" approaches to supervision. Few would quarrel with the notion that supervisees are entitled to our best judgment, guidance and expertise in exchange for their payment, whether direct or indirect. I feel, however, supervision by its nature is a more collegial endeavor than therapy, one that benefits from dialogue and free feedback from supervisee to supervisor.

Dr. T., a psychologist, pursued a program of family therapy training and supervision with me. In addition to his private practice, Dr. T. regularly provided consultation to a state agency responsible for evaluating allegations of child abuse and neglect and for protecting children who had been subjected to alleged instances of such abuse and neglect. As the consultant, Dr. T. was often asked for his input on the most difficult and complex cases. At times, Dr. T.'s views about what would be most beneficial for clients conflicted with those espoused by the agency. In a number of these instances, I strongly encouraged Dr. T. to take a stand on behalf of his clients and his beliefs. At that time, however, I was concerned that what I felt to be "encouragement" might have been experienced by Dr. T. as intrusive pushiness or as a demand that he see things my way. The case below provides one illustration of this situation.

Wally had been removed from his mother's home due to a history of parental neglect and placed in foster care. Supervision on this case, reflecting the supervisor's contextual orientation, (e.g., Boszormenyi-Nagy, Grunebaum, & Ukich, 1991; Goldenthal, 1993) focused on the value of being actively partial to Ms. Smith, Wally's mother, despite her past failings as a parent, as well as to Wally and to his foster family. As the result of her work with Dr. T., Ms. Smith made a great deal of progress, was able to see the ways she had unwittingly harmed her son, no longer used drugs or alcohol, and very much wanted to develop a better relationship with him. She recognized that at least for the short term he might benefit from the foster placement, but she hoped for visits, joint therapy sessions, telephone calls and other things that would facilitate their eventual reunification. Unfortunately, the foster parents were unable to see Ms. Smith's positive side, felt that she would continue to be harmful to her son, and hoped to adopt Wally at some point. They actively discouraged Wally from visiting his mother or from participating in the joint therapy sessions. In supervision, Dr. T. was consistently encouraged to maintain his stand that Wally could benefit from the support of his foster family and from a renewed relationship with his mother, and that any attempt to impede his mother from her wish for closeness might well backfire, ultimately harming Wally, his mother and the foster family.

The unanswered questions were, "What did Dr. T. experience through this process? Did he feel that I was supporting him in taking a firm stand? Or did he feel that I had pushed him into a confrontation with the agency he worked for, potentially creating a difficult working environment or even endangering the stability of his consulting relationship?" This issue was discussed between supervisor and supervisee (see transcript below) along with other similar situations in which the supervisor had encouraged the supervisee to take strong stands consistent with his own values and clinical judgment.

References

Boszormenyi-Nagy, I., Grunebaum, J., & Ulrich, D. (1991). Contextual therapy, In A. Gurman & D. P. Kniskern (Eds)., *Handbook of family therapy,* (vol. 2. pp. 200–238). New York: Brunner/Mazel.

Goldenthal, P. (1993). *Contextual family therapy: Assessment and intervention procedures.* Sarasota: Professional Resource Press.

Minuchin, S. (1993). Supervisors as social engineers: Creating family therapy friendly organizations, *Supervision Bulletin. VI,* (3).

Transcript of A Conversation About Balance Between Peter Goldenthal and Dr. T.

PG: *As we worked together on this case were there ever times when it felt like I was pushing you too hard?*

Dr. T.: Sometimes when we talked I was less assertive or unsure regarding the specific action I wanted to take. You made the point real clear. In this very complex system where there are a lot of other variables (e.g., my relationship with the agency, with other workers) sometimes it's not easy to see the most crucial, urgent issue.

PG: *I'm very interested in whether your reaction was one of being pushed or of being supported in taking a direction you were already headed in.*

Dr. T.: I think that some of the time I didn't realize at first the need to take action. In our discussions, you guided me to that realization adn to some steps. I knew something had to be done but I wasn't 100% sure or confident of the exact thing to do. I do think that if there were a point where you insisted and I felt strongly I would have moderated your input and done it my way, I ultimately have the responsibility of the consequences. I have thought about this before. There have been times that I've thought, "Oh boy, I'm going to do this, but, my God, what's going to happen?" Some of the things I've done have certainly sent the system spinning for a while. I didn't know how they were going to take it, sort of stirring up trouble, but the argument of what's best for the parent, the child, and the child's offspring was a very strong approach.

PG: *So would it be fair to say that you have felt both supported and pushed?*

Dr. T.: Yes, I would say so. I think that sometimes the most crucial issues are embedded in the system's complexity where we may not see or attend to them. Sometimes the "push" you give makes me focus on that central issue. I was missing the issue because I was thinking of the other psychologist seeing Wally and her concerns with doing the right thing in rigidly following the agency's instructions and in refusing to do any family therapy.

Supervisory Power as an Asset...

Brian Grant, Ph.D.

Published in the AAMFT Supervision Bulletin, Vol. VIII, No. 1, Spring 1995

The supervisor's power is typically what the supervisee is paying for. Surely it is a greater violation for supervisors to fail to exercise power for which they are paid, than to disproportionately overuse the air time and the hour, or under-attend to supervisees' growing mastery and feelings.

The issue is more: What balance of overt supervisor/supervisee power is most useful for the supervisee's maturation as a therapist? I suggest finding an answer to this question has been complicated in recent years by a growing belief, at least in the professional community, that it is always inappropriate and sadistic for someone with greater power to act in a way that makes someone with lesser power uncomfortable. This idea greatly complicates providing useful supervisory evaluations or suggesting that supervisees might have to learn to master behavior that currently makes them anxious. It interferes with assessment of whether some supervisees' ideas about human interaction are flatly in error. None of us likes running into situations in which our ideas are called into question, our behaviors are challenged or our personal maturity is visibly suspect. But I'm also confident that all of us remember situations in which precisely those experiences, when viewed from the distance of a few months or years, are seen as life saving and power enhancing. Hence, I argue that the best time for supervisees to evaluate their supervisors' usefulness to them is many months after the actual events being evaluated. As with parenting, or any other process focusing on the enhancement of another's development, some of the most important things that are done are painful to the recipients of the input. This does not necessarily make them either ethically inappropriate or technically useless.

It clearly is part of supervisors' responsibility to monitor supervisees' anxiety and distress, modify their own behavior so that the aforementioned anxiety does not debilitate the learning process, and refrain from humiliating or tormenting supervisees for gratification of supervisors' power needs or intrinsic sadism. Certainly supervisors have a responsibility for encouraging ongoing conversation about the extent to which this is happening, as well as monitoring unconscious communication that would suggest it is happening. But there does come a point in very effective supervision where what supervisors need to say to supervisees boils down to, "Your discomfort with our last interaction stems from your wanting something from me that it's not appropriate for me to provide. It requires some personal maturation from you, perhaps enhanced by your exchange with your own therapist, rather than a change in my behavior."

Such a statement from supervisors is subject to corrective feedback, from the trainee and from a broader community that oversees both of their work. But, if supervisors are not in a position to make that demand on supervisees, to use their power to call a student to accountability for ongoing growth, then the supervisory process cannot be of the rigor required to consistently upgrade the practice of this profession. On the other hand, if supervisees have no recourse when confronted with what feels like sadism or humiliation, then we merely reenact the political hierarchies of all of our nightmares. What is necessary to prevent both distortions is a community of discourse in which those who have experience and knowledge, and those who are seeking to get it, are honored; and in which the primary criterion is growth of therapists and clients rather than the comfort of either supervisors or supervisees.

Four Dimensions Deemed Essential to Quality Supervision: Theoretical, Personal, and Empirical Account

Stephen A. Anderson, Ph.D., Sandra A. Rigazio-DiGilio, Ph.D., Margaret Cochran-Schlossberg and Sylvia Meredith

Published in the AAMFT Supervision Bulletin, Vol. 10, No. 3, Winter 1998.

Faculty and students at the University of Connecticut explored the question of what comprises a good supervisory relationship. We wanted to determine the themes that would emerge when various sources of information on this question were examined. We decided to uncover these themes by first reflecting upon our own personal experiences as supervisors, supervisors-in-training, and supervisees. Additionally, we conducted a review of the supervisory literature across mental health disciplines. Finally, we collected survey data, asking supervisees at various stages of MFT training, to reflect upon the supervision experiences they had thus far encountered as part of their training. The survey was completed by 160 supervisees from 45 of the 52 MFT training programs—in the U.S. and Canada—that held COAMFTE accreditation or candidacy status. Using these three information sources, we were able to classify four dimensions that supervisees deem essential to ensuring quality supervision environments and experiences. As the four dimensions emerged from the responses of students at different stages of MFT training who had experienced both individual and group supervision as well as a variety of clinical and supervisory environments, we assume that these dimensions are seen as important by supervisees across all phases and components of MFT training. We recognize, however, that any supervisory relationship undergoes change as it evolves and as the needs of the supervisee change over time and in response to different circumstances. As such, we also assume that the importance of each dimension maybe weighted differently during differing phases of training, within various clinical and supervisory contexts, and in relation to the unique needs and learning styles of each supervisee (Rigazio-DiGilio & Anderson, 1994).

The first dimension that emerged as important to quality supervision was a sense of openness in the supervisory environment. This reflects the supervisor's willingness to foster a learning environment where mistakes are viewed as a likely and important part of the learning process (Ladany, Hill, Corbett, & Nutt, 1996), and where supervisees are encouraged to explore and experiment (Allen, Szollos, & Williams, 1986; Worthen & McNeil, 1996). This type of environment additionally promotes a reciprocal feedback process wherein supervisors regularly provide feedback to supervisees regarding their strengths, limitations, and progress, and supervisees provide feedback to the supervisor. Supervisors are seen as self-disclosing and as providing opportunities for supervisees to see one another's work. The propensity toward encouraging supervisees to expose their clinical work and to risk exposing their imperfections provides avenues that offer supervisees valuable feedback from their peers as well as their supervisors. Finally, this environment promotes an acceptance of differences in opinions, values, life experiences, and theoretical orientations.

However, it is important that an environment of openness be counterbalanced with a clear and definable structure for the supervision experience. It is important for supervisees to be clear about their supervisor's expectations and that the goals and tasks of the supervision be mutually agreed upon (Ladany & Friedlander, 1995).

The second dimension of importance related to respect, support and encouragement. This dimension encompasses the various ways supervisors communicate with their supervisees. MFT students found it essential that their supervisors convey the message that they as supervisees, are important and valued. This is accomplished, in part, by the supervisor regularly providing praise and encouragement.

Worthen and McNeil (1996) referred to this as

the supervisor, "conveying an attitude that manifested empathy, a nonjudgemental stance toward [the supervisee], and a sense of validation or affirmation" (p. 29). This dimension was also represented by the degree to which supervisors arranged a regular schedule for supervision sessions, and then adhered to this schedule. Maintaining a regular schedule of supervisory sessions demonstrates a respect for the personal time demands of the supervisee and communicates that the supervisor values the supervisee as a colleague. Respect, support, and encouragement also are perceived to be conveyed by the supervisor who is accessible to the supervisee outside of the regular schedule, should this need arise.

A third dimension seen as important to quality supervision was the personal growth of the supervisee. Despite the debate that has often engrossed the field as to the value of personal growth versus technical skills, available research suggests that supervisees value the personal growth dimension of the supervisory experience (c.f., Allen, et al., 1986; Nelson, 1978; Sumerel & Borders, 1996; Worthen & McNeil, 1996). This dimension involves the supervisor's own modeling of an investment in personal growth. It further entails supervisors' willingness to directly confront their supervisees' blind spots. Personal growth often involves such issues as increasing the supervisee's self awareness, capacity for empathy with clients, tolerance for a broader range and intensity of clients' affective expressions, and a willingness to process one's own emotional reactions to client behaviors (Anderson, Rigazio-DiGilio, & Kunkler, 1995; Aponte, 1994; Atkinson, 1997; Sumeral & Borders, 1996). Finally, personal growth entails understanding the connections between one's own family of origin experiences and one's reactions to clients (Anderson & Holmes, in press; McDaniel & Landau-Stanton, 1991).

The fourth dimension that emerged as important to quality supervision was conceptual and technical guidance and direction. This dimension involves the supervisor teaching supervisees various conceptual frameworks and assessment skills that can assist supervisees to understand clients seeking treatment. It further involves teaching supervisees practical intervention skills that help them to address specific clinical issues, as well as helping them to develop the necessary relationship skills to establish a working alliance of trust with clients. Although various "schools" of family therapy may differ in their views of just what skills are needed in order for family therapy to be effective, all acknowledge the importance of supervisees developing such skills (Anderson, et al., 1995; Avis & Sprenkle, 1990). And although the supervisees in our survey tended to place greater relative importance on the personal growth dimension than on the acquisition of specific skills, they too recognized the value of the skill dimension (c.f., Allen et al., 1986; Sumerel & Borders, 1996; Worthen & McNeil, 1996). Supervisees like to be taught practical skills and they appreciate receiving feedback and guidance that is direct and straightforward. They also prefer to have their supervisors demonstrate their own therapeutic skills directly (Allen et al., 1986).

In contrast to the above facilitative dimensions, a number of supervisor qualities were perceived by these students to be related to poor supervisory experiences. The first, mirroring the opposite of the first facilitating dimension, can be described as a sense of rigidity and conformity in the supervisory environment. This occurs when supervisors encourage unthinking conformity, do not tolerate divergent viewpoints, and emphasize traditional gender or sex role stereotypes. In such an environment, student weaknesses and shortcomings are more likely to be emphasized, along with a heavy emphasis on evaluation. A second negative quality, in juxtaposition to the second facilitating dimension, was the supervisor not valuing the supervision as important and significant. This is seen to be evident when supervisors frequently cancel sessions, seem preoccupied with personal problems or other matters, and allow frequent distractions and interruptions to occur during supervisory sessions. A third negative dimension is the supervisor operating in an intrusive or sexist manner. This occurs when the supervisor makes sexual advances, uses sexist language, devalues the supervisee on the basis of gender, or treats the supervisee like a sex object. It also occurs when the supervisor violates the supervisee's personal privacy by pressing for more personal disclosure than the supervisee is comfortable providing (Allen et al. 1986; Atkinson, 1996; Worthen).

Although others have proposed qualities that make the supervisory experience a positive or negative one, we believe that the dimensions described above capture much of what is essential. We have consulted a wide variety of sources in deriving these dimensions.

It is our hope that these will provide useful guidelines for supervisors and supervisees in determining what is and is not helpful in their own supervisory experiences.

References

Allen, G. J., Szollos, S. J., & Williams, B. E. (1986). Doctoral students' comparative evaluations of best and worst psychotherapy supervision. *Professional Psychology: Research and Practice*, 17, 91-99

Anderson, S. A, & Holmes, S. (in press). Personal mythologies: A framework for dealing with therapeutic an supervisory impasses. In S. Krippner, L. Gray, & M. Bova (Eds.), *The psychotherapeutic use of narrative*. New York: Irving Publishers.

Anderson, S.A., Rigazio-DiGilio, S. A., & Kunkler, K. P (1995). Training and supervision in family therapy: Current issues and future directions. *Family Relations* 44 489-500.

Aponte, H. J. (1994). How personal can training get? *Journal of Marital and Family Therapy*. 20, 3-15.

Atkinson, B. J. (1997). Risks and safeguards in person-of-the-therapist supervision. *The Supervision Bulletin*, 9(3), 4-5.

Avis, J. M., & Sprenkle, D. H. (1990). Outcome research on family therapy training: A substantive and methodological review. *Journal of Marital and Family Therapy* 16, 241-264.

Ladany, N., & Friedlander, M. L. (1995). The relationship between the supervisory working alliance and trainees' experience of role conflict and role ambiguity. *Counselor Education and Supervision*, 34, 220-231.

Ladany, N., Hill, C. E., Corbett, M. M., & Nutt, E.A. (1996). Nature, extent, and importance of what psychotherapy trainees do not disclose to supervisors. *Journal of Counseling Psychology*, 43, 10-24.

McDaniel, S. H., & Landau-Stanton, J. (1991). Family of origin work and family therapy skills training: Both-and. *Family Process*, 30, 459-471.

Nelson, G. L. (1978). Psychotherapy supervision from the trainee's point of view: A survey of preferences. *Professional Psychology*, 9, 539-550.

Rigazio-DiGilio, S. A., & Anderson, S. A. (1994). A Cognitive-Developmental Model for marital and family therapy supervision. *The Clinical Supervisor*, 11, 93-118.

Sumerel, M. B., & Borders, L. D. (1996). Addressing personal issues in supervision: Impact of counselors' experience level on various aspects of the supervisory relationship. *Counselor Education and Supervision*, 35, 268-286.

Worthen, V & McNeil, B. W. (1996). A phenomenological investigation of "good" supervision events. *Journal of Counseling Psychology*, 43, 25–34.

The MSU/FTQ: Obtaining Client Feedback About Theory-Driven Interventions

Robert E. Lee, Ph.D.

Published in the AAMFT Supervision Bulletin, Vol. 10, No. 2, Fall 1997.

A therapeutic alliance involves shared goals and enough of a relationship to support work on those goals. It can be cultivated by asking clients to help guide the process of therapy. This empowers clients relative to the other members of the training system, and allows them to say what they need and how the therapist is doing. Supervisors, therapists, and clients can benefit from the client's picture of what therapy looks like when it is going well. This picture reminds all parties of their positive synergism and alerts them to what should continue or be increased.

This is true throughout the course of supervision and treatment. Just as it is not unreasonable for a supervisor to periodically debrief the therapist, asking him or her what the supervisor is doing that the trainee finds helpful, the therapist should periodically consult the client. Supervisors and therapists may question how much to weigh and to implement what each other and the clients say, depending on the circumstances. However, it seems prudent to seek feedback.

Open-ended or Directive Questioning?

The nature of the information acquired depends on how the client is asked. If more or less open-ended questions are used (Bischoff, McKeel, Moon & Sprenkle, 1996: Quinn, 1996; Quinn, Nagirreddy, Lawless, & Bagley, 1996; Sells, Smith & Moon, 1996), clients reveal those things therapists do that *the clients think* are important to the resolution of their problems.

The Michigan State University Family Therapy Questionnaire (MSU/FTQ, Lee, Emerson, & Koch ka. 1997) is a more directive approach. It is a relatively exhaustive list of 74 generic, structural, strategic, brief, and transgenerational family therapy interventions culled from the literature and translated into layperson's language. Driven by theory and "accepted practices." It asks clients to evaluate things *theorists have said* are important to successful family therapy based on formulations about symptom formation, behavioral maintenance, and systemic change. Although some theorists (Anderson. 1993; Hoffman-Hennessy, 1993) would encourage therapists to do so, it does not seem prudent to overlook decades of reflection and practice, deconstruct therapy, and operate solely on what the client says. Instead, it is more reasonable to formally put clients in the context of the profession and its theory-driven assumptions and ask them their experience of these. The MSU/ FTQ does precisely that.

The marital and family therapy client uses the MSU/ FTQ to provide feedback about the effectiveness of therapy by indicating whether or not specific interventions occurred and their importance to the client. When the MSU/FTQ is used for training, the assumption is that if the client tells the therapist that something the therapist has been doing is "important," the therapist should pay attention to that and continue to do it. The MSU/FTQ also can alert the therapist to things not being done. In short, the MSU/FTQ is a checklist and a rating scale that clients can use to "train" therapists. In addition, the very perusal of the 74 items may remind therapist and supervisor how therapeutically rich the treatment session is and can be. Accordingly, the MSU/FTQ can be used as a checklist of interventions to guide one's own work and to teach others.

A Case Example

Emerson (Lee, Emerson & Kochka, 1997) has offered the following illustration of the MSU/FTQ as a supervisory resource from the marital and family therapy training program at the University of Nevada at Las Vegas. The therapist, a 39-year-old former teacher, seemed unusually hesitant and fearful upon meeting the "N" family, a single-parent household consisting of a mother and two daughters. The parents had divorced five years earlier, and the girls had no contact with their father. Mrs. N seemed clinically depressed and said that she was overwhelmed by the behavior of her youngest daughter, Martha who, at 13, was sloppy, uncooperative, surly, and under-achieving in school. Mrs. N. said, in contrast, that Susan, 17, was an almost perfect daughter. A senior in high school, she made good grades, helped her mother, and stayed out of trouble.

In the subsequent supervision session the therapist quickly demonstrated that she had accepted the family's diagnosis of its problem: Martha was a 13-year-old who needed an "attitude adjustment." "I need to work with her to get her motivated to do her school work, her chores at home, and to clean up her attitude." The supervisor cautioned against a hasty decision about "the problem," and suggested a more systemic view. Nevertheless, in subsequent therapy sessions the therapist continued to side with Mrs. N. and Susan relative to Martha. Like them, she questioned Martha about what she did after school, why she didn't do her homework, why she continued to talk on the phone to friends that her mother had forbidden her to see, and why she was generally making everyone else's life miserable. Typically, Martha responded with silence and a look of disgust.

Variations on this dance occurred each week despite the supervisor's remonstrations about linearity and identified patients, the supervisory team's observations, and the therapist's vow to try a different therapeutic role. Mrs. N spoke of how hard she had to work to feed her two daughters, how little help and respect she received from Martha and how with Susan leaving her at the end of the year, she would be stuck with this recalcitrant child. Susan would concur sympathetically, Martha would "tune out," and the therapist would take on the role of interrogating teacher.

In anticipation of a holiday break the family members were each asked to fill out the MSU/FTQ. The supervisor then went over the questionnaires carefully with the therapist. Mrs. N's and Susan's answers often were identical. They continued to express discontent with their family situation, but were happy with the therapist. They thought that the therapist was "both caring and firm," "really knew how to listen," and "helped us to define the problem clearly." They said that she had asked what led up to the problem, what solutions had already been tried, and "spoke

in a way that matched our moods and experience." In contrast, Martha was very unhappy with both the family situation and therapy. She used the MSU/FTQ to state that the therapist, her mother, and her sister did not listen, were not caring, and did not understand the problem. She did not feel that the therapist "appreciated how each of us is different and special, and accepted us as we are." Nor did the therapist show them "how everyone's behavior was connected to the problem," or stop "the shifting of the blame to others," making "...change the responsibility of every family member." Indeed, none of the responses of any of the family members indicated that the therapist had focused on the "we-ness" of the family, reframed problematic behavior, or worked to increase the family's adaptive resourcefulness as an ecosystem. In fact, on the basis of all three questionnaires one could reasonably ask whether or not family therapy actually was being done.

Since the therapist had insisted all along on dealing individually with Martha as the identified patient, the supervisor proposed that in one last session before the holidays, Martha be met with alone and asked to elaborate on some of her answers. An angry Martha went directly to an item regarding therapists showing respect for all family members. She stated that the therapist definitely had *not* shown her any respect. "You didn't want to hear anything from me, just like my mom. Your mind was made up, just like hers." She then went to an item which asked about the therapist insisting that parents be parents and children be children. Martha declared bitterly that this was not the case in her family. "Mom is out with her boyfriends practically every night after work. She sleeps all day on the weekends, and Susan bosses me around like she was my mom. Mom lets her, and says I have to mind her. It's not fair. She's not my mom. And you're just like them, telling me what to do and not listening to my side of things."

The supervisor used the contrasting opinions of the family members to show the therapist that a great many things indicative of systemic family therapy were not taking place. Instead the therapist had been inducted into the family system, clearly adopting the N family way: Mother and eldest daughter take no responsibility for the family disharmony and instead focus on Martha, who behaves badly and allows herself to be scapegoated. Upon reflection the therapist admitted that, although she intellectually comprehended systemic approaches, with this family she nevertheless slipped back into an old and familiar role as a teacher in a parent-teacher conference. That is, she was talking with the parent about what was wrong with her child and how to fix her. The supervisor suggested that, when therapy resumed, the therapist regularly review the MSU/FTQ before and after therapy sessions. She was to use it as a checklist to keep herself on track and to resist being inducted by the family system and thereby rendered ineffectual.

Her first session of the new semester with this family began with verbal reassurances to the rebellious Martha that her insights had impressed the therapist. This captured Martha's attention and confused her mother and sister. They encountered a "different" therapist who, over the course of several succeeding weeks, helped them discover that Martha's rebellion was neither mysterious nor maliciously intended. Some parts of it were normal for her stage in life. Some parts involved taking on traits expected of her. And some parts were a desperate cry from a lonely child who had "lost" both her parents at a young age. She had been only eight when her parents divorced, her father disappeared; and her mother became deeply involved in her work and her new social life. Concurrently, her mother and older sister had stifled their own grief and anger, accompanied by the parentification of Susan. In therapy Susan began to discover her own resentment and appropriately shifted the focus of her anger from Martha to her mother and father.

Therapy ended with Susan less interested in Martha and her mother, and more interested in senior activities, a new boyfriend, and going off to college. Susan also was planning to meet with her father. She wanted to get her own sense of how he felt about them. She speculated about a continuing relationship with him, including a financial one. Mrs. N was nervous about this initiative, but Martha was curious. For her part, Mrs. N took more daily time with Martha, but her guidance was more consultative than directive. Concurrently, Martha became more available socially to her mother and sister, her grades began to go up and she was investing in an acceptable group of peers.

References

Anderson, H. (1993). On a roller coaster: A collaborative systems approach to therapy. In S. Friedman (Ed.), *The new language of change: Constructive collaboration in psychotherapy* (pp. 323–344). New York: Guilford.

Bischoff, R. J., MeKeel, A. J., Moon, S., & Sprenkle, D. H. (1996). Therapist-conducted consultation: Using clients as consultants to their own therapy. *Journal of Marital and Family Therapy*, 22, 359–379.

Hoffman-Hennessy, L. & Davis, J. (1993). Tekka with feathers: Talking about talking (about suicide). In S. Friedman (Ed.), *The new language of change: Constructive collaboration in psychotherapy* (pp. 323-344). New York: Guilford

Quinn, W. H. (1996). The client speaks out: Three domains of meaning. *Journal of Family Psychotherapy*, 7(2), 71–73.

Quinn, W. H., Nagirreddy, C., Lawless, J., & Bagley, R. (1996). Utilizing clients' voices in clinical supervision. *The Supervision Bulletin*, 9(1), 4–8.

Sells, S. P., Smith, T. F., & Moon, S. (1996). An ethnographic study of client and therapist perceptions of therapy effectiveness in a university-based training clinic. *Journal of Marital and Family Therapy*, 22, 321–342.

The MSU/FTQ is available without charge from the author at 107 Human Ecology, Michigan State University, East Lansing, Ml 48824-1030 (E-mail: boblee@msu.edu)

Supervision Without Easy Answers

by Arnold Woodruff, M.S.

Published in the AAMFT Supervision Bulletin, Vol. VIII, No. 2, Summer 1995.

Editor's Note: The Standards Committee desires to bring in information and ideas from other arenas of human endeavor to help, in a narrative and postmodern way, to add perspectives on our work. This article, in the form of a book review, attempts to highlight ideas from the book Leadership Without Easy Answers (1994) by Ronald A. Heifetz that might relate to the practice of family therapy supervision.

Ronald Heifetz is a psychiatrist who directs the Leadership Education Project at the John F. Kennedy School of Government at Harvard University. He is also the author of *Leadership Without Easy Answers*. To his credit, his ideas, true to the title of the book, are not easy, nor easy to summarize, but I will try.

Heifetz, who admits to a strong systemic bias in his thinking, defines "adaptive work" as "developing the organizational and cultural capacity to meet problems successfully according to our values and purposes." He proceeds to elucidate the nature of adaptive work in a number of settings, including medical and governmental.

There are four major sections in the book: Part I, "Setting the Frame," Part II, "Leading With Authority," Part III, "Leading Without Authority," and Part IV, "Staying Alive." While I found Parts III and IV the most interesting and helpful, Part II "Leading With Authority," appeared to have the most to say to a family therapy supervisor who could be assumed to have authority in the supervision relationship.

Heifetz defines three types of situations faced by a leader with authority. He first describes clearly defined situations in which a technical fix is required and the leader is able to apply such a solution. Other situations involve clear problems, but solutions require learning to develop. In these situations, the leader and the supervisee (in our case) must work together to develop the solutions. In the third type of situation Heifetz describes, neither the problem nor the solution are clear and both the leader and the supervisee must learn, but with the supervisee taking on the bulk of the responsibility for achieving desired directions and outcomes. Heifetz outlines the specifics of how a leader helps achieve outcomes by following five basic principles of leadership:

1) Identify the adaptive challenge.

2) Keep the level of distress within a tolerable range for doing adaptive work.

3) Focus attention on ripening (developing) issues and not on stress-reducing distractions.

4) Give the work back to the people (supervisee), but at a rate they can stand.

5) Protect the voices of leadership without authority (i.e., the supervisee or family when they raise hard questions).

Heifetz's discussion of the nature of leadership and power and how they are, in fact, conferred either unconsciously or by force of personal or cultural habit raises many interesting discussion points for our struggles as an organization to overcome the racism, sexism, and other issues of diversity that are a part of our own cultural habits. He points out, for example, that "the inclusion of competing value perspectives may be essential to adaptive success."

In summary, this book provided me with many thoughtful moments when considering the enterprise of clinical supervision. I would hope that others in our field would benefit from reading it.

References

Heifetz, R. (1994). *Leadership Without Easy Answers.* Cambridge, MA: Belknap Press, Harvard University.

Supervision, Co-vision, Meta-vision and Alter-vision

Maryhelen Snyder, Ph.D.

Published in the AAMFT Supervision Bulletin, Vol. IX, No. 1, Winter 1996.

In my opinion, the word "supervision" is problematic, connoting a hierarchical vision in which one person oversees another. The actual practice of supervision may require certain elements of this hierarchical overview. To whatever degree the supervisor is legally, ethically, and institutionally responsible for the supervisee's behaviors, a hierarchical overview may have a strategic place. It is useful, however, in this era of "postmodern" reflection on the manner in which language constructs practices to examine some alternative (or additional) terms for the practice of supervision. The following explorations of language have grown out of my participation in discussions of supervision from collaborative and social constructionist perspectives. Each term that we might use to describe what we do as supervisors, gives rise to "interrogatives." Thus each is followed by some sample questions which logically emerge from the particular stance.

Co-vision

The word "co-vision" has the advantage of emphasizing the collaborative manner in which supervisor and supervisee (and therapist and client) look together at the process of therapy. In this context, the responsibility of the supervisor is to rigorously invite mutual exploration, and to provide openings, structures, and experiences for the exploration (deconstruction and co-construction) of meanings.

When I think of myself as a co-visor or co-visionary, do I act and think dialogically with those who consult me, maintaining consciousness of how meanings are understood and evolve collaboratively? Do I experience myself as changing in the interaction?

Meta-vision

The word "meta-vision" indicates the "second order of awareness in which the system can apply awareness to itself. The isomorphic processes of supervisor/supervisee, therapist/client, client/other clients, self/self, can all be addressed under the rubric of "meta-vision." For example, I have been struck by a recurrent observation in articles describing qualitative research on differences between client and therapist perceptions regarding what has worked in therapy. Clients often comment to the researcher that the process of reflecting on the therapy in conversation with the researcher has felt as therapeutic as the therapy itself.

As a meta-visor, do I invite, allow, and develop methodology for the continual reflection on process at all levels?

Alter-vision

Another form of "vision" that has been useful to me as a person, therapist, trainer, and supervisor could be called "alter-vision," or vision from "inside" the perspective of the other. A variety of methods can be used (*Family Process,* Snyder, 1995) to allow a dramatic shift in—and enlargement of—perspective. The capacity of human beings for taking the perspective of others is still a relatively untapped resource for change. A therapist, for example, who is asked to "become" the client about whom he or she is feeling critical, confused, blocked, or conflicted will often suddenly experience a clarification of what is going on and what is needed that didn't seem available prior to assuming the alternative identity. Another use of "alter-vision" is as a method for stepping into alternative models of therapy and viewing clients from "inside" a variety of theoretical frames.

As an alter-visor, do I have and use methodologies for allowing radical shifts in perspective out of dominant cultural "discourses" or other perceptual frameworks in which I or the other might be embedded?

These various terms are offered not as suggestions for actual usage but rather as linguistic tools for enhancing the co-creative practice of supervision.

Supervision as a Lifestyle

Philip Davis, M.Div.

Published in the AAMFT Supervision Bulletin, Vol. VIII, No. 1, Spring 1995.

There was a day when, working on professional credentials, supervision seemed like just another academic chore. Then the lights came on, and supervision, unlike coursework, seemed to be creating a lifestyle. It was stimulating a tendency to reach upward toward the meta level, to increase the size of the system. Some scientist commented that we don't understand the meaning of life because our context is too small, and used the example of a caterpillar on a leaf who does not understand that a metamorphosis is a good thing. The ability to reach upward for meaning is an acquired skill, however, not instinctual, like the caterpillar's reaching upward for a branch to hang its cocoon on.

Where supervisor and supervisee meet is in the common need to reach upward. Unlike the caterpillar, we need a hand reaching down as a transition point. It is not so much the expertise of the supervisor that is necessary, but rather the mutual understanding that "This is necessary."

In my responsibilities at a state agency in Hawaii, where I supervise therapists and staff, the question most often occurring is one of "Where do things connect?" Obviously, if something is an issue of family sequences, and it is wrongly interpreted as a gender issue, it will skew the treatment plan, and the family and the therapist will suffer. The supervisor enters this interaction to become part of the therapeutic system, and adds one further layer of interpretation. In a process of maturation that is intrinsic to systemic development, the observer reaches out for an observer, the supervisor, in order to reach the meta level context of meaning.

Conflicts occur in an agency setting where a therapist is accustomed to operating on a lower level of meaning, and clings for security to some pet context that is pulled out of the box whenever things get difficult. In such cases, even a supervisor can unhelpfully insist that a therapist "get back to the basics" even if the basics are not working. In one instance, the supervisor insisted that the therapist was in a cultural conflict with the client, but the problem was one of family sequences, in allowing a certain unchecked behavior to continue unchallenged.

The value of the systems perspective, in contrast to others, is this reaching up to the meta level, to eliminate burnout. I have often observed, soon after dealing with a traumatic family, the agency staff all catch the flu at the same time. Some families seem to feel more competent if they are able to provoke this kind of crisis. In one instance, all the staff fled...quit without warning. Monday came, but nobody came in.

Until good lines of accountability are established, no one can really function adequately as a therapist. I like healthcare reform because it creates such accountability. These changes are encouraging collegiality, and perhaps in that process we will discover how valuable we are to each other. The idea that anyone can be "PC" or correct or healing is flawed. Healing comes from the system and our interconnectedness. No one is an expert, but some have more access to resources than others. The traditional isolation of the mental health practitioner is coming to an end, inevitably resulting in the positive positioning of those who are accustomed to a team approach featuring superior supervision as an asset.

One more thing: family therapy is not marginalized. It is providing a model for supervision that keeps a human face on large, unwieldy healthcare conglomerates. We know how to keep the family from getting lost in the system, and thus we know how to keep the therapist from getting lost in the family and in healthcare conglomerates.

Words Make a Difference...

Anthony Heath, Ph.D.

*Published in the AAMFT Supervision Bulletin,
Vol. VI, No. 1, Winter 1993.*

I write to you all to urge a change in the discourse of family therapy supervision. Specifically, I suggest that the word "therapist" replace the word "supervisee" in oral and written prose including the text of all organization publications. This suggestion is based on my assumption that the people we supervise are more than recipients of our supervision. They are, at least, therapists; they deserve all the respect and privileges of this name.

I also believe that we supervisors have been guilty of treating therapists as less than competent. We generally have left them out of our meetings, failed to invite them to speak through our literature and diagnosed their motivations.

I suggest we start here. Words make a difference. Remember "patients?"

Chapter 4

Supervision Structure, Assessment and Technique

Contracting from the Top Down

Teresa McDowell, M.A.

Published in the AAMFT Supervision Bulletin, Vol. IV, No.3, October 1991.

As marriage and family therapists we pride ourselves in being aware of family systems even when working with individuals. Yet when we contract to provide supervision how often do we enter the supervisee's work system in a planful way which intentionally enhances the relationships between the supervisee, those she works with and ourselves?

Some time ago I received a call from a therapist at a local mental health agency. She stated that she and several of her colleagues were interested in group supervision. They discussed this with their director and he agreed to have her call me for more information. I found myself responding to her much as I would a child asking to set up an appointment for her family, encouraging her to ask the director to contact me. I wanted to make sure I had "parental" permission.

When the director and I eventually met we discussed the agency's goals, policies, and other relevant information such as the therapists' responsibilities in the area of case management As we reviewed who should be in the supervision group, I again found myself responding as I would when working with a family, considering how supervision could strengthen and clarify the existing holons in the agency. Our meeting allowed me an opportunity to explain the supervision process, clarify any discrepancies in philosophy or theoretical approach, delineate the roles of clinical and agency supervisors, determine the process of evaluation, and specify the procedure for notifying me of emergency situations and ethical issues. By the end of our meeting the director and I were in agreement and I believe he saw me as an ally he could trust with his "family." We set up a time to meet with the unit supervisor. I felt the supervision process was not likely to be undermined or triangulated by the system. If a problem arose, the groundwork had been laid for finding a solution.

Since this experience, I have begun keeping in mind a "supervision" map which includes the supervisee, members of her work system, the client family, and other relevant systems involved with any given case. This map helps direct many of my decisions, including those aimed at encouraging hierarchical congruence and clarity within the work system.

By recognizing supervisees as part of a system we can acknowledge the effect that system has on the supervision process and on the therapist's ability to work with families. We can also acknowledge the effect we as supervisors have on the work system and realize our responsibility for insuring that our impact is beneficial, eventually enhancing the supervisee's success in helping families change.

Supervision Contracting Tips— Coming From You

Published in the AAMFT Supervision Bulletin, Vol. IV, No. 3, October 1991.

Editor's Note: In our June 1991 issue we asked you to share your expertise on contracting with supervisees. Many of you did and below is a collection of your tips.
- Cheryl L. Storm, AAMFT Supervision Bulletin editor

Many supervisors include a statement in their contracts indicating supervisees agree to practice according to the *AAMFT Code of Ethics.*

Sandra A. Rigazio-DiGilio instructs supervisors-in-training to identify the scope of supervision, the supervisory context, the structure of supervision, the specific learning objectives, and the procedures for evaluation and feedback in her supervision course. She further notes the supervisory contract should be consistent with the supervisor's model of supervision.

Noting the evolving nature of contracts and the limited knowledge supervisors have initially about their supervisees, **Marshall Fine** revises his contracts periodically.

Tom Todd recommends including information about the steps taken if supervisors or supervisees discontinue supervision before the agreed-upon time.

Patricia Dwyer includes a summary of the administrative and clinical controls of the supervisees' setting, the amount of professional liability insurance carried, and a statement indicating supervisees are aware of the supervisor's legal responsibility for their caseload. She further defines the handling of dangerous situations as: *"I agree to inform my supervisor by phone within 12 hours of actions taken to protect clients from hurting themselves and/or others, to inform my administrative supervisor, and to record my actions in the clinical case notes. If my supervisor mandates an action on my part in a dangerous or unethical situation, I agree to comply with her instructions. If I fail to follow her instructions within the time she required, I agree that she will take the appropriate action and inform my administrative supervisor. Repeated failure to carry out my supervisor's instructions may necessitate that she discontinue supervision with me, notify my administrative supervisor, and/or notify the AAMFT Supervision Committee and Ethics Committee."*

Striking the Supervision Bargain

Cheryl Storm, Ph.D.

Published in the AAMFT Supervision Bulletin, Vol. IV, No. 1, February 1991.

Recently, a clinician, wishing to fulfill the AAMFT Clinical Membership requirements, approached me wondering if she could hire me to provide supervision of her private practice cases. As we began to talk, I was once again struck by how the differences in supervising in an institution versus a private context shape the supervision contract.

Within an institution, the terms of the supervision contract are relatively clearly outlined by the institution. The institution sets the framework for supervision by determining the way in which supervision is conducted, the overreaching goals of the process, when supervision occurs, and how long supervision lasts. Job responsibilities are formally outlined to the supervisor by the institution. For example, in my institution I am expected to provide a mixture of live, video, and case presentation supervision during practicum to two students who meet for one and a half hours each week for 15 weeks. I am required to provide an evaluation to each student on an instrument developed by the institution. A supervisee is told what he or she can expect from a supervisor and what is expected of him or her by the institution prior to entering into supervision. In my context, a supervisee is to complete requirements as specified in a syllabus, obtain a satisfactory evaluation, and complete the specified hours of supervision meetings and therapy contact hours. Although some contracting still occurs around individual issues of the supervisee, the primary contract is between the supervisor and the institution, and between the supervisee and the institution.

With a private practice supervisor, the contract is determined by the supervisor in conversation with the supervisee. The Commission on Supervision, in the description of the responsibilities for AAMFT Supervisors in the August 1990 edition of *The Approved Supervisor: Standards and Responsibilities,* states that "The supervisor and the supervisee must develop a contract delineating fees, hours, and time and place of meetings. The contract should be specific about case responsibility, caseload review, handling of suicidal threats and other dangerous clinical situations, etc." (p. 26). Although these are useful guidelines, the specific contract is the agreement that is reached between the supervisor and the supervisee. Thus, there is more freedom to individualize the supervision contract as well as less inherent structure to guide the process. The terms of the supervision contract are only as clear as the supervisor and supervisee make them.

In an institutional setting there is an existing authority structure. The supervisor is under the umbrella of an institution in which there are procedures for evaluating the supervisor's performance, usually procedures for processing complaints, and opportunities to discuss supervision issues. If the supervisor does not uphold his or her part of the contract, the supervisee can complain and the institution can take action ranging from mediating the disagreement to firing the supervisor. If the supervisor has upheld the supervision agreement but the supervisee has not complied with his or her part of the agreement or progressed satisfactorily, supervisors can receive the backing they need to stand their ground and push for the supervisee to take appropriate action to insure that only competent therapists receive Clinical Membership.

In contrast, in the private sector, there is no defined way to proceed if difficulties arise within the supervision process. Although the best resolutions are those that occur between the supervisor and the supervisee, the nature of the contract makes resolution at times difficult Because the supervisor evaluates the supervisee's competencies and a negative evaluation can seriously affect the supervisee's career, supervisees may be reluctant to discuss their concerns with the supervisor until late in the process or to terminate supervision and seek another supervisor. Similarly, a supervisor maybe less open with critical feedback since he or she can be fired. Over time, I have become increasingly aware of how an explicit supervision contract facilitates the supervision process while protecting both parties. As a private supervisor, I now put in writing the agreement that I strike with clinicians. By doing so, I believe I reduce the margin that exists for difficulties while increasing the potential for success, since my supervisee and I both can evaluate whether the supervision contract is being fulfilled.

Supervisors as Guardians of the Profession

Upon becoming an Approved Supervisor, one assumes not only the responsibility for the development and clinical work of supervisees but a significant responsibility to the discipline itself. Most supervisors are acutely aware of their responsibilities to supervisees and clients. Many may be less clear regarding their responsibilities to the profession.

I propose that supervisors assume significant responsibility as guardians of the profession in three major ways:

1. Supervisors are guardians of the MFT educational process. If supervisors endorse this process, MFT remains a distinct mental health discipline and the integrity of our profession is maintained.

2. Supervisors are guardians of the development of the individuals who will represent the discipline in the future. The degree of these individuals' professional knowledge, therapeutic expertise, and ethical standards will shape our profession in the decades to come.

3. Supervisors are guardians of the quality of services our profession provides to the public. Supervisors require supervisees to demonstrate the ability to provide services consistent with standards of practice of our discipline, and insure that marriage and family therapists are ready to practice independently.

Extension of the Commission

The Commission on Supervision (COS), the recognized supervision standard-setting body for the field, defines what constitutes supervision and sets the qualifications required of supervisors. The Commission designates individuals as Approved Supervisors, professionals who are competent to conduct supervision. Thus, Approved Supervisors are essentially delegates of the Commission. They insure that there is equivalency in the educational process within the field as they require their supervisees to participate in similar supervised clinical experiences.

Development of the Next Generation

Approved Supervisors assist supervisees in applying what they have learned in the classroom to the therapy room, the real test of becoming a therapist. Thus Approved Supervisors are responsible for facilitating the most crucial time in therapists' professional development. All supervisors, to the best of their abilities, assist supervisees in using their MFT knowledge, and developing therapeutic competencies and skills needed to practice marriage and family therapy. In their development of this next generation of therapists, supervisors determine the standards of practice for our profession. If supervisors take this responsibility lightly, supervisees with marginal ability in translating classroom knowledge into therapeutic action may be passed on, ultimately lowering standards of practice. Because professional standards of practice are passed from one generation to the next, the degree to which the Approved Supervisors of today promote the highest standards of practice will be reflected in the way their supervisees promote the same standards when they become supervisors and develop the next generation.

Gatekeeper

All supervisors continually evaluate the progress of their supervisees. On a regular basis, Approved Supervisors are expected to conduct formal evaluations of their supervisees' professional performance and competency and to maintain an ongoing tally of supervision completed. In addition, they are required to report this information to credentialing, certifying, and licensing bodies. Essentially, Approved Supervisors serve as gatekeepers to our profession. The gate is open to those who meet at least minimal standards for competency and closed to those who are below these standards. If supervisors are remiss in this responsibility and unqualified therapists are allowed through the gate, consumers suffer by receiving less than quality care.

Like guardian angels, Approved Supervisors watch over the profession. They insure that marriage and family therapists receive the education required to prepare them adequately, develop the therapeutic competencies to provide quality care to clients, and attain the professionalism to represent our profession well.

Clarifying Contextual Influences Creates Workable Supervision Relationships

Layne A. Prest, Ph.D. and Toni Schindler-Zimmerman, Ph.D.

Published in the AAMFT Supervision Bulletin, Vol. V, No.3, November 1992.

As we are ever more aware, the world, including the domains of therapy and supervision, is a complicated place. At first glance it might seem that ignoring some of the personal and contextual characteristics of supervisor-supervisee relationships would merely simplify what we do. And, in fact, many of us have operated that way for quite some time. Ultimately, however, we have found that this only causes problems and creates obstacles to productive working relationships. This is in part because, as the marriage and family therapy (MFT) supervision literature points out, there is a broad variety of supervisees and supervisors, discrepancies in terms of their expectations of supervision, and a multitude of contexts within which supervision is conducted. In addition, there are no specific guidelines for establishing an effective "contract" for supervision. And, until recently, the MFT supervision literature has lacked significant attempts to encourage an ongoing dialogue in which supervisors and supervisees discuss needs, agendas, styles, techniques, and goals in a systematic manner. This seems striking given the importance placed on establishing similar contracts with clients in therapy (Prest and Schindler-Zimmerman, in press).

As professionals who have had a great deal of experience as supervisees and a growing number of experiences as supervisors-in-training, we wanted to develop an instrument that would be comprehensive but easy to use. We envisioned an instrument that would provide some structure for clarifying the sometimes enormous number of issues involved in supervision, but one which would remain flexible enough to be used in a wide variety of situations. Therefore, we conducted interviews and focus groups involving supervisees and supervisors concerning the important elements of the supervisory relationship and contract for supervision. These responses became the basis for the Initial Supervisory Session Checklist (IS SC).

The ISSC is a set of guidelines for use by supervisors and supervisees in constructing a comprehensive contract for effective supervision, regardless of the theoretical orientation and developmental level of those involved. We have used it to guide the development of the initial supervision contract, as well as in reassessing the supervision process along the way. A copy of the checklist may be obtained by contacting either of the two authors.

The ISSC has several sections: education and training, previous experiences in supervision, philosophy of supervision and change, theoretical orientation, supervision goals and techniques, legal and ethical considerations, and characteristics of supervisees' workplaces. This broad coverage allows those involved to discuss, among other things, the important contexts within which supervision occurs, including gender, racial, economic, and ethnic contexts.

For example, in reviewing the section on previous supervision experiences, a supervisee (who may be an Hispanic male) would have the structured opportunity to inquire about his potential (Caucasian female) supervisor's previous therapy and supervision experiences with Hispanics. Similarly, a supervisor working with a new supervisee in an agency serving the poor and underinsured would be stimulated to discuss the various social and political effects of differences in socio-economic status on the therapeutic and supervisory relationships and process when addressing the characteristics of the supervisee's workplace. In general, the ISSC helps create an environment to discuss difficult issues we may otherwise tend to ignore.

Excerpt From the ISSC

In order to assess the range of the supervisee's competence, the following points should be discussed:

- Previous supervision expereince (e.g. format, setting).

- Strengths and weaknesses as therapist/supervisee (as indicators of developmental level).
- Supervisee's competence with stages of therapy process: initial call, intake, joining, middle phase, termination and referral.
- Supervisee's level of development in terms of case planning, notes, collateral support and networking.
- Supervisory competence with various issues (e.g. ethnicity, gender, age, alternative lifestyles, abortion, models, techniques, populations, therapy groups and family form.
- Methods for managing supervisor-supervisee differences.

References

Prest, L.A., Schindler-Zimmerman, T., & Sporakowski, M. (In press). The initial supervision session (ISSC): A guide for the MFT Supervision Process. *The Clinical Supervisor.*

Proactive Supervisors Required: For Therapists Working with Violent Families

Chris Sand-Pringle, Ed.S.

Published in the AAMFT Supervision Bulletin, Vol. VII, No. 3, Fall 1994.

The competence and strengths of supervisors are particularly challenged when supervisees are working with violent families. Considering the supervisory goal to empower supervisees, it may appear paradoxical that the more violent client situations, the more proactive, directive, flexible and visible supervisors need to be. However, if supervisors are not willing to match the severity of situations with a level of planful involvement, supervisees may feel unsupported, unsure, frightened, intimidated and liable in working with a violent family. If this is the case, not only will supervisees be ineffective, they may inadvertently contribute to the potential for violence. I have identified seven themes to be addressed by supervisors that respect the vital role of supervisors in the therapeutic context and depict the isomorphic nature between supervisor/supervisee relationships and therapist/client relationships. These themes are designed to be utilized in working with violent families and from the perspective of empowering supervisees. I implement this framework with out-patient and home-based supervisees.

Structure

Supervisors address safety issues and the need for structured therapeutic contexts at the onset of supervisees' work with violent families. For example, a supervisee may be encouraged to utilize no-harm contracts, no-use contracts, leverage from other professional systems and session rules.

Predictability

Supervisors do not create an atmosphere of ambiguity or unpredictability within the supervisory relationship. Supervision contracts are established; goals and expectations within the supervisory relationship are clarified. Within this context, supervisors use an empowerment approach from which supervisees can then focus on clients rather than be preoccupied or distracted by: When will they see their supervisor? or What do their supervisors expect?

Making the Covert Overt

Underlying issues that may block or sabotage therapists' work with violent families are addressed in supervision; family of origin issues, supervisees' fears and concerns, supervisees' feelings about abusers and victims of abuse. Supervisors guide supervisees in how and when to address covert issues (violence, secrets, hidden agendas) with family systems.

Perpetuating Crisis

Supervisors are not crisis-oriented and do not perpetuate crises by only responding to supervisees' dramatic client situations. Supervisors regularly protect time for supervision and give positive feedback when things are going well.

Hierarchy and Boundaries

Supervisory relationships model clear, professional boundaries. Structurally, supervisors are in charge of and responsible for the overall treatment context and empower supervisees to take charge of therapy with violent families.

Maneuverability

Supervisors and supervisees strategize ways to use supervisors during treatment with violent families to create therapeutic maneuverability. Examples include videotape review, live supervision, the reflecting team approach, co-therapy, framing supervisors as "experts" with violent families or accessing the supervisor as "leverage" in a way that protects supervisees' relationships with families.

Metaperspective

Supervisors guide supervisees in maintaining a metaperspective with violent families so that supervisees can maintain the position of facilitator of positive change. In supervision, systemic hypotheses and treatment strategies are developed that enable supervisees to impact the families' destructive patterns.

As supervisors are challenged to match what supervisees need in working with violent family systems, supervision cannot be limited to case reports in the office. Using the above themes to enhance planful involvement, supervisors empower supervisees to maintain safe and therapeutic positions with violent families.

References

Gelles, R.J. & Cornell, C.P. (1990). *Intimate violence in families.* Newbury Park, CA: Sage.

Kagan, R. & Schlosberg, S. (1989). *Families in perpetual crisis.* New York: W. W. Norton.

Liddle, H. A. (1991). Training and supervision in family therapy: A comprehensive and critical analysis. In A. S. Gurman & D.P. Kniskern (Eds.) *Handbook of family therapy,* Volume II. (pp. 638–697). New York: Brunner/Mazel.

Zarski, J., Sand-Pringle, C. & Lindon, C. (in press). Critical issues in supervision: Marital and family violence. *The Family Journal.*

Assessing Supervision: Social Validity and Invalidity of Evaluation

D. Eugene Mead, Ed.D.

Published in the AAMFT Supervision Bulletin, Vol. VI, No. 2, Summer 1993.

The primary goals of supervision are to help supervisees become more effective therapists and to safeguard the welfare of clients. Therefore, supervisors, therapists and clients should be involved in evaluating supervision. In addition, since supervisors play a major role in the socialization of therapists, members of systems outside of the supervisor-therapist-client system also have an interest in the evaluation of supervision. Therefore, evaluation of supervision should include all the consumers of the supervision process to determine if (a) the supervision goals are relevant, (b) the techniques supervisors employ are acceptable and (c) the outcomes they achieve are satisfactory. This form of evaluation is not outcome assessment nor is it simply assessment of consumer satisfaction. Wolf (1978) and others (Fawcett, 1991; Schwartz & Baer, 1991) have described it as social validity. Social validity assessment is aimed at determining if a program of intervention, such as supervision, is acceptable to consumers.

An equally important form of evaluation is social invalidity assessment (Schwartz & Baer, 1991). In social invalidity assessment the evaluator attempts to determine if any of the consumers are unhappy with the goals, processes, or personnel involved and if they plan to do something about it. This form of assessment is aimed at immediate detection and correction of problems related to supervision which could damage clients, therapists, supervisors and the profession. The purpose of this paper is to discuss the who, what, where, when, how and why of supervision social validity and invalidity assessment.

Who Should EvaluateSsupervision?

As already stated, supervision should be evaluated by all the consumers of supervision. Recent discussion of social validation has identified four types of consumers: direct and indirect consumers, and immediate and distant community consumers (Fawcett, 1991; Hawkins, 1991; Schwartz & Baer, 1991). The direct consumers of supervision are therapists. One group of indirect consumers of supervision are the present and future clients of supervisees. Another group of indirect consumers of supervision are the administrators, insurance carriers, government agencies and family members who pay for therapy.

Other consumers of therapy supervision are found in the community. Immediate community consumers include family members of supervisees, boards of directors, accrediting bodies and representatives of other government agencies in the community such as the police and the courts.

More distant community consumers of supervision are other members of the profession, public officials, citizens and journalists. All of these consumers of supervision should be assessed, as they all may have the ability to control the viability of supervision.

What Should be Evaluated in Supervision Assessment?

As noted earlier, customer satisfaction and dissatisfaction should be assessed when evaluating supervision. This assessment should be prospective, actively seeking out consumer likes and dislikes related to supervision goals, techniques, outcomes and personnel (Schwartz & Baer, 1991).

Where Should Supervision Evaluation be Done?

Supervisors, therapists and clients can be assessed about supervision in the clinical setting where supervision takes place. In keeping with the proactive stance recommended above, evaluation of supervision by other consumers should be sought by supervisors rather than waiting for them to come to us.

When Should Supervision be Evaluated?

Schwartz and Baer (1991) recommend that social validity assessment should be done early and often. In order to prevent problems, supervision assessment should be. done as close as possible to tasks of therapy and supervision (Mead 1990). These include: (1) gathering information; (2) establishing the problems and goals; (3) forming a treatment plan; (4) carrying out treatment; (5) assessing processes and outcomes and (6) terminating treatment. Note the distinction between social validity assessment and assessment of supervision processes and outcomes. Social validity assessment is aimed at determining current consumer satisfaction and dissatisfaction as it is occurring rather than assessing the effectiveness of techniques or the success of outcomes after it has happened.

How Should Supervision be Evaluated?

The questionnaire is the most frequently used form of social validity assessment (Bornstein & Rychtarik, 1983; Hawkins, 1991). Questionaires will continue to be used for cost-effectiveness reasons. A number of questionnaires for evaluating supervision are reviewed in Liddle, Breunlin, and Schwartz (1988) and Mead (1990). Further research into supervision validity should be attempted using observational methods as well (Fawcett, 1991; Hawkins, 1991; Schwartz & Baer, 1991).

Why Evaluate the Social Validity and Invalidity of Supervision?

There are two reasons to continuously evaluate supervision. First, survival of supervision may depend upon early determination of consumer satisfaction and dissatisfaction. Problems which are detected early and immediately corrected may prevent resistance, defection and/or criticism by therapists and other consumers. Furthermore, when consumers' suggestions are solicited and heeded they often feel more committed to supervision. Second, listening to consumer suggestions can lead to improvement of supervision.

References

Bornstein, P. H., & Rychtarik, R. G. (1983). Consumer satisfaction in adult behavior therapy: Procedures, problems. and future perspectives. *Behavior Therapy*, 14, 191–208.

Fawcett, S. B. (1991). Social validity: A note on methodology. *Journal of Applied Behavior Analysis,* 24,235-239.

Hawkins, R. P. (1991). Is social validity what we are interested in? Argument for a functional approach. *Journal of Applied Behavior Analysis*, 24, 205–213.

Liddle, H. A., Breunlin, D.C., & Schwartz, R. C. (1988). *Handbook of family therapy training and supervision*. New York: Guilford.

Mead, D. E. (1990). *Effective supervision: A task-oriented model for the mental health professions*. New York: Brunner/Mazel.

Schwartz, I. S., & Baer, D. M. (1991). Social validity assessments: Is current practice state of the art? *Journal of Applied Behavior Analysis*, 24, 189–204.

Wolf, M. M. (1978). Social validity: The case for subjective measurement or how applied behavior analysis is finding its heart. *Journal of Applied Behavior Analysis*, 11, 203–214.

Using Dramatic Enactment in MFT Supervision

Daniel J. Wiener, Ph.D.

Published in the AAMFT Supervision Bulletin, Vol. 10, No.1, Summer 1997.

Enactments are techniques which use physical movement and dialogue to represent or explore social interactions. Role-play is probably the most widely known and frequently used type of enactment. Although many supervisors report using role-play, they usually employ only "realistic simulation," the retrospective recreation of part of the therapy session.

Enactments are useful in clinical supervision and training because they create highly impactful learning experiences that anchor imagery kinesthetically, by doing rather than talking-about. Dramatic Enactment (DE) techniques, which employ fictional roles and/or non-conventional scenarios, offer the additional advantage of shifting the social context of the supervisory session to a more playful mode, thus facilitating exploratory behavior by lessening fears of the "real life" consequence of change.

The author, a trainer and supervisor of MFTs at one hospital-based, three agency-based, and an AAMFT-accredited, university-based training program during the past fifteen years, has developed and experimented with a variety of DE techniques that may enhance supervisee training, irrespective of theoretical orientation. Below are ten examples of DE techniques that supervisors might employ:

1. An exercise that teaches how we co-construct realities and demonstrates how we persist in seeing what we have convinced ourselves is there. Participants experience the effects of dealing with their own initial disconfirmed expectations.

2. An exercise in which one player discovers his identity through the way other "family members" interact with them.

3. A role-play that teaches the practical use of status choices (behavior signifying the relative importance of self and others), which strongly affect "family member's" individual perceptions of the "therapist," their degree of anticipated cooperation, and whose therapeutic issues are addressed.

4. A role-play demonstrating how hidden status agendas engender intrafamilial conflict.

5. A game in which players discover the power of the therapist-as-listener to validate/invalidate client narratives.

6. A fantasy role-play to try out feared or forbidden responses as a way of helping the trainee detoxify those limiting, painful, or taboo reactions that arise in all therapists.

7. A technique for heightening supervisees' awareness of the degree of cooperation operating between family members and themselves as therapists.

8. A game that lessens competitive strivings among supervisees in group supervision by having them "stand in" for one another in rapid succession during simulated MFT sessions.

9. A role-play that lessens supervisee fears of making mistakes by "intentional blundering."

10. A use of role reversal to enable supervisees to gain empathy for family members' experience of a problem.

When contemplating the use of DE, it is important that the supervisor consider practical issues regarding appropriate and ethical conditions under which to employ such techniques in training. Another important consideration concerns which uses of the self of the therapist are activated by DE. However, by moving beyond the use of role-play to simulate therapy situations, the supervision process may be enhanced through the use of Dramatic Enactment to address a wide variety of issues.

Self-Supervision Using Discourse Analysis: Playing With Talk About Talk

Diane Steiden

Published in the AAMFT Supervision Bulletin, Vol. VI, No. 2, Summer 1993.

In private practice or when isolated from colleagues, we bump up against difficult situations—with limited options to research how we operated at the moment and how to do it differently. Using discourse analysis as a mode of self-supervision, it would be possible to reconsider actions, through language.

Self-supervision is deliberate thinking about one's actions, independent of others. This evaluative or reflective activity is performed to better understand how we operate as therapists and/or supervisors and to offer opportunities to take a different view or position in the clinical context. Self-supervision is a relatively recent idea (Anderson & Goolishian, 1990; Steiden, 1992; Todd, 1992) which has not been part of traditional training in family therapy.

Discourse analysis is an ambiguous term, however, simply put, discourse analysis can be described as *talk about talk*. It can vary from looking at the multiple meanings of a single complex word (Empson, 1989) to considering patterns of talk throughout the session (Stubbs, 1983). Discourse analysis can be done by reviewing tapes (audio or video) or the transcripts of tapes. Some (the very experienced) can analyze talk during a session.

The process of discourse analysis invites the clinician to look at different ways to interpret the "text" from a session. My first experience using discourse analysis as self-supervision helped me to see ways I had made assumptions about the clients concerns based on literal interpretations of their talk. Repeated *re-searching* of the text continued to open my eyes (and in the future, my ears) to ways in which I had accepted and not understood underlying themes and concerns. I then began using discourse analysis as a method of self-supervision in other challenging clinical situations.

In the process of teaching self-supervision using discourse analysis (thanks to Janet Chevalier, a Master's student at the University of Guelph for her curiosity), I listened to about 15 minutes of a segment ending five months of therapy, recording words and phrases that spoke to me as shared between client and therapist. Discussing a specific "word" and the connected phrases with the therapist it became evident that "fear" was a dominant theme throughout the course of therapy. Fear, in fact, organized much of how this woman led her life. Yet, in the therapist's brief description of the client, prior to our teaching/learning session) fear and the concern for safety (physically and emotionally) were not presented, even though they were addressed during the course of therapy.

Next, consider how using discourse analysis as self-supervision in the process of supervision might be useful. What if there is a "dissensus" or moment of unresolved negotiation/understanding between participants (Ratliff, 1991)? Rather than leave the dissensus dangling, the use of conversational and/or discourse analysis process might offer the clinicians opportunities to renegotiate and/or close these unresolved moments. Either participant could offer the other a different interpretation of the situation from a new position of understanding.

The pragmatics of in-depth discourse analysis would mean that sessions were taped, transcribed and then analyzed. As this is unrealistic for most of us, other options would include: replaying the tape (audio or video) and listening for words, phrases, or looking for patterns that were not obvious during the session. Then, trying *"to play with the talk"* in a way that is different from the initial interpretation (e.g. taking the literal meaning and seeing what figuratively or metaphorically fits, looking for patterns of talk—who talks most, least, who says what after whom, etc.) If taping cannot be done, then the therapist could jot down words that seem to be repetitive or themes that reoccur as the session(s) proceeds. Each individual and every situation will be unique and the method used should allow space to play with the talk in a way that opens up the clinical context for new interpretations.

Evaluating our clinical work, as supervisor or supervisee, requires a variety of skills and experience. Integrating the idea of self-supervision as a deliberate activity, and establishing methods to accomplish this may provide professionals with more options to respond to challenging situations. The use of discourse analysis in a therapeutic context is but one way to self-supervision.

References

Anderson, H.. & Goolishian, H. (1990). Supervision as collaborative conversation: Questions and reflections. In H. Brandau (Ed.). *Von der supervision dur systemischen vision.* Salzburg: Otto Muir Verlag.

Empson, W. (1989). *The structure of complex words.* Cambridge, MA: Harvard University.

Radiff, D.A. (1992). *Dangling dissensus in family therapy supervision.* Paper presented at International Communication Association Conference, Miami, FL.

Steiden, D. (1992). *Discourse analysis as self-supervision* Unpublished manuscript. Nova University. Ft. Lauderdale, FL

Stubba, MJ. (1983). *Discourse analysis: The sociolinguislic analysis of natural language.* University of Chicago Press. Chicago, IL.

Todd, T.C. (1992). Self-supervision? A goal for all supervisors. *Supervision Bulletin,* V, 3.

Family Supervision: Co-constructing Basic Therapy Skills

Jon L. Winek, Ph.D. and Liza M. Shaw

Published in the AAMFT Supervision Bulletin, Vol. 11, No. 1, Summer 1998.

Family supervision is an innovative technique for advancing family therapy trainees' skill development by inviting their significant family members in for an interview. Personal experiences of trainees are important training issues in Marriage and Family Therapy. Nichols (1993) has identified having trainees study their own families of origin as one of the current trends in family therapy. Bowen's now-classic article in which he worked with his family to differentiate himself (Anonymous, 1972) seems to have started this trend. Others have followed suit and have suggested course work, genogram construction, written assignments, psychodrama, and individual and group therapy to in-corporate trainees' own families into their training (Coopersmith, 1980; Dulll, 1983; Hawkins & Killorin, 1979; Kane, 1996; Liddle & Saba, 1985; McDaniel & Landau-Stanton, 1991; McGoldrick & Gerson, 1985; Smith 1993).

Incorporating the supervisees' family in their training is a logical extension of current training procedures, especially from the perspective of systems theory. The challenge which faces supervisors who use this approach arises out of the issue of dual relationships. Within the field of marriage and family therapy it has been made very clear that conducting therapy with trainees constitutes a dual relationship. According to accreditation standards, "Supervision will be distinguishable from psychotherapy or teaching" (AAMFT, 1997, pg. 12).

The dual relationship is a significant issue that may be addressed when working with trainees and their families. It is important for supervisors to be sensitive to trainee vulnerability, which tends to be similar in form to the vulnerability clients experience. This position of vulnerability is an inevitable reality inherent in the supervisor/trainee relationship. All supervisors—whether providing family supervision or not—must understand the power differential which exists within this relationship (Kaiser, 1992).

In many cases, students are being evaluated for their work in supervision by supervisors who must assign a grade for their performance. They are often encouraged to share openly with their supervisors, yet must keep in mind that even their open and honest sharing may be evaluated and sometimes even graded (Ryder & Hepworth,1990). Many times students are participating in supervision with professors with whom they have had courses, and/or with whom they will again take courses in the future. This brings up concerns regarding personal sharing on the part of students given existing or anticipated academic relations—a confusing gray area for both trainees and their supervisors and one which can lead to the very vulnerability discussed thus far. The complexity of this relationship ideally should be discussed within the supervisory context in order to shed light on any potential complications and avoid what has been non-specifically classified as a "dual relationship" (Ryder & Hepworth, 1990).

There must also exist a foundation of trust and respect between the trainees and the supervisors in order to successfully navigate and transcend these many shades of gray. Trainees need to know that in the supervisory capacity, their supervisors are acting in the best interest of the trainees' educational/clinical experience and are not going to abuse their position of power. In addition, although it is recognized that an abuse of power is possible in supervision due to the vulnerability of students, this does not mean to suggest that students are powerless. In our opinion, students have a responsibility to themselves and their supervisors to address the complexity of the supervisory relationship as issues which warrant such a discussion arise. In systemic fashion, we also believe that trainees and supervisors should be held equally accountable in maintaining personal and professional boundaries. After all, by the time marriage and family therapy students have completed the requirements necessary to participate in supervision, they are considered professionals. In our experience most of our students are healthy, adjusted individuals and family members. They are capable of recognizing the complexities which could lead to inappropriate dual relationships with their supervisors.

Jacobs (1991) addressed this responsibility of students in their supervisory experience by including a list of questions social work trainees could use to identify areas of concern in their relationship with their clinical supervisors. These appear to be valid and important questions which certainly could be applicable for marriage and family students as well. Particularly relevant are issues such as: whether or not students feel comfortable with their interactions with their supervisors, whether or not students feel judged by their supervisor, and whether or not supervisors are able to acknowledge their roles in conflict, should any arise (Jacobs, 1991).

In family supervision, the problem of duality can be avoided by carefully structuring involvement with the families so that the interviews address only the issues related to the clinical competency of the students. Thus, the goal of family supervision is not to help with the life adjustment of the trainees but to assist with their development into competent practitioners. We concur with Ryder and Hepworth (1990) who state, "One way to understand supervision is similar, i.e., as a process of helping a neophyte therapist evolve, at least partly, into a colleague and, perhaps, friend" (p.129). If a student is having difficulties as a result of family issues, a referral to an autonomous clinician is still the correct procedure. However, when utilized well, an interview with his/her family can help with the development of the student's competence and confidence as a professional.

Development of Family Supervision Interview

The idea of bringing trainees' families in for supervision sessions originated from the *first* author's training during his doctoral program. My supervisor invited me to bring my parents m for a supervision session. I can still, some eight years later, recall that session, which had a significant impact on my development as a family therapist. That single hour-long session went a long way to solidify my personal identification as a professional. Likewise, that session helped legitimize my training from my family's perspective. Their perception of my decision and commitment to my training shifted as a result.

It is interesting that I remember in detail how that session came about. My supervisor made a comment in passing (it's ironic how sometimes the most meaningful comments in supervision and therapy come in passing) that if students were really interested in getting supervision they would bring their families with them to the supervision sessions. One day, when my parents were visiting me, I took the opportunity to invite them to my supervision session. As I expected, my father was immediately glad to attend and my mother expressed some reservations. I recall simply expressing to them how important it would be to me if they attended and my mother's reservations dissolved. Since then I have lost the details of the session but still recall with fondness its impact.

Theoretical Foundations of Family Supervision Interview

When conducting the family supervision interview, a constructionist lens is applied. As Hoffman (1990) summarizes the approach, "As we move through the world, we build up our ideas about it in conversations with other people" (p.3). Our experience has shown that the significance of the conversations is often a function of the significance of the relationship between participants. Our experience also has shown that profound conversations occur between people in significant relationships. In most instances the strongest relationships exist between family members. This theoretical approach applies well to the family supervision interview because of its non-judgmental, supportive stance.

The constructionist stance has been critiqued for the not-knowing position of the therapist (Hoffman 1990). In the same way that one cannot not behave, it is logical to believe that one cannot not have an idea. In the family supervision sessions we have a clear idea of what drives the interviews: This is the idea that trainees have skills as family therapists. The goal of the interviews is to ask family members, in the presence of the trainees, to explain the origins of the trainees' therapeutic skills and to describe how they are applied. By sharing such views and tracing their history in a narrative story the reality of perceived skills becomes more vivid. Thus these interviews seek to fix competence in the trainees' views of themselves and their therapy.

Process of Family Supervision

This technique has been utilized with several trainees. At the start of a term an open invitation is extended to the students to attend a family supervision session. The supervisor simply explains to the students how the interview is structured and shares how s/he has found this process helpful. Since the interview is entirely a choice for the students, many do not select this option. The most common reason for not choosing such an interview is simply geographic distance between the students and their families. In some instances, the family supervision interview has been conducted with students and their current partners. However, given the nature of our program, most of our students are younger and without committed partners so these types of interviews are less common.

When a student accepts an offer to bring her/his family in for supervision the supervisor and student have a pre-session discussion of the interview. In this session they discuss issues having to do with the potential for problems relative to dual relationships. The student is asked if s/he has specific goals for the session. Most students do not but are simply excited to have a session with their family. In addition, the student is asked about any concerns s/he might have about the upcoming interview. If some are raised, they are processed. In all instances where this technique has been utilized it has been made clear to the students that this interview is focused on the students' therapy skills and development as family therapists. Likewise, the student is reminded not to disclose any information about her/his clients during the session. The pre-session is always closed with the supervisor asking if there is anything the student would prefer they not discuss during the session. In no instances thus far, have students had anything they wanted held back. However, we believe it is still important to ask this question so it can be assured that the session does not cross any boundaries for the students in this regard.

As stated above, the goal of the family supervision interview is to provide a format in which trainees can co-construct with their family members therapeutic competence. From the constructionist perspective the trainees are encouraged to create with their family members stories about their journeys toward becoming competent family therapists. This is quite simply accomplished by asking the trainees to trace with the family their decision to start training as marriage and family therapists. Parents often point to issues in the trainee's' childhood where they demonstrated early promise as future family therapists. If trainees bring their partners, there is often a discussion of how the decisions were made to seek graduate education.

Not only do these sessions support trainees but they also provide support for their family members as they seek to incorporate the changes that occur in the supervisees as a function of their training. The field has been slow to address the stress that training as an MFT has placed on the families of its students. From our systemic perspective and experience we know all too well that when a member of a family experiences a rapid period of growth, family members are affected. It is common for students who are unmarried to experience stress in their families of origin and for married students to experience marital stress and even divorce as a result of this strain. It is interesting to note that there is a whole body of literature on the self of the therapist but very little published on the therapist as family member. Having family members present allows the families an opportunity to support the supervisees' development and to understand changes in supervisees.

Outcome

While family supervision has just begun, we have some anecdotal feedback regarding the family interview. Consistently we are told how supportive the experience is. The trainees report that they feel their training gets legitimized. Trainees have reported that it is also significant to see a non-pathologizing family interview modeled for them. One trainee was having a difficult time getting his required family hours due to a feeling of insecurity about working with families. Alter he volunteered for a session with his wife, the impasse dissolved. In a later session he reported that since he had the experience of an interview with his wife he felt entitled to work with his clients' families.

Family supervision has been shown to be an excellent tool for the therapist-in-training in developing competence and confidence. Both students and their families benefit from the experience in many ways. In our opinion, in light of today's post modernist, social constructionist epistemology, this co-creative process is the next logical step in the evolution of training from a systemic perspective.

References

American Association for Marriage and Family Therapy (1997). *Manual on accreditation (version 9.0).* Washington, DC: Author.

Anonymous. (1972) On the differentiation of self in one's own family. In J. Framo (ed.), *Family interaction: A dialogue between family researchers and family therapists* (pp.111-173). New York: Springer.

Coopersmith, E. (1980). The family floor plan: A tool for training, assessment and intervention in family therapy. *Journal of Marital and Family Therapy, 6(2), 141–145.*

Dulil, B. (1983). *From the inside out and other metaphors: Creative and integrative approaches to training in systems thinking.* New York: Brunner/Mazel.

Hawkins, J. L., & Killorin, E. A. (1979). Family of origin: An experiential workshop. *American Journal of Family Therapy, 7(4), 5–17.*

Hoffman, L. (1990). Constructing realities: An art of lenses. *Family Process, 29(1), 1–12.*

Jacobs, C. (1991). Violations of the supervisory relationship: An ethical and educational blind spot. *Social Work, 36(2), 130–135.*

Kaiser, T. L. (1992) The supervisory relationship: An identification of the primary elements in the relationship and an application of two theories of ethical relationship. *Journal of Marital and Family Therapy, 18,(3), 283–296.*

Kane, *C.* M. (1996). An Experimental approach to family-of-origin work with marital and family therapy trainees. *Journal of Marital and Family Therapy, 22(4), 481–487.*

Liddle, H. A., & Saba, G. W. *(1985).* The isomorphic nature of training and therapy: Epistemological formulations for a structural strategic paradigm. In J. Schwartzman (Ed.), *Families and other systems* (pp. 3–11). New York: Guilford.

McDaniel, S. H., & Stanton, J. (1991). Family-of-origin work and family therapy skills training: Both-And. *Family Process,* 30,459–471.

McGoldrick, M., & Gerson, R. (1985). *Genograms in family assessment.* New York: W. W. Norton.

Nichols, W. C. (1993). Introduction: Critical issues in marital and family therapy education. *Contemporaiy Family Therapy, 15(1),* 3–8.

Ryder, R., & Hepworth, J. (1990). AAMFT ethical code: "Dual relationships." *Journal of Marital and Family Therapy, 16(2),* 127–132.

Smith, R. L.. (1993). Training in marriage and family counseling and therapy: Current status and challenges. *Counselor Education and Supervision, 33(2),* 89-1-1.

Risks and Safeguards in Person-of-the-Therapist Supervision

Brent J. Atkinson, Ph.D.

Published in the AAMFT Supervision Bulletin, Vol. 9, No. 3, Winter 1997.

I believe that supervision is most useful when the focus moves back and forth between the professional and personal functioning of the therapist. Professional aspects include learning how to apply theory and technique to assessment, interviewing, case planning etc. It involves knowing what to do next, where and how to direct therapy, what to give attention to and what to ignore. The personal functioning of a therapist is much more complex, involving internal and interpersonal processes that are not always under the therapist's conscious control. Indeed, therapists' reactions to clients are often so automatic they may not even be aware of them. I have come to believe that the effectiveness of each therapist is determined largely by the extent to which she or he is successful in becoming aware of these reactions, listening to them, learning from them and helping them change when change is needed.

As a supervisor, I observe therapists interacting with clients and help them identify automatic interpersonal and internal reactions that occur regularly. As therapists refine awareness of reactions set in motion during therapy sessions, they also generally choose to explore them during supervision. Often, this involves accessing and attending to these reactions directly during the supervision hour. Thus, a portion of supervision becomes a context for practicing the art of listening to, accepting, receiving suggestions and eliciting cooperation from aspects of oneself that sometimes operate at a tacit level. As supervision progresses, therapists generally experience greater sensitivity to the nuances of their reactions to clients, a greater ability to use this information effectively in therapy and a greater sense of internal harmony as they become more skilled in exploring and calming uncomfortable aspects of their experience with clients. Sometimes therapists are interested in discussing aspects of their personal histories or present circumstances in supervision, particularly if it occurs to them that some of the reactions they are having with clients parallel the ones they are having (or have had) in their own lives. Therapists are never pressured to discuss such information, but often chose to do so as they seek to give attention to automatic processes that operate in their relationships with clients.

Risks

It is common for therapists to feel some apprehension about exploring the personal aspects of their professional functioning with a supervisor. This often has to do with the fact that part of a supervisor's responsibility is to evaluate therapists at various points during supervision. It is natural for therapists to be hesitant to disclose their internal experience to someone who has organizational authority over them. There is a possibility that the supervisor could become biased and/or use personal information against the therapist in an evaluation. Conversely, the therapist may *feel* that their supervisor's evaluation was biased by personal information, even if the therapist made every effort to be honest and objective. There is also a risk of psychological distress if therapists disclose aspects of their internal experiences with their supervisor, then feel judged, rejected, disapproved of; or betrayed by this person whom they have come to trust and respect.

Safeguards

Before giving supervision, I discuss the potential risks with therapists, including several safeguards that I believe work to prevent misunderstanding and the potential for exploitation in the supervisory context.

First, I believe that supervisors who intend to facilitate person-of-the-therapist exploration should have been previously engaged, or be currently engaged, in supervision or supervision-of-supervision that focuses on their own reactions to others in the professional context. Risks are most minimal when supervisors place a high priority on maintaining awareness of their own reactions to therapists during supervision and are able to ascertain when subtle emotional states are influencing their reactions as supervisors. Supervisors should model the kind of internal awareness that they are attempting to facilitate with therapists. This requires a certain amount of vulnerability on the part of supervisors, but I believe this is essential for supervisors who intend to help therapists with person-of-the-therapist exploration.

Second, I take the position that the *person-of-the-therapist portion of the supervision is entirely optional,* and I will proceed only to the extent that therapists feel comfortable with such a process. If a therapist is hesitant to begin person-of-the-therapist supervision as described above, I suggest that we talk it over and see if we can come to an agreement about what might work. For example, the therapist might be comfort-able using supervision as a context for identifying internal and or interpersonal reactions that take place during therapy, but not comfortable exploring them in the context of supervision. I express flexibility (within a certain range) and optimism that we can work something out. If we simply cannot come to an agreement, I suggest that we meet with other clinical supervisors, discuss the situation, and decide where to go from there.

Third, I encourage therapists to wait to explore their personal experience in the therapy room until they are confident that (a) I have a strong commitment to maintaining awareness of my own reactions during supervision and would be able to recognize and willing to acknowledge any of my reactions to them that were more extreme than a situation warranted, and (b) I really care about their well-being and have their best interest at heart. How can therapists develop this kind of confidence about a supervisor before beginning supervision? I know of two methods that help. Supervisors can provide names and addresses of former supervisees who are willing to discuss what supervision was like for them. Prospective supervisees can be encouraged to contact former supervisees to inquire about their experience with the supervisor. Both the act of offering names of former supervisees and the discussions therapists may have with former supervisees can help establish an initial level of confidence as supervision begins. Supervisors can also demonstrate their commitment to self-awareness in the supervisory process by expressing a willingness to talk about their own development as supervisors and to discuss what they have learned about themselves through their own supervision (or

supervision of supervision). If they feel comfortable, supervisors might even discuss cutting-edge aspects of their own process they are presently exploring in their development as supervisors. In initiating such discussion, supervisors demonstrate their commitment to responsible self-awareness and receptivity in the supervisory process.

Fourth, I never push therapists to explore aspects of their experience that (a) they don't think are important to explore, or (b) they don't feel ready to explore. I encourage therapists to operate according to their own sense of what is right for them, not my sense.

Fifth, I have an open policy regarding inviting a third party to supervision meetings. If a therapist should ever feel too uncomfortable to talk with me about an issue one-on-one, or feel unsuccessful in attempting to do so, I would encourage the therapist to bring another person with him/her someone with whom the therapist could feel safe. This could be another supervisor, a colleague, or whoever the therapist would like.

Finally, I put all of this in writing and discuss it with therapists before supervision begins. Therapists sign an in-formed consent document indicating they understand the risks of person-of-the-therapist supervision and are comfortable with the safeguards I have suggested. I do not begin the person-of-the-therapist aspect of supervision unless the therapists have explicitly indicated that, should they become confused or uncomfortable with anything that happened during supervision, they would be able to discuss it with me, and they are confident that I would respond appropriately. Of course, this is a necessary precondition for any good supervisory experience, but I believe it is absolutely essential in supervision that involves person-of-the-therapist exploration. Sometimes supervision touches on areas that are highly personal, and there is a potential for therapists and supervisors to misread the actions or attitudes of the other. Unless therapists feel free to check out their perceptions and express confusion or discomfort, they may be at risk for feeling violated, even in situations in which supervisors place a priority on being supportive and responsive to expressed confusion or discomfort. A hypothetical example will help clarify: During the third week of supervision, while reviewing a videotape of a session, it became obvious to both therapist and supervisor that the therapist had become frustrated with a client, then distanced emotionally during the session. At an appropriate point, the supervisor asked if the therapist would like to explore these reactions further during the supervisory hour. Because of his stress level on this particular day, the therapist felt too vulnerable to be comfortable exploring his emotional reactions. But the therapist was hesitant to say this to the supervisor, thinking the supervisor might be disappointed or disapproving (he didn't yet know from his experience with the supervisor it was safe to draw personal boundaries). Consequently, the therapist tried to minimize the feeling of hesitation, and instead said "yes" to the supervisor's offer. Had the therapist expressed reluctance (verbally or nonverbally) to explore the reactions, the supervisor would have been understanding and supportive, recognizing that the therapist must feel free to control the timing and limits of his vulnerability in supervision. Fortunately, the supervisor picked up on the incongruence in the therapists answer and questioned him more closely about his level of comfort. The therapist finally did express his hesitation, and they agreed to postpone the exploration for another day.

If therapists are unable to say, "I'm uncomfortable," or "I'm not up for exploring my feelings today," in response to such situations, they may feel pushed or invaded, even in situations in which supervisors are careful about respecting therapists' boundaries. This is why I feel it is critical, before supervision begins, for the supervisor and the therapist to discuss the therapist's ability and willingness to express to the supervisor any discomfort or confusion that might arise during the supervisory process. Good supervisors can often pick up on nonverbal signs of discomfort on the part of therapists, but ultimately the safety of the supervisory experience requires an ability and willingness on the part of therapists and supervisors to speak openly about their level of comfort in supervision, throughout the course of supervision.

Discussion

The safeguards described above serve several positive functions. First, discussing them with the supervisor before supervision begins helps therapists think through potential risks involved in supervision and become more sensitive to their level of comfort with the kind of supervision being proposed. Second, discussion of risks and safeguards assures therapists

that the supervisor is aware of the potential risks involved in supervision and is concerned about the safety of the supervisory context. Third, by being invited into a discussion of risks and safeguards, and by being asked to assess their initial level of comfort and choose the extent or manner in which they wish to begin exploring personal aspects of their professional functioning, therapists generally feel empowered and assured that their level of comfort with the process is absolutely critical and will be respected and honored during the supervisory process.

While candid discussion about the risks and safeguards is necessary, it is not sufficient to guarantee the safety of the supervisory context. In the end, the safety of the supervisory context rests with the emotional maturity of the supervisor. Is it safe for therapists to express discomfort or confusion with the supervisory process? Will the supervisor be direct about his/her thoughts and reactions during supervision? Can the supervisor be supportive of differences of opinion or style that arise between the supervisor and therapist? Is the supervisor aware of his/her reactions to a therapists that are more extreme than the situation warrants? These are probably some of the most important questions to be considered.

Conclusion

Because of the added level of vulnerability involved when therapists use a portion of supervision to explore their own experience in the therapy room, additional safeguards and measures must be taken to ensure that therapists feel safe. I have attempted to provide some suggestions about how to proceed. I welcome comments, ideas and descriptions of other practices that supervisors have found useful in establishing a safe context for exploring the personal functioning of therapists in their work with clients.

References

Aponte, H. (1994). How personal can training get? *Journal of Marital and Family Therapy, 20, 3–15.*

Atkinson, B. (In press [a]). What is the difference between personal therapy and person of the therapist supervision? In C. Storm and T. Todd (Eds.), The reasonably complete systemic supervisor resource guide. Boston: Allyn & Bacon.

Atkinson, B. (In press [b]). Entering supervision with both eyes open: Informed consent in supervision. In C. Storm & T. Todd (Eds.). *The reasonably complete systemic supervisor resource guide.* Boston: Allyn & Bacon.

Atkinson, B. (1993). Hierarchy: The imbalance of risk. *Family Process, 32,* 167–170.

Kantor, D. & Mitchell E. (1992). Letter to the editor. *The AAMFT Supervision Bulletin, V(2).*

Storm, C. (1991). Changing the line: An interview with Edwin Friedman. *The AAMFT Supervision Bulletin, IV(3).*

Tomm, K. (1993). Defining supervision and therapy: A fuzzy boundary? *The AAMFT Supervision Bulletin, VI (1).*

Utilizing Clients' Voices in Clinical Supervision

William Quinn, Ph.D., Chandra Nagireddy, M.S., John Lawless, M.S., and Rob Bagley, M.S.

Published in the AAMFT Supervision Bulletin, Vol. IX, No. 1, Winter 1996.

This article provides a brief description of a client feedback centered supervision model. The model incorporates the clients' voices and the supervisee's concerns. Supervision in marriage and family therapy (MFT) has yet to catch up with the current advances in clinical practice particularly regarding the role of clients in the design and delivery of their treatment. As the field of mental health care becomes more competitive and subject to greater influence from the consumer, delivery of therapy has to become more responsive to the concerns of clients. In addition, concepts of cultural relativism, in which attitudes, perceptions and behavior are situated in a cultural context, and social constructionism, in which creation process does not occur in isolation but through human exchange as persons endeavor to derive mutually agreed upon meanings, have received no more than minimal attention within the context of training. This model of feedback centered supervision grows Out of several previous projects at our clinic in which client voices are privileged, including the ethnographic interview to assess the client's experience of therapy (Quinn, in press), Interpersonal Process Recall (IPR) as a method for researching therapy process (Gale, Odell, & Nagireddy, 1995) and IPR to conduct supervision in MFT.

Normally, supervision involving video or case presentation by the therapist includes the supervisor and the supervisee engaging in interpretation and analysis of supervisee's actions and intentions in the context of the clients' problems. However, in the absence of any feedback from the clients who are the object of clinical intervention, both the supervisee and the supervisor have to rely on their own observations of the client. This may often involve second guessing clients' reactions to a specific intervention. In this context, both the supervisor and the supervisee may have their own unique observations of therapy events depending upon their theoretical perspectives and subjectivity. In the absence of the clients' feedback, there may be a struggle for legitimacy of perspectives when the supervisor and supervisee have competing perspectives. When the client is a couple or a family, different members of the client system may have divergent goals for therapy and may react differently to a therapy event. In working with couples and families, both the supervisor and the supervisee face a greater challenge in rendering therapy responsive to the competing needs and goals of the family members. This is the problem of inadequate data and an incomplete feedback loop. The issue can be resolved by directly obtaining feedback from the clients about their experience of the therapy events and the therapist actions. The feedback data can serve as the basis for supervision dialogue.

In supervision dialogue, both the supervisor and the therapist bring their respective agendas into play. The therapist and the supervisor may envisage certain outcomes for the client system, may prefer certain interventions, and may accord differing importance to the mastery of certain skills and competencies. When the supervisor and the supervisee differ in their agenda for supervision, struggle for dominance may become a theme in the supervisory process. While in most circumstances the agenda of the supervisor may prevail, it is often at the cost of the supervisee's motivation and agency. When the supervisor and the supervisee have the benefit of feedback from clients about their priorities, needs, reactions and interpretations, the supervision process can become focussed on clients' concerns. The supervisee's learning goals and the supervisor's instructional goals now can be in the service of explicit goals for the client, thus rendering the supervision process responsive to the clients' needs. When the therapist's developmental goals emerge in the context of the stated needs of his/her clients, learning can be more exciting.

We see this model as accommodating the developmental needs of the therapist's professional position in that it is responsive to the client system and the desire for change. With the active participation of the therapist-in-training in his/her own learning, via the request to identify parts of the video record that stimulate curiosity or reflect bewilderment, the conversation remains located within the parameters of the therapist's intellectual and emotional processes. Perceived "errors" that conversations are irrelevant or power-based are minimized.

Thus, in this model, rather than the supervisor being viewed as the origin of clinical observation, insight and supervision agenda, the clients' needs and priorities, problems and frustrations, as revealed through feedback interviews, provide the context and the goals for the supervision process. The supervisor's role is to enable the therapist to respond to his/her clients in a manner that best challenges his/her clinical competencies and meets the clients' goals most effectively. The critical role of the supervisor lies in providing a safe climate for the therapist to remain open to the feedback from his/her clients. The supervisor acts as the resource person willing to assist the therapist as and when such help is solicited. The goals of feedback centered supervision would be better realized when it is situated within the context of a broader contract between the supervisor and the supervisee. The contract may involve supervision focus on a particular model of therapy, a specific set of skills and competencies, a particular problem condition, or a supervisee's need to articulate his/her theory of therapy

Generating Feedback From Clients for Supervision

It is the responsibility of the therapist to seek the cooperation of his/her clients by articulating the purpose of the feedback interviews, how the information will be processed and how it might impact their therapy. When the clients sense that their therapist is genuinely interested in what they have to say and understand how their feedback can help their therapy, they usually consent to provide feedback. If the client is a couple or a family, it may be important to interview the members separately and assure them that any information revealed about the other family members will be used with discretion in future sessions. The therapist requests either his/her supervisor or a colleague trained in qualitative interviewing techniques to interview his/ her clients.

The most important task of the interviewer is to translate the therapist's intent of eliciting clients' experience of therapy events in a manner which does not jeopardize the therapist-client alliance. When the supervisor interviews a supervisee's client, it is crucial for the supervisor not to cross into the role of a therapist or a therapist-critic and to demonstrate respect and regard for the therapist in their presence. Ideally, the interviewer will assume the role of a researcher who is solely concerned with eliciting the clients' experience of the therapy.

We have used two methods of interviews in generating feed-back from clients. One is the open ended in-depth interview and the other is the Interpersonal Process Recall (IPR) interview. Open ended in-depth interviews generally tend to be evaluative and elicit global impressions about the therapy and its impact on the clients. At the beginning of the interview, the interviewer reiterates the objectives of the interview and his/her role as the interviewer and how the feedback information will be used by their therapist. The interviewer can begin the interview with a statement like, "Can you please share your thoughts and feelings about your therapy sessions so that your therapist can better understand what has been accomplished and what needs to be accomplished?" or "Can you share any thoughts about your therapy which you think will help your therapist and your therapy?" The interviewer should ask questions which invite clarification or articulation or elaboration on issues referred to by the client and avoid leading the client into areas that may interest the interviewer.

In an interpersonal Process Recall (IPR) interview, the client is presented a video record of a therapy session or a session event and asked to recall his/her thoughts and feelings while playing back the tape. Generally, the client is given control of the playback and is requested to stop as often as possible and share his/her thoughts and feelings about the events reviewed. The interviewer can also request interruption of playback of the therapy tape at points where he/she may become intrigued by events in the session. In such instances, the interviewer makes an open-ended request for the client's comments. The session or the event is selected by the therapist in consultation with his/her clients. The session may represent a significant positive shift or may signify impasse or a negative experience for either the clients or the therapist. A non-eventful session may also be selected for review as a starter simply with the goal of gaining comfort with this supervision process.

Processing Clients' Feedback in Supervision

Feedback interviews are video recorded and presented to the supervisee in a separate session by the supervisor. The supervision session is modeled along the same lines as the Interpersonal Process Recall interview with the clients. However, the goal of this session is to help the supervisee review and respond to his/her clients' feedback on the therapy session. The supervisor's role is to facilitate supervisee articulation of his/her reactions, thoughts and feelings in response to the clients' feedback. The supervisee plays back the video record of the feedback interview and stops at points to articulate thoughts and feelings as well as his/her interpretations and inferences. This also provides a point of departure into supervision dialogue as it normally occurs. However, such a dialogue now occurs in the context of the feedback data from the clients, the supervisee's reactions to the feedback, and his/her perspective of therapy events. Supervision dialogue may focus on making sense of the feedback data, integration of perspectives, challenging previous conclusions, reviewing intervention strategies and ultimately, arriving at a new understanding of the therapy processes and events in the case. Feedback centered supervision may lead to new learning goals for the therapist and new instructional tasks for the supervisor while introducing a new twist into all the relationships in the arena.

The feedback centered model of supervision can be utilized as the mode of supervision or can be integrated with the ongoing supervision process, whether it is video assisted supervision or live supervision. However, learning is most facilitated when the relationship between the supervisor and supervisee is open and supportive. This supervision model can also be instituted where the goal for the supervisor is to move away from authority oriented supervision to a more collaborative supervision. The structure provided by this model facilitates the supervisor's sensitivity to the unique distinctions and interpretations which a supervisee may bring to his/her role as a therapist, as a function of such factors as one's gender or ethnicity. This model of supervision can also be used to gain insight into therapy events and processes which are opaque, to understand how certain changes occur in therapy, or to clarify why the therapy process is stuck. It also produces therapy that is responsive to the clients. The penetrating voice of a client can serve to engage the learning process.

References

Quinn, W.H. (in press). The Client Speaks Out: Three Domains of Meaning, *Journal of Family Psychotherapy.*

Gale, J., Odell, M., & Nagireddy, C. (1995). Marital therapy and self-reflexive research: Research and/as Intervention. In G. H. Morris and R. J. Chenail (Eds.), *The Talk of the Clinic.* Hillsdale, N.J.: Lawrence Erlbaum Associates.

Highlight Success in Groups: An Empowering and Energizing Exercise

Carla Pond, M.A.

Published in the AAMFT Supervision Bulletin, Vol. VIII, No. 1, Spring 1995.

The practice of therapy requires an ongoing source of energy and support without which therapists often find themselves tired, drained, frustrated, and bored. Those especially prone to this burnout may be therapists who work in larger systems (agencies, hospitals, etc.) where they have little or no control. However, private practice can also engender these feelings when it is isolating or stressful. The group supervision exercise below can help energize supervisees.

The exercise, which developed out of the solution-focused model of therapy, highlights the competence of each supervisee. Supervisees, I found, often arrived at supervision with a distinct lack of energy and sometimes even tried to convince me that their cases were hopeless. As a reaction to this I decided, in an isomorphic way, to apply to supervisees the same solution-focused approach I was trying to teach them to apply to clients. At the beginning of a supervision group I asked each supervisee in turn to describe a successful intervention that they had used since our last meeting. It was acceptable to highlight any successful interchange in therapy, however slight or seemingly insignificant. The rest of the group was asked, each in turn, to respond to the person who had just presented their intervention. Responses varied from simple praise or affirmation, the report of similar interventions, or the invention of new ideas. Often therapists commented that they could use the idea on one of their cases. Interest and excitement began to build regarding cases.

Before the end of each turn, each supervisee was also asked to talk about what is was like to present their idea, to receive reactions and to respond. Often, lively discussions followed. This processing turned out to be a crucial part of the exercise. Comments like "I forgot I could do this" surfaced. Follow up questions were asked when appropriate: How could you stay in touch with your successes on an ongoing basis? What could happen that could get you to forget you are competent? What could get in the way of building on your successes? How could you sustain the feeling about your work that you have right now?

Noticeable results emerged immediately from this process. Supervisees had not been used to, generally speaking, having time to focus on their success, usually only stopping to process cases when they are stuck. When given the chance, supervisees natural resources surfaced, often putting them in touch with their original reasons for becoming a therapist, and reminding them how exciting it can be to positively affect clients' lives. As supervisees experienced themselves as competent, anxiety subsided.

Another benefit of directly hearing about others' successes was the broadening of viewpoints. Supervisees developed self confidence as they received public acknowledgement. The exercise helped normalize difficulties supervisees might have been having and helped them transfer their focus from how they were feeling to skill building and problem solving.

One supervisee made the following comments about participating in the exercise. She felt that it helped her to be empowered as a therapist... "and to recognize the things that can get ignored...it's easier to have an awareness of clients but not ourselves...it's helpful to hear other people energizing us and developing us...the process put value on what I do...I felt encouraged, challenged and anxious to keep going...put me back in focus."

This exercise can be repeated often, even weekly, with a group. As the group gets used to presenting ideas and is able to sustain energy, the format can be shortened to simply highlighting and sharing techniques. When used sporadically it is best to use the entire exercise and allow ample time so supervisees can experience the shift in their self-perception and get their creativity flowing. It can also be used in individual supervision where the amount of attention from the supervisor hopefully offsets the loss of the group interaction.

The process presented here, as is true of all solution focused work, is more than just "focusing on the positive" because it is designed to energize supervisees without denying or ignoring the negative. It is clear to supervisees that this exercise is not a substitute for presenting difficult cases or situations that they are grappling with, but rather a way to prepare them to tackle challenges.

As we see supervisees become increasingly competent therapists, we, as supervisors, isomorphically experience ourselves as capable. This approach requires us to believe that each supervisee has the ability and potential to be an effective therapist, according to that person's own style. We can define our own competence as the ability to facilitate this process.

Energy, on the surface, is a concept that may seem nonsystemic or intrapsychic. But perhaps it might be useful to look at it as a reaction rather than a condition. If we are energized as a response to a stimulus then energy can be seen as an interactional process. As supervisors we can commit ourselves to behaviors that elicit energy from supervisees, helping to produce therapists who may be described as self-confident, able to generate appropriate custom-made interventions, and who know when to ask for help and how to get help. This exercise is one way we can train supervisees to be self-energizing, competent therapists.

Chapter 5

Supervision Modalities— Live, Videotape, Etc.

Perspectives on Live Supervision: Supervisor, Therapist, and Client

Published in the AAMFT Supervision Bulletin, Vol. VIII, No. 2, Summer 1995.

The Supervisor's View

Eric McCollum, Ph.D.

I began my live supervision "career" without the benefit of mirror or phone. I sat in a corner of a small room at a youth center while the therapist worked with the family. If I had an idea or direction for the therapist to go in, I'd wave or nod and we'd step into the other room to confer. It was there that I learned the first of many important lessons about live supervision. First, families will put up with all kinds of odd things (like a stranger sitting in the corner of the room while they discuss their problems) if they have faith in our wish to help them. No family refused our in-the-room brand of live supervision. We had one child, however, whose mission in life was to make such grotesque faces at me that I would laugh. Several times he succeeded. Now, of course, in the age of reflecting teams and more therapeutic candor, I'd likely not find silence so necessary. The second thing I learned in the comer of that little room is that live supervision is not so much a matter of mirrors and wires as it is a matter of blending together different points of view.

Like therapy, doing live supervision has pushed me to grow in all kinds of ways I never expected. Perhaps most intimidating is the confidence my students place in me. As we interview students for admission to practicum, over and over again they tell us supervisors how they expect to look for us for the answer when they run into trouble. Over and over again I tell them that I don't have all the answers, that I often struggle with not knowing what to do myself Over and over again, they don't believe me. I've even had students get angry in supervision, claiming that I knew the answer to their questions but purposefully withheld it. I tell them that I wish I could usher them into a textbook world of therapy where everything always goes the way it is planned and where supervisors always have the answer. But I can't. I think that world only exists in textbooks. And facing that fact is one of the sad steps of growing up as a therapist.

The other dilemmas I face in live supervision array themselves on a continua for me. How active should I be versus how restrained? How much do I tell a student what to do versus how much do I let them struggle toward their own solution while I do my best to safeguard the client? How do I keep my own anxiety under control and curb my own oldest-brother wish to take over and make things "right" versus letting student and clients stew with their troubles? The dilemmas of supervision remind me all too clearly of the dilemmas of therapy.

But along with the dilemmas come the satisfactions. The other afternoon I sat behind the mirror and watched a student at the end of her first year do a wonderful termination interview with a woman who had gained a great deal from therapy. It was one of the finest interviews I'd seen in a long time and a pleasure to see my student so clearly demonstrate how much she'd learned in our program. There is something deeply satisfying about teaching what I know—and in watching students use it so well.

But this work is daunting too. I want to give my students the (nonexistent) answers, shelter them from the ambiguity and conflicts of our profession, hide them from my human flaws. I know that some of them will be better therapists than I am. It is obvious even now. I'm excited by their talent and enthusiasm and a little jealous too, wishing I was young again, and just starting out.

Working Live

Jerome Adams, Ph.D.

As I sat behind the mirror watching Frank interview the couple, it was clear he was sinking fast. The husband had not completed the previous week's homework assignment as instructed. Frank took this as a sign the husband was not committed to his marriage, and hinted the therapy may be failing, even though both partners said they were getting along much better. Frank was getting more pessimistic, the couple more discouraged.

I called Frank on the phone and had him ask the husband if he had done the homework, or had changed it to make the assignment "his own." The husband replied that he had, and went on to recount several things he had done for his wife he was feelings very good about. At a break later in the session, Frank and I discussed ways he could compliment the husband's creativity and the couple's excellent progress in treatment.

Helping a therapist change direction quickly is one of the things "working live" does best. Live supervision put Frank on a more optimistic course almost immediately. He felt better and so did the couple.

Among the many ways of working live, I particularly like the Milan concept of the multi session. I conduct a short pre-session with the therapist to review goals for the session, observe the interview which may involve calls from the team, discuss the team's ideas with the therapist at a mid-session break, and then meet with the therapist after the family has had a chance to hear the therapist's observations and ideas in a post-session wrap-up.

The interview is a time of intense concentration, I must pay attention to the dynamics of the family and help the therapist make a sound assessment. But I must focus my attention on the activities of the therapist as well. For example, the therapist may have asked me during the pre-session for advice on how to develop a particular interviewing skill. Telephone call-ins to the therapist are especially tricky. If I make a suggestion, I usually offer a brief rationale. For less experienced therapists, call-ins have the potential to add confusion. Beginning therapists are prone to view call-ins as criticisms, a sign they are not getting it right. Too many phone calls can overwhelm the therapist. How many is too many? That depends on the therapist, and is again something I need to be aware of as a supervisor.

In Frank's session I didn't have a lot of time to explain the change in direction. I had a good relationship with him and knew he would trust my judgement. But I also knew Frank would need an explanation. This is where the post-session wrap up is extremely valuable. I typically take up to half an hour with the therapist and team reviewing what happened in the session.

In my experience, the post-session is where trainees ask the best questions. They have more time to reflect on how an interview fits with the overall treatment objective. I have an opportuntiy to explain its relationship to the family's larger institutional context. Trainees see for themselves how theory is put into practice.

Live supervision can't do everything. But it is the best way for me to see for myself what the trainee is doing, correct mistakes if I need to, ans assure no harm comes to families. For the trainee, it is the best way to witness the immediate positive effect of a procedure done correctly.

A Student's Eye

Stephanie Jester, M.S.

"Breathe, Stephanie, breathe" siad my supervisor from the other side of the one-way mirror. It was a difficult session with my client, a paranoid schizophrenic, who was telling me about the three different voices she heard inside her head. My supervisor and I had prepared for this session during the previous week, but nothing could have prepared me for the way the client presented that night. My supervisor waited for me to catch my breath, and then encouraged ne to treat each voice as a "person." I was then able to work with the voices as an "internal family system" and help the client gain more control over her experience. This frame became a very powerful tool that I was able to use throughout the course of the therapy, even when my supervisor did not observe the session "live."

I was truly thankful for the support of live supervision that night. However, my supervision needs changed over the course of my 2-year internship. My personal and professional growth during those two years necessitated a constant shift in the way that my supervisor and I worked together. My supervisor's ability to adjust to my growth was the key to our successful live supervision experiences.

On the afternoon of my first live supervision session, I met with my supervisor to plan for the case. When she asked what I needed from her, I said, "PLEASE don't let me get stuck with nothing to say." I met with the couple, whose marriage was on the verge of a breakup. Halfway through the session, I felt as hopeless as they did. I wanted to say, "go ahead and split up...I really don't know what else to tell you." I knew I couldn't say that. "Please call and tell me what to do" I thought to myself as I said to the client, "what attracted you to your husband in the first place?" BEEEEEEP...the phone rang...my supervisor was going to save me. Because my supervisor knew I was stuck, she not only told me what to do, but she also gave me the words to use. She said, "Give me an example of a time when your husband remembered to do something for you." I used her words and the session was up and running. By the end of the evening, the clients had decided to try to save their marriage.

As I grew more confident, I needed something different from my supervisor during live supervision. I became much more aware of my clients' reactions to the one way mirror and the beeping telephone. I worried that my clients would think I had said something wrong when the telephone rang, and that they would question whether or not I could handle their case.

My supervisor, thankfully, attended as much to our relationship as to the relationship between my clients. We discussed my growth and changing needs, and modified our working relationship during live supervision. We became a working team, and started to inform my clients that we were a team during their first session. This allowed me to gain credibility with my clients and allowed my supervisor to sit back and recognize that I didn't need her as much anymore.

When I think back now about my experience with live supervision, I can't imagine what it would be like to train without it. Live supervision allowed my supervisor to know more about my first sessions than I knew myself. If she hadn't watched the sessions live, she never would have known what truly happened in the sessions, because I did not know enough at the time to describe everything to her. In addition, she was able to guide me through real life situations with clients that I really wasn't ready to handle on my own. If I had a personal reaction to a client, she was able to observe it, and process the reaction with me after the session. Without live supervision, she never would have known about my reactions and how they were affecting the therapy.

The only negative reaction I had to live supervision was the difficulty in switching from supervisor to supervisor. Each one had a very different supervisory style, and this was often hard to adjust to during the middle of a session. If I had it to do over again, I would discuss these differences more openly so that I could anticipate their impact prior to my therapy sessions.

During my first six months as a newly graduated marriage and family therapist, I was constantly reminded of the value of live supervision. My employer continually told me that I was much better prepared to see clients on my own than graduates of other training programs that did not use live supervision.

I am thankful for the learning opportuntiies that live supervision provided me. I believe that it made me a better therapist, and gave me the opportuntiy to work with a supervisor that I now consider a trusted mentor. Today, as I practice privately in a small marriage and family therapy clinic, there are times when I wish the phone would ring and my supervisor's voice would come over the line to give me a gem of advice.

A Client's Voice

Anonymous

Q: The Lay of the Land [Your experience of live supervision]

A: "I didn't always know who was back there... [behind the mirror]. It was disconcerting and would have been less ambiguous if they had told me the process beforehand. I often wondered how many people were behind the mirror."

Q: Were you conscious of the supervisor's presence behind the mirror?

A: "There was an obvious difference when the supervisor made a process comment as opposed to telling the therapist to go in a totally different direction. At times I was waiting for the phone to ring...other times, [the phone] pissed me off. Like when the supervisor said we weren't talking loud enough. And sometimes I thought the therapist missed something [that was important to me.] There was clearly a senior/junior position between the supervisor and the therapist. Sometimes the supervisor was somewhat intrusive...and sometimes the therapist appeared to be waiting for a call."

Q: Did the presence of the two professionals (supervisor and therapist) make you feel more comfortable?

A: "I did assume I was getting the beset quality of care. The supervisor was sort of a safety net."

Live Supervision as a Window: An Interview With Braulio Montalvo

Interview conducted by Cheryl Storm, AAMFT Supervision Bulletin editor, with Braulio Montalvo, M.A.

Published in the AAMFT Supervision Bulletin, Vol. V, No. 2, June 1992.

Storm: *You are the author of the now classic paper (Montalvo, 1972) on live supervision.*

Montalvo: When I wrote that paper, I was proposing live supervision as a supplement to other supervision methods. It was developed because we were looking for other windows for viewing therapists' work. Our original intention was to find a way to get closer to the therapy when our supervisees were needing our help. I am surprised it has become such a single tool. It has been perverted and for many is now the only way.

Storm: *So you believe other methods of supervision are valuable?*

Montalvo: Live supervision should not be the only tool used in supervision but used with others. Supervisees learn different skills from what I call synoptic supervision, supervision in which supervisees summarize several of their therapy sessions with a case, than from live supervision. There is tremendous value in contrasting what is learned through synoptic supervision with live supervision of a case. It is the contrast between "talking about" or abstracting from the "raw stuff" and "seeing in the real world" that provides supervisors with something to work on with supervisees. Each method is a window to help supervisors and supervisees gain information to understand families and to refine the tools of the therapist. Supervisors should think about using a variety of methods. Sometimes seeing less is seeing more. Observing every other therapy session enables supervisors to see broad patterns. Many supervisors get too wrapped up in one or two themes because they get too close and miss the bigger picture. All windows are needed. Synoptic supervision taps what therapists think, live supervision accesses what they do and once a month sporadic supervision shows their overall professional development.

Storm: *You state in your article that the rela-tionship between the supervisor and supervisee is "vertical" yet "a model of mutual consent and collaboration" [p. 344].*

Montalvo: I was focusing on the nature of the supervision contract. The relationship is vertical by consent. If you are going to be responsible for shaping a profession by facilitating appropriate use of abilities, those with experience must lead the way. I believe assuming supervisors and supervisees are on equal footing is unethical. In fact, I even believe that the relationship of supervisor and supervisee should *not* be too isomorphic to the relationship of the therapist and family. Without differentiation of form and function it is hard to work.

Storm: *Probably the major criticism of live supervision is that therapists can become "puppets," dependent on their supervisors, and fail to develop as unique professionals.*

Montalvo: Robotization is a honest pitfall of the method. Live supervision can lead to the flat-footed supervisor who continuously interrupts and detracts from the autonomy of the supervisee. This method was developed based on the model of the good attending physician who helps you over the hump. He or she leaves you standing, in control. Therapists who have supervisors that misuse the method to exhibit their expertise or to gain control are crippled by live supervision and should escape. However, this can also happen from other methods of supervision such as when supervisees "sit in" with their supervisors. This method too can fail to produce the agile, flexible supervisees we aim to train.

Storm: *Do you have any advice for supervisors to prevent robotization?*

Montalvo: Live supervision is an art. My model was Haley, who by the way encouraged me to write that paper. He could say three words and you would know just what to do. Supervisors' should be cryptic and economical in their comments, have an unobtrusive way of operating and leave their supervisees standing on their own. Thus, good live supervisors do not interrupt constantly and allow themselves the flexibility to not intervene.

Storm: *Some supervisors have "taken the mirror down" and supervision occurs in the presence of families and with input from clients. Do you have any reactions to these new developments?*

Montalvo: I have seen variations on this method. I am not sure whether what I have seen is the method or the method not used well. I was called in recently to disentangle a case in which this method resulted in a disaster. Each member of a team of therapists shared their views with a family based on the idea that therapy is a democratic smorgasbord of ideas and that all participants, clients and professionals, are equal. It seemed that everyone was afraid of leaving someone out, which resulted in confusion. I question the outcome of therapy with this method. In this particular case, no one seemed to be concerned about the adolescent's continuing truancy and drug use. I believe responsible hierarchy is essential in therapy and to learning therapy. People, whether clients or therapists, come to us because we are "humble" experts and we should respond with a direction, even if the direction is "I don't know."

Storm: *Does it surprise you that your paper has had so much influence in the field?*

Montalvo: I see live supervision, when used carefully, as a symbol of family therapy's strong traditional respect for the immediacy of the family's presenting problem, for what's observable and has to be empirically addressed, in order to be helpful. Live supervision, despite its flaws, helped us to move one step closer to the ground of family work, and away from philosophic and ideologic cobwebs, which abound in our field's explanations of what it does.

Storm: *What changes do you see occurring in the process of supervision?*

Montalvo: Attention to helping supervisees become open and respectful of contributions from members of surrounding institutions such as the school, health providers, etc. Supervision must occur at these interfaces. Skill in the problem-solving with strictly intrafamilial issues is seldom enough in dealing with the complex problems we see. Supervisors must help therapists to enhance their skills at dealing with the interfaces.

References

Montalvo, B. (1972). Aspects of live supervision. *Family Process*, 12, 343-359.

Technology in Live Supervision

Lewis L. Moore, Ph.D., Adrian Hickmon, Ph.D. and Vann Rackley, Ph.D.

Published in the AAMFT Supervision Bulletin, Vol. VIII, No. 2, Summer 1995.

Harding University's master's program in marriage and family therapy focuses on an intense clinical experience. The program's goal is to train clinically competent marriage and family therapists (MFTs). Based on this perspective, the program demands a heavy concentration on live supervision. The ability to do live supervision anytime with a trainee working in any therapy room is imperative. The following description of facilities, equipment, and technology identifies the system the program developed to provide such training.

Installation of the recording and communication network cost approximately $50,000. The technology provides high quality and efficient advantages for live supervision and client comfort. The most important aspects of this setup include a remote control system, an easy-access control room, client-oriented work space, and discreet camera and microphone placements.

The greatest benefit of the facility's technology comes from the ability to monitor several cases, live, in a single setting. This allows the supervisor to choose the case or therapist needing the most attention and is an efficient use of supervision time. When a client doesn't show up for an appointment, supervisors can do live supervision with another MFT and MFTs can join a live supervision group.

The Harding University marriage and family therapy clinic has ten fully equipped therapy rooms. Three rooms have pan-tilt/zoom cameras that can take broad angle shots of large families or groups and yet is sensitive enough to focus on eye color of a particular individual. Camera mountings are in the ceiling corner above the office door. They are discreet and do not present a distraction for clients. The three pan-tilt/zoom cameras allow the therapist or the supervisor to: (1) change the field of vision to be sure all clients and the therapist are included in the picture, (2) adjust to seating movements of clients during the session, and (3) during live supervision, focus more closely on an individual client or the therapist for part of the session. This prevents the monitor from displaying a partial picture of the therapy room. Each therapy room, the control room, and the three clinical faculty members' offices are equipped with an intercom phone system for immediate supervisor-therapist communication. Therapy room equipment includes a very sensitive pressure zone microphone. The microphone is ceiling-mounted and not intrusive.

Additionally, each therapy room has a remote control panel that initiates taping in the control center. Again, this allows the MFT to go on with little technical requirements, remaining in the therapy room to control recording instead of walking to the control room. The control center has ten video recorders and corresponding monitors. Supervisors can monitor all therapy rooms. One can be selected for routing to a 19-inch monitor in the control room, a 19-inch monitor in the director's office, or a 27-inch monitor in the group room. From either of these positions, a supervisor can connect to any of the therapy rooms for live supervision. The control room routing system has been so facilitative in the director's office that the program is installing the system in the other two clinical faculty members' offices. The router system creates a unique opportunity for supervision of supervision as well. Live supervision of supervision can be set up even when the supervision of therapy is live. MFTs can be involved in therapy in either of nine therapy rooms. The control room router system directs the therapy picture to the group room monitor for live supervision. The group room picture of the supervisor and the monitor showing the therapy session can be routed to the director's office for live supervision of supervision.

There are several advantages to this setup compared to a one monitor per therapy room or the one-way mirror. This setup allows the supervisor to push a button on the router system to switch from one therapy room to another. Presently, by using the one-way mirror, three supervisors can be doing live supervision simultaneously without scheduling problems. With the upcoming addition of the routing system in the other two offices, four supervisors can do live supervision simultaneously from the three offices and the control room. Supervisors can talk with MFTs participating in live group supervision without the concern of intruding in the therapy session as with the one-way mirror. The one-way mirror system is impractical as the sole means of live supervision. It would demand ten separate supervision rooms to match the ten therapy rooms to provide the same live supervision potential available to Harding's program.

Clients read and sign a therapy agreement form at the beginning of the first session. This form notifies clients that they may be observed by a supervisor and a student supervision group. MFTs verbally inform clients at the beginning of a session if observation and supervision will occur. The advanced setup of the clinic is very professional and comfortable. Like clients in all training programs, there are a small percentage that do not want to be videotaped or observed in live supervision. However, the first eight months of operation has shown a positive response by hundreds of clients. The professional atmosphere and advanced technology have given a very poignant message to clients concerning the quality of care provided by the clinic. Technology can be the center of attention at first, but as it becomes familiar, the focus quickly shifts to the individuals, marriages, families, and learning. Harding's MFTs simply view the program's technology as tools that enhance their learning experience and the quality of care provided to clients.

Reverse Live Supervision: Leveling the Supervisory Playing Field

D. Blake Woodside, M.D.

Published in the AAMFT Supervision Bulletin, Vol. VII, No. 2, Spring 1994.

For many, live supervision has become a critical portion of the training stream. The usual benefits of this type of supervision appear obvious—direct observation of the supervisee's performance and interventions, and the opportunity to provide instantaneous corrective feedback. One of the problems that this sort of arrangement can engender is that such sessions can become performances, stilted and artificial—especially in settings where time is short and the opportunities for live observation are few. Because many supervisees have never had the experience of having their clinical work directly observed, anxiety about it may heighten the unnatural nature of the experience. Add the effect of a "team" of supervisees plus supervisor behind a mirror, a team who may hastily deliver interventions, usually in a darkened room to the anxious supervisee.

In our setting, we have had the luxury of regular access to live sessions as part of a family therapy clinic in a comprehensive inpatient, day hospital and outpatient program for the treatment of eating disorders. The family therapists attached to these units hold a joint clinic weekly, where families from any one of the units are seen. The therapists and their supervisees function as a "team." This arrangement is useful from a programmatic point of view, as patients are often transferred across the treatment programs, and from the point of view of training, it increases the mass of therapists and students providing a superior educational experience. Because this has been a working clinic, as opposed to a supervisory forum, I went through a stage where I was having some difficulty in formulating treatment plans for my cases. My supervisor, perhaps in desperation, hit upon the idea of asking me to function as the voice from the team when she was seeing families. Thus, she forced me to think actively about this particular aspect of the work. While it was first awkward to be giving my supervisor "direction," this reverse live supervision led to a demystification of the whole process. Previously, commentary from the team had come as a rather mysterious, intimidating event. It also forced me to think actively about what my supervisor had been doing while I was in front of the mirror. Thus, I began to think in a much more focused way about how treatment plans were to be formulated, and about how to monitor the process of change in a family.

There is a significant difference in observing one's supervisor as compared to being behind the mirror observing another supervisee. In the latter circumstance, one's supervisor is almost certainly present. Despite all efforts to the contrary, the supervisor ends up leading any discussion or commentary. Difficulties observed in the conduct of the session will be interpreted differently—usually as evidence of the supervisee's lack of experience. This can enhance supervisees' fear of exposing potential problem areas. Viewing tapes of the supervisor's work usually suffer similarly since tapes are almost always chosen to highlight the supervisor's competence or brilliance. When was the last time any of you saved a tape of a really bad session to show your supervisees?

I presently use reverse live supervision as a standard part of my supervisory repertoire and believe that it has a number of benefits. By allowing supervisees to experience the process from a different perspective, this technique breaks down some of the artificial barriers in the supervisory relationship, particularly those relating to the inherent power differential between those in front of the mirror and those behind it. Demanding that supervisees periodically provide such commentary also allows a more rapid development of the ability to observe oneself. Supervisory dialogue tends to become more collegial and two-way after such an experience. Supervisees are much more likely to feel comfortable expressing opinions which may not match those of their supervisors. The effect of observing their supervisor struggle with a difficult case, appear at a loss or just come behind the mirror and say, "Boy, I wish I hadn't gotten out of bed today" cannot be overstated. It will almost inevitably leave the supervisees feeling more at ease with their mistakes, and improves the quality of material brought for supervisory sessions. Finally, such experiences may simply help to humanize the experience of supervision a bit more. It is really hard to remain too formal when your supervisees have just observed you making one of those classical errors that you have been warning them about for months!

Systemic/Strategic Team Training: An Abridged Research Update

Robert-Jay Green, Ph.D. and Mary Herget, Ph.D.

Published in the AAMFT Supervision Bulletin, Vol. II, No. 3, October 1989.

Since 1984, we have been conducting a three-year outcome study of systemic/strategic "Milan-informed," team consultations. In this brief summary of our work, we will attempt to describe the project and its implications for training. However, we encourage readers to examine the original work; references are provided below. We fear that condensing a three-year project into a report this brief is like translating *War and Peace* into a haiku... something gets lost in the translation.

Eleven therapists in training (interns and externs) were asked to select two of their most difficult ongoing cases. While all cases continued in regular therapy, one of each trainee's cases was selected at random to also participate in a three hour, five part team consultation. The trainee's other difficult case continued in regular therapy only.

The outcome measures one month after consultation included Goal Attainment Scaling (GAS), therapist global ratings of change, and client global ratings of change. Three years later, the GAS was administered again.

At one month post-consultation, the team condition yielded superior results on clients' main and composite goals (GAS) and on both therapist and client global ratings of change *(p<.05)*. At the time of the three year follow-up, these superior GAS results were maintained. On other treatment goals, the majority of team clients showed substantial improvement, while the majority of non-team clients showed minimal or no improvement.

Also at one month post-consultation, 64% of the therapists reported using a systemic/strategic orientation with the case they had brought to the team. In contrast, only 27% of these same therapists were using a systemic/strategic orientation with their non-team cases. This finding implies that team consultations only selectively alter a trainee's theoretical orientation.

Overall, our results showed that trainees' "stuck" cases had very poor outcomes in the absence of live team consultation. Furthermore, a single team consultation had powerful effects on goal attainments over a three year follow-up period. Thus from an ethical standpoint, live team consultations with trainees seem imperative for the welfare of clients whose therapy is at an impasse.

References

Green, R-J. (1988). Impasse and change: A systemic/strategic view of the therapeutic system. *Journal of Marital and Family Therapy,* 14(4), 383–395.

Green, R-J. (in press). *The therapeutic system.* New York: Basic Books.

Green, R-J. & Herget, M. (1989). Outcomes of systemic/strategic team consultation: I. Overview and one-month results. *Family Process,* 28(1), 37–58.

Green, R-J. & Herget, M. (1988). Outcomes of systemic/strategic team consultation: II. Three year follow-up. Manuscript submitted for publication.

Live Supervision of All Therapy Sessions: A Must for Beginning Therapists in Clinical Practica

Karin B. Jordan, Ph.D.

Published in the AAMFT Supervision Bulletin, Vol. 9, No. 2, Fall 1996.

In my opinion, live supervision of all sessions during the clinical practicum experience should be provided for beginning trainees who are making the transition from student to professional provider. Beginning trainees are "faced with complex situations where nuance flourishes relative to their responsiblity to themselves, their clients, the legal system, and the professional ethical standards" (Boyland, Malley & Scott, *1995,* p. xi). During the clinical practicum, it is the trainee's responsiblitity to obtain practice in psychotherapy, whereas the role of the Approved Supervisor is to evaluate the supervisee's knowledge base and readiness for supervision, assuring that the client receives at least minimal care (Cormier & Bernard, 1983; Mead, 1990). The AAMFT *Code of Ethics* mandates that Supervisors do not permit their trainees/supervisees to perform and/or present themselves as able to perform services beyond their training, level of experience, and competency. The question then arises: How can the Supervisor assure that the beginning trainee is adhering to these standards without providing live supervision of all sessions?

Van Hoose and Kottler, as early as 1977, reported that the leading cause for malpractice suits has been the failure to supervise therapists adequately. Since it is the Approved Supervisor's responsibility to determine if the trainee is "in over his/her head," she must go beyond consultation, video supervision, and occasional live supervision. How else but through live supervision of all sessions can the supervisor be familiar with the trainee's entire caseload and "blind spots," in order to provide timely supervision?

Slovenka (1980) reminds us: "Without the locus of clinical responsibility resting squarely on the supervisor's shoulders, there would be little justification for troubled people being assigned to partially trained students." Approved Supervisors, then, assume a central position for helping beginning trainees to increase their therapeutic effectiveness while minimizing client risk. When assuming this position, supervisors should give careful consideration to providing live supervision of all sessions. This will allow them to fulfill their ethical responsibility to the profession and to the trainee, helping ensure the trainee's readiness to move on into the field as a competent therapist. Additionally, this practice will significantly lower the supervisor's risk of liability for future errors and omissions.

By providing live supervision of all sessions, we as Approved Supervisors can greatly increase our effectiveness, thereby sending out highly qualified therapists.

References

American Association for Marriage and Family Therapy. (1991). *AAMFT Code of Ethics.* Washington, D.C.: Author.

Boyland, J.C., Malley, P.B. & Scott, J. (1995). *Practicum & internship: Textbook for counseling and psychotherapy. 2nd ed* Accelerated Development.

Cornier, L. & Bernard, J. (1982). Ethical and legal responsibilities of clinical supervisors. *Personnel and Guidance Journal,* vol.60, 486–490.

Mead, E. (1990). *Effective supervision: A task-oriented model for the mental health professions.* New York: *Brunner/*Mazel

Slovenka, R. (1980). Legal issues in psychotherapy supervision. In A. Hess (Ed.), *Psychotherapy supervision theory, research, and practice,* 453–473. New York: John Wiley & Sons

Van Hoose, W. & Kottler, J. (1997). *Ethical and legal issues in counseling and psychotherapy.* San Francisco: Jossey-Bass

Process of Family Therapy Live Supervision: A Brief Report

Barbara R. Frankel, Ph.D.

Published in the AAMFT Supervision Bulletin, Vol. III, No. 1, January 1990.

This report is a brief summary of an exploratory study that examined the process of live supervision. The focus of the project was two-fold: to learn about the immediate impact of supervisory phone-in interventions on both trainee and family behavior; and to explore the validity of the concept of isomorphism as it relates to training and therapy. The two behavioral categories which were primarily of interest in the examination of isomorphism were relationship and structuring skills.

This research project took place in two family therapy training contexts, the Institute for Juvenile Research in Chicago, Illinois and at the Purdue University Marriage and Family Therapy Graduate Program. The subjects included supervisors (12), trainees (42) and client families (84). Of the supervised family therapy videotaped sessions collected, two were randomly selected from each trainee. All supervisory phone-ins were video-taped and dubbed onto the videotapes at the point at which they occurred. This was done so that it would be possible to examine the supervisory process that occurred before, during, and after each supervisory phone-in intervention. In addition, trainees reported their independent perceptions of the supervisory experience. The intent of this paper and pencil procedure was to determine possible difference in supervisor and trainee ideas about what constituted effective and ineffective phone-in interventions. The ceding systems employed for supervisor and trainee behavior enabled observers to code the presence of specific behavioral components and then rate their effectiveness on a five-point scale. The client coding system enabled observers to distinguish between client cooperation and non-cooperation. The reliability for the coding schemes ranged from good to excellent.

The results of this study suggest that supervisors employed primarily directing statements (i.e., providing instructions, commands, and suggestions) and less frequently, behavioral categories such as reframing, supporting, questioning, and confronting statements in their phone-in interventions during the process of family therapy supervision. It was not surprising that supervisors mainly used phone-ins to direct trainees to take some action with a family subsequent to the in-session interruption. However, it was unexpected to find that supervisors employed supportive behaviors only about one-third as often as they used directive behaviors in their phone-ins. There was no appreciable change in supervisory behavior across gender or experience level of the trainees. The overall trend was for supervisors to behave similarly toward females and males, experienced and novice trainees.

When only examining those phone-in interventions that supervisors and trainees considered as effective and ineffective, there were significant differences in two out of seven behavioral categories. The phone-ins that trainees chose as "most effective" contained support components significantly more often than those of supervisors. Trainees were twice as likely as supervisors to designate a phone-in as "least effective" when the supervisor failed to provide support. Further, trainees were twice as likely as their supervisors to identify phone-ins with challenging statements as "least effective." Finally, supervisors chose phone-ins that included challenging statements twice as often as trainees.

These results indicate that trainees would rather receive more support than challenges from their supervisors during a therapy session. Yet supervisors appear to have focused their energies on more instructive phone-in interventions and used less supportive behaviors. Further, although supervisors did not use phones-in regularly to confront or challenge a trainee on therapeutic behavior to change the course of therapy (17.2% of the time), even that frequency was perceived by trainees as too often for the particular situation.

The concept of isomorphism was addressed by investigating the concordance of supervisor and trainee supportive and directive behaviors. The findings indicate that while therapist behavior did not significantly change as a result of the presence of supportive and directive phone-ins, trainee behavior change was predicted when the effectiveness of those supervisory interventions was examined. For example, when supervisors were effectively supportive, trainees were more likely to improve their support with clients. Similarly, when supervisors' support was ineffective, trainees' support tended to deteriorate. These results suggest that there was an isomorphic relationship between supervisor and trainee for both supportive and directive strategies when the dimension of quality was examined.

This study also examined whether congruent supervisor and trainee behavior had an impact on client behavior (i.e., level of cooperation). Generally, the research findings suggest in those phone-ins when both supervisor and trainee supportive and directive behaviors were judged effective, client behavior positively changed under certain conditions. While it is difficult, in so brief a report, to specify those circumstances in which the isomorphic relationship between supervisor and trainee behavior became apparent, the results of this study provide some empirical evidence for the idea that supervisors have influence on subsequent trainee and client change. More specifically, with these findings, there is support for the concept of isomorphism as valid and it appears that supervisors do have immediate impact on trainee and client behaviors.

References

Frankel, B. R. & Piercy, F. P. (1990). Isomorphism in family therapy supervision: A study of the relationship among selected supervisor, therapist, and client behaviors. Manuscript submitted for publication.

Frankel, B. R. (1990). Congruence between ratings of supervisors and their respective trainees in live supervision. Manuscript in preparation.

Research: Trainees Talk About Effective Live Supervision

Linda Wark, Ph.D.

Published in the AAMFT Supervision Bulletin, Vol. V, No. 1, February 1992.

Trainees and supervisors were interviewed after therapy sessions regarding their views about the helpful or not so helpful aspects of live supervision. Five trainees and their supervisors participated as dyads for six therapy sessions with one client couple each. Three methods were used to understand what comprises effective supervision: separate interviews with trainees and supervisors, the critical incident technique (a highly focused interview question about discrete incidents during supervision), and the observations of the researcher documented during each therapy session. This research approach, known as triangulation, provides validity for phenomena under investigation by comparing the data from several methods. Outside raters participated in the analysis which converged the data from all three methods into one picture of effective supervision.

What did supervisors do that trainees found most important? (Generally, supervisors were viewed as enhancing trainees' work when they could maintain connectedness, comfortableness, and compatibility with trainees. Supervisors did this by validating trainees, being responsive to their needs, and allowing them to choose the direction of sessions and then working with it. Trainees appreciated working *with* supervisors rather than just following their directions. One trainee said, "The supervisor was understanding of my style. He didn't provide a new frame but added to what I was doing. I feel like I'm leading, and he's in step with me."

In this study, the most striking theme for supervisors' consideration may be trainees' cry for independence. Trainees with less than one year experience were as vocal about wanting autonomy as those with over five years experience.

Despite this call for autonomy, trainees were grateful for help in planning sessions and reviewing what happened afterwards. The balance between helping and autonomy is exemplified in a statement from one trainee. She said, "If someone can build on what I know, I'll learn more. If the experiential model is one that I want to get really good at, then I need somebody to supervise me who can use that language."

Supervisors were not always viewed as connecting well with trainees. This was considered a problem by trainees and supervisors. Trainees were left feeling preempted and wondering if the supervisors really knew what was going on with clients.

The data also indicates supervisors can be helpful by also stepping back from supervisory involvement (e.g., reducing the number of phone calls during a live therapy session); collaborating with trainees (e.g., supervisors were collegial rather than hierarchical); and helping trainees feel comfortable with trying something new (e.g., the supervisor adapted a new skill to specifically fit the trainee).

Glasnost Supervision: Removing the Mirror in Live Supervision

Ben Furman, M.D. and Tapanl Ahola

Published in the AAMFT Supervision Bulletin, Vol. V, No.2, June 1992.

During the first two years we trained therapists at the Brief Therapy Training Center in Helsinki, our training model was based on the concept of direct supervision. Trainees invited one of their own clients, individuals or families, to come to the center for supervised interviews. Sessions were observed by training groups in the next room through closed circuit TV. Trainees interviewed clients while trainers gave directives through an intercom telephone.

All sessions followed the same format. Before sessions there were brief consultations during which a plan was made for the interviews. Therapists then interviewed clients for about an hour. After the interviews, clients were sent out for coffee and therapists met with the observing groups to discuss ways of explaining what the problems were all about. We used to favor functionalistic explanations, the problem served some positive or protective function within the context of the clients' families. Whatever explanation we came up with, it was used as the rationale for the final interventions, assignments that therapists gave clients at the end of sessions. After the session was over and the clients had gone, training groups met again and trainees were given a chance to ventilate and ask questions. Sometimes we saw the same clients more than once, but usually we followed up on the clients indirectly through therapists.

We gradually began to experiment with modifications to this conventional supervision model as we developed a style of working with people that could be characterized as the joint negotiation of solutions. Examples include:

- we went into therapy rooms to consult with therapists instead of calling them on the phone;
- we conversed through the telephone with clients rather than therapists and supervised them to ask questions from the other family members and even therapists;
- we interviewed clients and therapists together as if they together formed couples who had requested consultation;
- we invited clients to observe our conversation rather than sending them out for coffee.

The increased openness reflected in these and various other experiments required us to abandon the pejorative way of talking about clients that is commonplace when professionals discuss cases among themselves. We had to learn to talk about clients and their problems in a way that was respectful of all parties involved with the problem including those not present at the session.

In the fall of 1988 we decided to move from direct supervision to what we playfully called "glasnost supervision"; we decided to invite our clients and accompanying persons to sit in the same room with the training group for the whole session.

When we announced this new procedure to our trainees, some of them were hesitant. They voiced apprehension that their clients might not agree to come in for a session knowing that there would be some twenty strangers present. However, we soon found out that, when clients were given the option of either sitting together in the same room, they invariably chose the latter. Clients seem to find it more agreeable to be able to see the people who take part in the meeting. We have used the open format since, not only at our training center but wherever we teach and supervise, and have found it to have many advantages. It is preferred not only by clients but also by therapists, who no longer have to be in charge of interviews, and the other trainee who have a chance to participate in the conversations. At the end of these joint solution negotiations we regularly ask our clients and the accompanying persons how they felt about the meetings. Invariably the response has been positive. This, we believe, can be attributed to the solution-oriented way in which we talk about problems.

We believe that people should feel comfortable and at ease whenever they meet with the intention of solving problems or resolving conflicts. For this reason we deliberately promote the emergence of such an atmosphere by behaving informally ourselves, offering coffee to clients, using people's first names, readily giving compliments, encouraging openness and encouraging laughter by kidding and joking.

In our view the conductor of the session should lead the conversation in such a way that the emphasis is on solutions rather than problems. By this we mean that the problem and other issues should be discussed in a manner that tends to generate and encourage optimism, collaboration, and trust in one's own resources, whether supervisee or family member.

The growing awareness of the importance of the way one thinks about a given problem has paved the way for a new view of therapy and supervision as an art of helpful conversation. Therapy and supervision are no longer thought of as technologies for change, but rather as an event where professionals (both supervisors and supervisees) and clients jointly search for productive ways of thinking and talking about problems.

The Performance Metaphor in Family Therapy Training

Richard Baldwin, MFA, Claire Fialkov, Ph.D., and David Haddad, Ed.D.

Published in the AAMFT Supervision Bulletin, Vol. VIII, No. 2, Summer 1995.

Our family therapy training group is experimenting with new and exciting ideas about performance and reflection-in-action. Reflection-in-action (Schon, 1983) occurs when we practice supervision training and intentionally think about our performances (conversations and physical actions) *while* we practice. Our group uses video as a way to intentionally re-process our performances and collectively bear witness to these new events. Much in the same way that studio artists understand that new meaning is created each time they enter their studios or each time that something is "performed," our knowledge is also modified by the interaction between supervisors, trainees, and the medium of video. Implicit in our postmodern model is the recognition that one's expertise is a way of looking at something which was once constructed and may be reconstructed (Schon, 1983).

The use of video has traditionally reflected a modernist paradigm, a representational model which retains the notion of a universal truth and uses observation as a way to "capture reality." The camera is in a fixed location, with camera motion either eliminated or accomplished by an outside-the-system technician. Participants implicitly agree to act as if the camera is not there, thus perpetuating media illiteracy by pretending that it is not relevant. This practice masks the potential of media to become a powerful postmodern tool, and makes invisible the "politics of observation (Foucault, 1977)." Comments tend to focus on the content of what has been taped or captured, not the process of taping itself. No attention is given to the subjective editing that occurs, e.g., why does the camera zoom in on the face of the crying client? Participants often regret that the camera failed to capture the "really important moment," or the moment of "truth."

In contrast, our model stresses that "there are only accounts of truth within differing conversations, and no conversation is privileged (Gergen & Kaye, 1992)." We use video in a proactive and intentional way to practice reflection-in-action, by regularly passing a hand-held camera around the group while in conversation or during a group experiential exercise. The presence of the camera is apparent as it is passed from hand to hand, becoming a tangible other voice and vision in the room. We view the tape and reflect on what we hear and see, sometimes re-making a segment of the conversation or exercise. Video becomes an integral part of the conversation we have with each other. Sometimes we watch a person listening to someone else speaking, or we wonder why one person chooses to focus in one area, and another person somewhere else. We have the opportunity to check out what our language means to others, restate our words, and play with the language we use, which increases our awareness of the importance of words. Conversations about our experiences holding the camera and being watched and recorded further encourage media literacy.

We use a Panasonic VHS camcorder as well as a VHS-C camcorder, palmcorder type. A TV/VCR combination is available for immediate playback. A tripod, extra batteries for the camcorders and extra blank tapes are available as needed. The action proceeds uninterrupted. Recording starts when the group begins to discuss its intentions. In this way we have a record of our attempt to define and perform actions as we attempt to reach a goal. This use of media is referred to as process media. It is done cheaply, involves no post shooting editing, and is intended for immediate play-back.

"Video-in-action" enhances our awareness of our participation in the performance of constructed knowledge. This process stimulates imagination, facilitates play, enhances improvisational abilities and infuses training with new life and relevancy.

References

Foucault, M. (1977). *Discipline and punish.* New York: Pantheon Books.

Gergen, K.J. & Kaye, J. (1992). Beyond narrative in the negotiation of therapeutic meaning. In S. McNamee & K. J. Gergen (Eds.), *Therapy as social construction, (pp.167-185).* London: Sage.

Schon, D. (1983). *The reflective practitioner: How professionals think in action.* New York: Basic Books.

Therapy and Supervision in the Age of the Internet

Heather Ambrose, Ph.D.

Published in the AAMFT Supervision Bulletin, Fall 2000.

Access to the Internet has opened up a realm of possibilities for marriage and family therapists. In a day of instant communication and knowledge gathering, it has become possible for therapists to expand their practice beyond their office walls. It has also become possible for therapists to consult with other therapists in a more expedient fashion. In the same way, therapists in training may now have a bigger network from which to receive supervision and supervisors can expand their base of supervisees. With the constant advancements in technology taking place, there is no telling how the field of family therapy and the practice of supervision will look in the next few years. As exciting as the possibilities are, it is also important to be aware that growth and innovation bring along many unknowns and potential problems that can arise from jumping too quickly on the technology bandwagon. This article will begin to examine some of the implications associated with using the Internet in the practice of therapy and supervision.

Implications for Therapy

The questions of "How can we ethically and effectively do therapy on the Internet?" or "What services can ethically and effectively be provided on the Internet?" have often been asked. Ruiz and Lipford-Sanders (1999) suggest that perhaps these are not the types of questions we should be asking. Instead, we might first want to address our own definitions of what therapy is and the goals of therapy. From there, we can begin to ask ourselves what we believe effective therapeutic services consist of and the best way to deliver these services. Ruiz and Lipford-Sanders further state that regardless of whether we are doing therapy online or in person, we need to be clear about what it is we are doing (i.e., therapy, coaching, giving advice) so that we do not practice outside of our areas of training and competencies.

Not surprisingly, there are some very positive aspects of conducting therapy online. For instance, clients who have limited access to therapy for various reasons (location, transportation, physical condition) are more likely to take advantage of therapeutic services offered over the Internet (Ruiz and Lipford-Sanders, 1999). Online therapy can also be more cost effective for clients and may give clients an enhanced sense of security because they can control the flow of information they share with their online therapist (Haas, 2000).

Just as there are positive points to conducting online therapy, there are also some negative ones. One of the biggest criticisms of online therapy is the lack of nonverbal cues. However, according to Haas (2000), online therapists can deal with the lack of nonverbal cues by teaching clients to use emotions and acronyms to express their feelings. Therapists must then be able to identify word cues that clients use to express themselves, because the way a client writes can give a therapist clues as to how the client is thinking about something. Other criticisms of online therapy include potential ethical problems such as confidentiality, security, and implications associated with treating clients in a different state than the one in which the therapist holds a license to practice therapy (Ruiz & Lipford-Sanders, 1999, Caudill, 2000). While these issues are important to consider, they are too broad to be addressed within the context of this article. However, it will be important for clinicians to monitor how these issues are being addressed by law, state-licensing boards, and by the AAMFT Ethics Committee.

Implications for Supervision

Online supervision is breaking the boundaries of the traditional supervisory relationship. This may be especially true for post-degree supervisees who are working toward licensure. Many clinicians seeking licensure as a LMFT have found themselves in a position of either forgoing the LMFT licensure, because there was not an AAMFT Approved Supervisor within a 50-mile radius, or they have had to engage in long-distance supervision over the phone. Long distance supervision can be very costly because supervisees must not only pay their supervisor, but must also pay the phone bills for the supervision. Therefore, the Internet may prove to be a more cost-effective way of conducting long-distance supervision. The advancements in technology occurring almost weekly can potentially make the long distance supervisory relationship as effective as weekly face to face meetings.

Online supervision can occur in a variety of ways. For starters, supervisors and supervisees can engage in supervision on an ongoing basis by corresponding through email. Supervisors and supervisees may also conduct more of a real time supervisory session through instant messaging or through Internet Relay Chats (IRC) (Lumadue & Wilson, 1997). With IRC, a supervisor can create his/her own chat room and conduct either individual or group supervision in a more private live chat format. However, it is important to note that no online communication is completely confidential. Therefore, supervisors and supervisees must do everything in their power to protect the identity and confidentiality of the clients being discussed during online supervision.

Microphone and camera software also presently exists and is becoming standard equipment with newer model computers. Using microphones and cameras during online supervision can simulate a face to face supervisory session and is much more cost effective than video tele-conferencing.

As exciting as the future for online supervision is, there are some potential problems to be aware of, as well. The issue of online confidentiality has already been addressed. In addition, we must also consider that technology breakdowns or the expense of technology for both the supervisor and supervisee may make online supervision more difficult. It is also important to remember that at this point, online supervision does not allow the supervisor access to raw client data. Therefore, occasional face to face meetings for supervision may still be required, regardless of geographical distance between the supervisor and supervisee.

Narrative Interventions Via the Internet

I have been practicing online supervision on a small scale for the past three years. The supervision I have conducted online with my supervisees has mainly consisted of what I refer to as narrative supervision, based on Narrative Therapy (White & Epston, 1990). I use online narrative interventions as an adjunct to the face to face collaborative supervision I conduct on a weekly basis. After meeting with a supervisee, thoughts, questions, or comments often arise from our discussions that did not occur during the actual supervisory meeting. When these thoughts arise, I email my supervisee and share my ideas with him/her. Many times my emails comment on the supervisee's skill at handling a difficult or sensitive situation. I also wonder about certain dynamics occurring with the client, the supervisee, or both. After receiving the letter, the supervisee will often respond with his/her thoughts, and our written dialogue may occur until the next face to face supervisory session in which we further discuss our ideas. I find that these communications add a richness to the supervisory process and relationship. When conducting group supervision, I invite all the members of the group to participate in the narrative.

For my own personal development and supervision, I participate in online consultation groups. I find it very helpful to be able to ask questions and exchange ideas with other professionals in an expedient manner. I have also found that online consultation groups help keep me connected to other MFTs as we continue to struggle with the changes occurring in the mental health field.

Conclusions

The 21st century will definitely force the field of marriage and family therapy and supervision to expand and grow in ways, which up until now were only possible in our imagination. Technology will continue to allow us to provide therapy and supervision in more expansive and creative ways and contexts. It is no longer a matter of when online therapy and supervision will occur, but a matter of how we will embrace the newness and challenges of this medium and use it to serve our clients and supervisees in better ways.

References

Caudill, O.B. (2000). Let your fingers do the walking to the courthouse: Long distance liability. *Family Therapy News, 31* (1), 10-12.

Haas, C. (2000). Online counseling presents challenges for mental health experts. *Counseling Today, (February)*, 18 & 31.

Lumadue, C.L. & Wilson, S. E. (1997). Graduate student's guide to research on the Internet. Class Reader. St. Mary's University.

Ruiz, N.J., & Lipford-Sanders, J. (1999). Online counseling: Further considerations. *Counseling Today, (October)*, 12 & 33.

White, M., & Epston, D. (1990). *Narrative means to therapeutic ends*. New York: W. W. Norton.

Chapter 6

Problems and Special Issues in Supervision

Steering Clear of Potholes: Avoiding Problems in Supervision

R. duRee Bryant, M.S. and Larry Frank

Published in the AAMFT Supervision Bulletin, Vol. VI, No. 2, Summer 1993.

As supervisors in an internship program that trains students from master's and doctoral programs, we have been interested in the wealth of clinical supervisory literature that warns of supervisory impasses with trainees who are often described as dependent, resistant, or just plain difficult to train (e.g., Caust, Libow, and Raskin, 1981; Liddle and Schwartz, 1983; Mazza, 1988; Protinsky and Preli, 1987). Our collective lack of experience with problems of this nature led us to wonder about possible reasons we have not encountered these same difficulties. This is not meant as a promotion of our program or even our way of doing things, though admittedly we feel our program is unique in a number of ways. Instead, it is more of an inquiry into what we, and other programs like ours, are doing right to successfully avert those problems.

Internship Selection Process

Vital to the success of our training program is the selection process for intern candidates. As a team, we prepare a group presentation to potential candidates, provided within the context of a series of internship program presentations, offering a first-hand view of our team in operation, as we describe various aspects of the training year. In many ways this provides the first screening, albeit self-screening, by the candidates themselves. Our belief is that if we are not the right place for their needs, they should be aware of this, even before the first interview. The presentation highlights the following areas: introduction and history of the agency; philosophy and expectations; the theoretical orientation being taught; a typical day in the life of an intern; short reports from our current trainees; the application process and opportunity for discussion or questions. Following the presentations, resources for further readings, paralleling our theoretical views, are made available. We have found that by inserting this step, many who would have been seeking an interview primarily to find out general information about our operations eliminate themselves by not applying.

The interviews themselves are again conducted as a team, giving all of us who would potentially supervise the students an opportunity for input. Following first interviews, a staff discussion of each candidate ensues, and attempts are made to agree upon three students. If complete agreement cannot be reached, second interviews are considered. After the grumbling about second and third interviews has subsided, we typically recognize the overall benefit and can ultimately celebrate the formation of our "new team."

Since our agency budget is not dependent on bringing in fees (there are none), we are free to be very selective about who we take on as interns. Although we have the capacity to take three supervisees, it is feasible that we would take no interns if we felt all the applicants' needs would be better served elsewhere. Training programs whose budgets depend on revenue from interns must fill all of their slots. Thus, there is more of a temptation to accept one or more candidates who perhaps aren't suited to that particular program; hence the possibility of problems down the road.

The Internship/Externship Distinction

Our experience in working with graduate interns with little to no previous therapeutic training can be characterized by their seemingly universal zest for knowledge and overwhelming desire to learn, in our case, a brief strategic model of therapy. At the same time, we might assume that the postgraduate, with extensive training in another model of therapy, could be ripe for such supervisory problems. While the graduate intern is working from a nearly clean slate, even the most devoted of externs with previous experience in one or more modalities has, at minimum, a more complicated training background impacting supervision. Problems highlighted in the literature, such as ambivalence in accepting a theory model (Haley, 1976), blasé expert therapists who insist they know

129

more than their supervisor (Mazza, 1988), and outright refusal to utilize the approach being taught (Protinsky & Preli, 1987) have been side-stepped in part by our supervisees' limited training backgrounds.

Our Philosophy

We are fortunate to be part of a system that supports a somewhat uncommon philosophy. Actually, we had not been aware of its rareness until our interns started telling us about their classmates' experiences at other placements. The elements of our outlook on training include:

Supervision, supervision, and more supervision. Interns in our program participate in live supervision behind a one-way mirror on all of their cases. In addition, they take part in three hours each week of face-to-face supervision of their cases (one hour with three different supervisors). They also join in presenting cases at a weekly case conference with all staff and their days conclude with a post-case discussion.

Case planning time. Limits are placed on the number of cases assigned, so that the therapist will have time to think through the case and make session plans. Case planning is seen as part of doing therapy.

Interns + supervisors = team. Interns are seen as part of the therapy team. Their ideas and input are solicited and valued. The collegial relationships among supervisors and interns, and among the interns is quite evident. In fact, visitors to our center have difficulty distinguishing the difference.

Emphasis on the positive. Supervisors' "method

of choice" is complementing those skills and abilities that we would like to see trainees continue. We find that interns are so accustomed to criticism-based models of teaching that our positive approach takes some getting used to, but at end-of-the-year interview, it is one of the aspects of the program they say they learned from the most.

We acknowledge that there is likely much more contributing to our apparent lack of supervisory problems than discussed above. This discussion has hopefully served to amplify what we consider to be potential pre-determinants for lessening problems in supervision, raised room for discussion of other possibilities, and made some sense, for the authors, of a phenomenon which probably exists more often than we know.

References

Caust, B. L., Ubow, J. A., & Raskin, P. A. (1981). Challenges and promises of training women as family systems therapists. *Family Process, 20,* 439–447.

Haley, J. (1976). *Problem-solving therapy.* San Francisco: Jossey-Bass.

Liddle, H. A., & Schwartz, R. C. (1983). Live supervision/consultation: Conceptual and pragmatic guidelines for family therapy trainers. *Family Process, 22,* 477–490.

Mazza, J. (1988). Training strategic therapists: The use of indirect techniques. In H. A. Liddle, D. C. Breunlin, & R. C. Schwartz (Eds.), *Handbook of family therapy training and supervision* (pp. 93–109). New York: Guilford Press.

Protinsky, H. & Preli, R. (1987). Intervention in strategic supervision. *Journal of Strategic and Systemic Therapies, 6,* 18–23.

Errors in Therapy

Mark Odell, Ph.D.

Published in the AAMFT Supervision Bulletin, Spring 2000.

Novice therapists often approach therapy with a sense of trepidation about "messing up." Indeed, in working with graduate students in an MFT training program who are approaching systemic practice for the first time (even if they have some individual therapy experience), there seems to be very commonly a significant fear of making a mistake. There are those who might suggest that there is no such thing as a mistake; cybernetically, all information is feedback that is inherently useful (Becvar & Becvar, 1999). That is all well and good theoretically, but it is not terribly practical, and it ignores the reality that certain actions on the part of the therapist increase the likelihood (sometimes approaching certainty) that therapy will not progress. Errors in treatment do occur—I confess, I am pretty adept at making them—and one element of good supervision is helping supervisees to become aware of the situations and issues with which they are more likely to err.

First, it is necessary to understand where errors can be identified. For example, it is not hard to imagine that one person's error is another person's brilliant move. Clients' views of what is useful or meaningful in therapy and therapists' views are not that similar (e.g., Gale, Odell, & Nagireddy, 1995), and it follows that such a disparity of perspectives would pertain to errors as well. I suggest we be open to the possibility of detecting errors from the perspective of any participant in the therapy system. It is also important to recognize that the attribution of error by one participant does not automatically render such an evaluation accurate for the entire system. The acting out adolescent whose parents are being coached by the therapist to take a more powerful and proactive stance would likely characterize such work as a big mistake.

Second, it is not always easy to determine when an error has been made because therapy is a process. Clients may not let the therapist know when they believe an error has been made (Odell, Butler, & Dielman, 1998), and they may not even become aware of an error until sometime after the fact. This may be because the clients have expectations about treatment that are not met or because there is a lack of fit with the therapist. Unfortunately, if you cannot tell a mistake has been made, you cannot fix it, and the longer it goes unaddressed, the likelier it is to become unrecoverable. I believe one of the reasons that planned terminations in therapy are somewhat unusual is partly because errors have been made and never addressed. It is more common for the client to simply discontinue attending sessions, and the therapist may never spend much time thinking about why, simply chalking up another case to "the way therapy often goes."

It might be useful to think of errors as being of a number of types. I often view errors from the specific to the general, from the level of intervention, to theoretical, to philosophical. These different domains are not mutually exclusive and in fact are interrelated. Still, it can be useful to track errors by attempting to locate their source. Once a pattern of errors becomes noticeable, then a deliberate effort at addressing them becomes possible.

Interventive errors are usually the least serious in terms of therapy outcome. They rarely damage the therapeutic relationship to the degree that it is irreparable, and they rarely produce harm. More likely, they often end up being impotent. They have little impact and nothing changes. These are usually errors in timing—e.g., trying to move too soon before clients' participation and motivation to change has been secured, or errors of magnitude—e.g., inappropriately mild or limited, or overly demanding interventions. The common end result is the clients generally being positive about the therapist and vice versa, but not much movement is noted. Nobody is really sure why.

The supervisee who seems to make mostly interventive errors can be identified by examining the process of many of his or her cases. They start off fine, develop decent rapport and a good working relationship, but the goals of therapy may be a bit fuzzy (i.e., the explicit agreement about what goal is being pursued is assumed, not obtained), and after a few sessions, therapy seems to stall. The therapist may assume the clients share the goal, but when therapy seems to become mired down, it may be that the assumption is wrong. It also may be that the therapist and the client have agreed on the goals, but the therapist has not created the necessary context within which the clients are ready to consider change. Often, asking clients to be explicit about their experience in therapy thus far can help to reveal why things have become stuck. Specifically, inviting the clients' feedback in supervision via videotape or in live conversation can sometimes free up the whole system to move forward.

The next level of error is theoretical or conceptual. Errors of this type can be recovered if they are caught early enough, but often they are not and therapy simply stops when clients fail to attend. Theoretical errors occur when a therapist embraces a therapeutic model too strongly, and tries to mold the client system into the model, or when a therapist adamantly avoids a particular model or set of models. Such rigidity can often look like a strength, because a therapist who is very comfortable in a particular model often is fluent in that model's language and can present a case quite eloquently from that point of view. However, key elements of the case can either be ignored or misapprehended in such a presentation, and so I like to ask supervisees to be able to discuss a given case from at least three different theoretical perspectives simultaneously, and if necessary generate a plan of action consistent with each.

Supervisees who tend to err in this way are not usually very hard to see. They are quite able to discuss their theoretical preferences and are good at mapping out what needs to be done with a case to move it forward. Unfortunately, they do not seem to be as successful as their model would suggest they should be, especially with cases that do not readily fit with their model. When they are asked to consider an alternative model, they may blanch a bit. What they need to realize is that they do not necessarily have to subscribe to a model in its totality to make use of the interventive strategies it uses. The question is how they can make use of what might help without necessarily getting caught up in a higher level conceptual or theoretical discussion.

The level of error that is of greatest concern is the philosophical. This is where a fundamental discrepancy occurs between the therapist and clients around basic values and orientations to healthy living. Discerning such a problem may sound as though it would be easy, but in practice it is not because the underlying values that orient people's lives are usually not explicitly articulated in therapy. Furthermore, therapists tend to assume a greater degree of commonality than may actually be there with clients, especially if the clients seem fairly similar to us ethnically and demographically. Doherty's work (1995) on the moral dimensions of therapy addresses some of the results of philosophical errors.

The supervisee prone to philosophical errors can be seen by the likelihood of their having rather strong responses to clients who do not share their assumptions, or in their reluctance to change their underlying agenda for therapy's outcome, even in the face of client wishes. This is the supervisee who knows what is really in the clients' best interests, and is committed to seeing that outcome through. The arguments made in service of the supervisee's agenda may be quite sound, especially if one grants the validity of their pre-existing assumptions. However, such a choice may be ill-advised. For example, domestic violence may only happen once before a couple comes for therapy. To assume (or worse, demand) that it has happened before, or that it permeates their relationship, may be a very harmful thing to do, and in fact the therapist who insists on such a view runs the considerable risk of driving the client away at the very moment they are most open to change. The same is true for such issues as infidelity and substance abuse, among others.

For supervisors wanting to help supervisees see their commonly made errors and turn them into positive experiences, the supervisor must first come to see his or her own common errors. Isomorphism occurs with frequency (Todd & Storm, 1997), especially when supervisee and supervisor are prone to similar errors. Then, supervisees need to explicate their underlying mission for doing therapy; this will address their philosophy of therapy and allow the supervisor to discuss with them its meaning and implications. Supervisees need to be able to articulate their preferred orientations and models, including why they prefer them, in the safety of a strong supervisory relationship. In the end, they need to understand that there are many ways to work, and many ways to err. If they are aware of their own unique pitfalls, they will be in a much better position to avoid them.

References

Becvar, D., & Becvar, R. (1999). *Family therapy: A systemic integration (4th ed.)*. Boston: Allyn & Bacon.

Doherty, W. (1995). *Soul searching: Why psychotherapy must promote moral responsibility*. New York: Basic.

Gale, J., Odell, M., & Nagireddy, C. (1995). *Marital therapy and self-reflexive research: Research and/as intervention*. In G. Morris & R. Chenail (Eds.), *The Talk of the Clinic* (105–129). New York: Lawrence Erlbaum.

Odell, M., Butler, T., & Dielman, M. (1998). *Therapeutic alliance and outcome in solution-focused marital therapy*. Unpublished manuscript.

Todd, Thomas C., & Storm, Cheryl L. (1997). *The complete systemic supervisor: Context, philosophy, and pragmatics*. Boston: Allyn & Bacon.

Exuberance vs. Wisdom: Observation from America's Farmland on Supervision of Family Therapy

Charles P. Barnard, Ed.D.

Published in the AAMFT Supervision Bulletin, Vol. IX, No. 1, Winter 1996.

For more than 20 years the author has been training aspiring family therapists with the assistance of one-way mirrors and video equipment. Throughout these years "behind the glass" there has been a deep appreciation of the enthusiasm and zest reflected in the efforts of developing therapists. Their enthusiasm is often translated into elegant and theoretically sound hypothesis that generate strategies and sometimes a bountiful number of interventions. One would think that in the midst of such conditions, even the most troubled and therapeutically cautious of families could hardly help but secure their desired changes. Unfortunately, this is not the case. This brief article is thus designed to describe what the author believes is one of the primary reasons more families do not change more significantly and swiftly in response to the observed enthusiasm, energy and well crafted ideas of these developing therapists.

A Recent Example

During a recent supervisory session, the author was observing, with one of the cotherapists involved, a videotape of the tenth session with a family. The therapist had indicated that this family had entered the session discussing termination in apparent response to their frustrated hope for more significant and rapid change.

Briefly, the family consisted of mother, dad, and their 15-year-old adopted son. They had entered therapy in hopes of narrowing the distance mother and dad were experiencing between themselves and their son, and had hoped that a reduction in the numerous "power struggles" and verbally explosive exchanges would accomplish this. The cotherapists were of the belief that progress was being made over the first nine sessions and expressed surprise by the family's stated desire to terminate therapy. In fact,

the cotherapists had entered this session with a well-developed strategy, including related interventions that were designed to facilitate even more change. This well-developed plan was turned on its ear by the family's opening declaration.

Mother and dad started the session by presenting the fact that recent discussion between the two of them had culminated in their considering termination. They reported that they were operating with the belief that change should have been more dramatic and secured more quickly. Mother then noted that in spite of their concern, change in the desired direction had been observed. She also reported that "...the peaks (good times between parents and son) and valleys (unpleasant times) had changed and the time between the peaks had lessened." To this report one cotherapist responded by saying in his best solution-oriented style, "Great, and I wonder how you can do even more of what you are doing to make the distance between the peaks even less?" Mother replied with, "That's a really good question!"

My initial reaction to this brief exchange was positive, as I thought the therapist was on target. This question, and mother's response, created a context that was conducive to identifying more solution talk that might advance even greater change. This interaction was then followed by a few explanatory comments by dad regarding how the son could be "so good," supported by a few recent examples. Son interrupted these apparent affirmative comments by dad with, "That's right, I'm never always perfect." The other cotherapist then followed with: "I wonder what seems to all too often come between you guys and keep your apparent good intentions from being received without distortion?"

Again, I was impressed with the response of the cotherapist and how it seemed to prepare fertile ground for externalizing the problem between dad and son and then encouraging them to attack "this enemy" that resides between them, or some other potentially helpful intervention. Instead, what I observed was a continuing sequence of cotherapist responses stacked one on top of the other. In and of themselves, the therapists' interactions were appropriate and potentially very facilitative. Unfortunately, the potential usefulness of their utterances fell victim to what I have so often observed among developing family therapists. Their exuberance and enthusiasm had taken over and essentially contaminated or neutered the beneficial impact of their therapeutic involvement by stacking one intervention on top of the other without proper cultivation of any of them.

Unlike more experienced therapists who regard their utterances and interventions as seeds in need of fertile soil and other elements necessary to nourish and advance the promotion of growth, developing therapists all too often seem prone to putting too many seeds in one place and not sufficiently tending to them in order to promote their full yield. Instead of regarding the potential that resides in one seed and the subsequent need to tend to its development, developing therapists seem to believe the seed is sufficient in and of itself. They too often fail to recognize that their well-placed question or observation, like the seed, is only representative of potential. They forget about the value of promoting its growth to full yield by such means as encouraging other family members to comment, or simply sitting back and engaging in reflection on the possible meanings and implications with all of the family members.

Perhaps through viewing the multiplicity of available training videotapes of luminaries in the field, and studying published case studies, we as trainers direct attention too extensively to the apparent artfulness and craftsmanship of a particular intervention, instead of what is done to more fully activate and capitalize on what has been offered. The appropriate silence, encouraging comment from other family members, artfully short-circuiting the distracting behavior, the subtle relationship-building skills employed from start to finish, the way a follow-up response is crafted and offered more to fully promote the potential of the initial utterance; these and other important cultivating acts may all be allowed to fade into the background in such a fashion that it is only the one statement or intervention that is noticed. Thus, the illusion is unintentionally created that all that matters in working with families is "the intervention," or a well-crafted question or statement. All the other variables of cultivation and nourishment about which trainees may learn from observing the videos and other forms of study fade into the background.

The beauty and effectiveness of the works of so many of the grandparents of family therapy reside in the parsimony and simplicity of their work, but this is all too often missed in the learning process. The experienced therapist recognizes that a few well-placed and appropriately nourished seeds yield far more than do wildly scattered or overly crowded and undernourished seeds. The deliberate and wise will reap far more from what they sow than the enthusiastic or "busy" who do not take the necessary time and effort to tend to what has been planted.

Conclusion

Time and again I am reminded of the simple fact that in doing family therapy it is indeed true that "less is often more." That is, doing more does not automatically translate into productivity. Enthusiasm and busyness often can and do promote low yield with clients, while simultaneously promoting the sense of exhaustion often reported by therapists in early stages of their development. The wisdom to slow down and properly nourish that which has been therapeutically sown will typically result in greater yield for the family, and with less wear and tear on the therapist.

As trainers and therapists we can probably all benefit from remaining mindful of the wisdom reflected by slowing down, cultivating and properly nourishing that which we sow, and then reaping the increased enjoyment of our greater yields from less effort. In this regard, exuberance should be encouraged and celebrated, but wisdom and its rewards also should be sought after and treasured.

Special Issues in Supervision: The Abusive Man

Brian Jory, Ph.D.

Published in the AAMFT Supervision Bulletin, Vol. 9, No. 1, Summer 1996.

This article focuses on supervisory issues and needs of therapists-in-training who are conducting therapy with abusive or violent men. Typically, this kind of therapy involves physical violence directed at the partner, but psychological abuse may also be evident. Tolman (1992) describes seven types of psychological abuse: creation of fear, isolation, monopolization, economic abuse, degradation, rigid sex role expectations, psychological destabilization, emotional withholding and contingent expressions of love.

Special Assessment Issues

A study conducted in a university clinic by O'Leary, Vivian and Malone (1992) indicates the need for a multi modal assessment for violence. This study found that only 3% of couples listed violence as a presenting problem on intake forms. But when specifically questioned in the intake interview, 36% indicated there had been physical violence in the last year. Scores on the Conflict Tactic Scales for the same couples indicated that more than half of the women had been physically assaulted by their partners in the last year. It was the conclusion of the researchers that abused women are often afraid to divulge their experiences to therapists because they fear retaliation by their abusers. This explanation can be coupled with other studies which indicate that abusive men usually deny and minimize their behavior (O'Leary & Arias, 1988; Edleson & Bryggei, 1986). For these reasons, therapists-in-training might be encouraged, in conducting assessments, to use a standard checklist such as the Conflict Tactic Scales or the Spouse-Specific Aggression Scale and to make specific inquiries about the abuse and violence in assessment interviews. This will often involve bolstering the safety of victims and potential victims by conducting separate interviews and insuring that information about abuse will be handled discretely. Some victims of abuse will reveal it only on the condition that the disclosure not be revealed to the abuser; in this case the therapist might recognize the dangers and find ways to address the issues of safety.

While intimate partner violence often appears on the surface to be mutual or bi-directional, a different picture emerges when understood in terms of frequency, lethality, motivation and impact. Therapists-in-training should be encouraged to focus on these factors in clinical interviews. Violence can be infrequent yet still have significant impact in terms of the fear it creates and the power it invests in the abuser. Since most abusive men project blame for their behavior onto the partner, it is not unusual for women to blame themselves. Women who have been targets of violence often act out of retaliation and fear, which gives the impression that they are aggressors. Motivation comes into play by realizing that men typically use violence to accomplish specific goals, while women may be acting in self-defense of past, current or future violence. It has been suggested that women who know a violent episode is imminent will sometimes initiate the violence to relieve the interpersonal tension and bring it to a conclusion. Also, women sometimes initiate violence in order to protect children from being the targets of abuse at the hands of a violent man. By taking time to understand the context of abuse, therapists-in-training will gain insight into the relational complexities involved and may find an answer to the worn-out question, "Why doesn't she just leave?"

Special Issues in Focusing Treatment

The propensity of abusive men to deny, minimize and rationalize their behavior often leaves therapists-in-training confused about where to focus their interventions. Concepts of justice can be used to confront, challenge, explore, and educate abusive men about violence and abuse (Jory, 1995). Four areas of intervention include:

1. Abusive men should be confronted about how they disempower and abuse power with their partner. This includes directly confronting all physical vio-

lence even that which is often minimized such as pushing, grabbing, shoving and the use of psychological tactics such as verbal threats, intimidation, coercion, isolation and degradation. Therapists should attempt to establish a no-violence contract with abusive men.

2. Internalized beliefs about male entitlement, rigid expectations for gender-typed behavior and the use of aggression to command respect should be challenged. This includes exploring internalized beliefs about the role of empathy, nurturing and attachment in relationships. It is important for therapists to hold aggressive men accountable for self-examining how they have psychologically constructed their own internalized beliefs and to change self-serving beliefs.

3. Therapists should explore how internalized beliefs may have evolved from experiences in the family of origin, particularly experiences as a childhood victim of parental violence, sibling abuse or witnessing domestic violence. It is important for abusive men to recognize that those who abused them were wrong and are accountable for their behavior. It is also critical that men understand there is no direct line between experiences in the family of origin and their own beliefs, but they may have interpreted these experiences to justify their own abusive behavior.

4. Therapists should seek to develop an awareness in violent men about the links between intimate violence and social injustice. This includes issues like gender domination, glorified images of violence in the media, gang violence and stereotyped expectations of masculine and feminine behavior.

A technique for focusing interventions with abusive and violent men (Jory, Greer, & Anderson, 1996), the intimate justice question, is particularly useful for beginning therapists to structure therapeutic dialogue with abusive and violent men. The therapist in training asks the man, "Suppose that something happened, and you were suddenly transformed into your partner. Knowing how you treat her, how would you feel? What would it be like to be in an intimate partnership with you?" The goal of the intimate justice question is to help abusive men consider the impact of their actions, to take ownership of the behavior and to reflect on the possibility of change. By creating a safe, yet firm, therapeutic environment, the therapist-in-training can challenge and confront denial, minimization and rationalization and gain leverage for therapeutic change with most clients.

Special Needs of Therapists-in-Training

The special needs of therapists-in-training can be illustrated by the experiences of two students in a COAMFTE-accredited masters degree program. One therapist, a female, was expecting a client she would have to draw out. However, the client spoke incessantly and loudly, with a commanding voice, pointing his cellular phone at her as he talked. Whatever the therapist said, Joe had his own track and was stuck on it, blaming his wife for everything, calling her whiny, a loser and a wimp. When his violence was discussed, Joe blamed his wife, stating that he was leaving her because he did not want to stay married to a violent woman. When questioned about a clandestine four-day gambling excursion he had recently taken, Joe pointed this out as an example of his wife's nagging and insisted that she forget about it. Although the therapist conducted the session professionally, in several instances Joe tried to discredit her by pointing out, "I know you are just a student."

In a second example, Ron, a client of a male therapist, explained how the police had arrested him for battering his wife on a technicality. He described how he "helped her go by" him, and then "accidentally stepped on her face" after she "accidentally" fell on the floor. Like Joe, Ron also described his wife as a violent woman badly in need of therapy. Ron verbally attacked the therapist at the end of the second session when he learned that the amount of counseling fee had been arranged with his wife. Ron began swearing in front of everyone in the payment area, drawing an analogy that letting his wife arrange the fee was like a waiter asking your wife what you want to order for dinner. After the therapist graciously invited Ron to return to the therapy room to discuss his concerns, Ron became more hostile, and loudly insisted, "You screwed up didn't you? You just can't admit you screwed up. I just want to hear you admit that you screwed up." Although the therapist had made no mistakes and had handled the situation professionally, Ron tried to discredit him by saying, "Dammit, that's not very professional."

These kinds of client interactions can arouse strong emotional reactions in experienced clinicians, but therapists-in-training are especially vulnerable. Supervisees may struggle with three types of internal dialogues. First, supervisees may wonder about their own physical safety, and this may expand to worries outside of the session. As the female therapist put it, "That energy is contagious. You are sitting next to someone that is big, making himself look bigger by waving his arms. He is louder, bigger and hyper." Second, supervisees may be concerned about maintaining their composure in relation to the client. The struggle is not fair; the therapist-in-training is supposed to remain professional while the client can act as he wants. Supervisees may worry about lashing out, shaking, crying, their voice cracking, or trying to out shout the client. They may have trouble sleeping following traumatic sessions. Third, supervisees may internalize the criticism of aggressive men and begin questioning their own competency and, in group training sessions, they may worry about peer judgement. As the female therapist explained, "I just kept thinking he [Ron] is trying to make me look stupid."

Three guidelines can be suggested to help supervisees meet the special needs of therapists-in-training in such situations. First, the COAMFTE Standard Curriculum (Area 2) lists violence among the seven areas of assessment and treatment that should be covered in marriage and family therapy training. Course work on violence should address the special issues of assessment and treatment. Videotapes and case presentations on work with abusive men can influence supervisee expectations, give them a sense of control and increase their ability to remain assertive and composed in the face of a client who appears out of control. Supervisees are taught how to draw out inhibited clients through empathy, questioning, probing and other techniques. But the experience of containing clients through effective challenge and engagement is rarely viewed in training videos or discussed in the case presentations.

A second suggestion is to insure that the trauma visited upon supervisees by aggressive men is handled in a pyschologically safe, supportive and caring supervisory environment. The negative comments of clients can be countered by an increase in confirmatory feedback from the supervisor. Supervisors who offer corrective feedback may contribute to the negative internal dialogue and self-judgment already at play in traumatized supervisees. Most supervisees already possess appropriate assertion and conflict resolution skills, and supervisors would do well to support the trainee in maximizing existing skills in challenging and confronting. This may involve using the hands to cut

off aggressive men who interrupt or become verbose, or sitting forward to get the attention of a man who refuses to listen. Supervisees may expand their repertoire of challenging skills at a later time when their confidence levels are higher. In group training situations, peers should be encouraged to offer supportive feedback as well.

A third suggestion is to explore supervisee reactions in the context of the emotional system of his/her family of origin. This should be attempted only in a supportive, caring supervisory environment away from the stress of the session itself. While supervisees may not be victims of abuse or violence in their families of origin, all have experiences with aggression and conflict which can be processed. This may help supervisees clarify their emotional reactions and may help them with internalized conflict such as guilt, self-judgement and shame and may bring about an understanding of how they can externalize these reactions with effective assertiveness and confrontation. Therapists-in-training who have unresolved issues as victims or witnesses of childhood abuse should be encouraged to address these issues and resolve them to the degree possible. It is particularly helpful for supervisees to explore how accountability was addressed in their own family of origin. Supervisors also will want to monitor these students to insure that unresolved issues are not projected onto clients.

References

Edelson, J. & Brygger, M. (1986). Gender differences in reporting of battering incidents. *Family Relations, 35,* 377–382.

Jory, B., Greer, C., & Anderson, D. (1996). Intimate justice: Confronting issues of accountability, respect, and freedom in treatment for abuse and violence. Unpublished manuscript.

O'Leary, K. & Arias, I. (1988). Assessing agreement of reports of spouse abuse. In G. Hotaling, D. Finkelhor, J. Kirkpatrick, & M. Straus (Eds.) *Family abuse and its consequences: New directions in research* (pp. 117–218). Newbury Park, CA: Sage.

O'Leary, K., Vivian, D., & Malone, J. (1992). Assessment of physical aggression against women in marriage: The need for multimodal assessment. *Behavioral Assessment, 14,* 5–14.

Tolman, R. (1992). Psychological abuse of women. In R. Ammeran & M. Hersen (Eds.), *Assessment of family violence* (pp. 291–310). New York: John Wiley.

Children's Art and Narratives: An Opportunity to Enhance Therapy and a Supervisory Challenge

Shirley Riley, M.A.

Published in the AAMFT Supervision Bulletin, Vol. 9, No. 3, Winter 1997.

Therapists and their supervisors are often in a situation in which client-created art work is a component of a case involving children in treatment. Often neither supervisee nor supervisor has had the training that would make it possible to take advantage of this form of enrichment in the therapeutic dialogue. Either in family or individual sessions, the chances are high that a child will use any paper and marking tool available to make drawings or scribbles. The question of what to do with these offerings, what value to put upon these marks, is often a puzzle for the therapist. Often children hope that their message will be understood by the adults, and too often their non-verbal comments are either ignored or inappropriately interpreted by the therapist or family members,

The following brief article is written with a narrative approach to treatment in mind, a natural mode in which children may tell stories about their world and about their drawings. However, the fundamental therapeutic tools of respect and restraint from interpretations, either verbal or non-verbal, combined with an empathic attitude of learning from the child, fit with most theories of family practice. The basic principles and attitudes about the use of art expressions in therapy, discussed below, hold true for adolescents and adults as well.

The Supervisor/Therapist Dilemma

The child's view of the world is irretrievably lost when abstract reasoning replaces the concrete thinking of childhood. This change generally comes about in adolescence (Bloch, 1995). Children see the world in a unique manner that is concrete and individually constructed. "Education" (socio-familial and peer-school) gradually erodes the individualistic meanings young children ascribe to events and objects, and prepares them for the generalized and socialized meanings imposed by the world at large. Their unique view gradually gives way to the common meanings that society attributes to events and lives. Therapists, however unconsciously, contribute to this loss of "innocent creativity" if they fail to appreciate the way a child views his/ her world.

The Child's View

There is a way that children commonly share their stories with an adult, one that is both spontaneous and laden with content. Children draw! It is difficult to keep them from drawing if art materials are offered and a permissive environment is established by the adult. Why are these art expressions so valuable to the therapist? First, the image is an externalization of an inner perception or dialogue the child is having around some specific event of thought. Second, only through this image can we adults regain some of the ability to recapture a modicum of the lost concrete thinking we once had. Imagery and symbols are retained in our memory bank in a distinct way, one that is more archaic than verbal memories (Tinnin, 1990). The image comes forth in a singular form (non-verbally) that is less contaminated with the compound meanings that lie within our complicated method of verbal communication. It is important to take advantage of this is primary avenue of expression, which may access the material repressed or "forgotten" by the client.

The therapist can step into the child's drawings, and let him/her teach the meaning of this visual narrative. The art is a form of personal externalization (Riley, 1994), an extension of one's self, visible projection of thoughts or feelings. When the art is accepted, honored and validated by the therapist, the creator is (through identification with his/her product) equally accepted, honored and validated. The client, in this case a child, can better understand through these actions than through words that he/she has been confirmed and valued. When the problem or anxiety has been externalized by the child in a drawing, it is the perfect time to confront the problem-laden behavior and still validate the worth of the creator (the child artist). Separating behavior from the child is a basic intervention that can be done gracefully when observing the problem rendered on the page and simultaneously validating the youngster who created the image. In the "real world," language may have been used in confusing ways, or carried paradoxical double messages to the child. In many cases of abuse or family shame, the child has been cautioned not to reveal information to the therapist. The art is a safe way to "tell" what has been forbidden to be talked about, a language of it's own. The art is the bridge between the child and the adult.

The supervisor may have to go over with supervisees some developmental information regarding drawing skills (Malchiodi & Riley,1996, Oster & Montgomery, 1996). Knowing the "normal" skills that most children attain on their way to competency in rendering imagery may forestall the tendency to find pathology in the art products. In addition, the supervisor and the supervisee may recognize, through the art, possible delays in developmental growth if the drawings are grossly out of "synch" with those of other children's of the same age. Sometimes the therapist has the fascinating experience of seeing parents drawing images with the same skills as their young children. The supervisor might then question, with the supervisee, whether there might be some difficulties with the parent's capacity to operate in other areas as a mature person. The art is a loaded vehicle for communication, both to the art-maker and to the observer (the therapist).

The supervisor is usually not a trained art therapist. Therefore, by departing from the usual issues of therapy and speculating on the meta-message in the artwork, this approach can provide a rare opportunity for a stimulating discussion and challenge the creativity of both parties. Supervisor and supervisee might even recall their own first drawings as a child and find, in this phenomenological manner, a way of understanding and empathizing with the young client in a unique manner. A question might be posed regarding whether the supervisee ever felt in the same position as the child attempting to communicate but not understood. Has the supervisor restrained him of herself when receiving these misunderstood messages from the supervisee, or has he/she projected his/her own interpretations without waiting to hear the message offered in an unfamiliar mode? The latter is a situation parallel to the example given about misunderstanding children's art.

Art and Narrative

Exploring an art expression allows both the therapist and the youngster to use metaphor and fables to broaden the scope of the conversation. The client/child may have greater comfort when answering questions based on the art piece rather than being quizzed about reality situations (Malchiodi, 1990). Significant success will be forthcoming if the therapist is play oriented, creative, not convinced that he or she has the answer (Anderson & Goolishian, 1988) is an adult open to learning through the eyes of a child. Children do not have grown-up vocabulary and do not assign the same meaning to words that adults have acquired. Children only understand the events within the limited scope of the years they have lived and the experiences they have had. They have not been around long enough to be able to evaluate successfully present events based on past experiences.

Caveats, Developmental Markers and Interpretations

Many adults feel that they can evaluate the meaning of a child's drawing by interpreting the form and (what they believe to be) the message. This is dangerous and disrespectful of an individual, of any age. Drawings mean what the creator reveals. If the meaning changes over time, that leads us to believe that the creator has changed. Imposing adult standards of communication and content on a child's product is exactly what will lead the therapist to false conclusions. This does not rule out the possibility that therapist and child can come to the same discoveries about the visual narrative, but when explaining the art, the originator of the artwork must be the leader.

There is an assessment component to the art. Children demonstrate, in general, their developmental growth through the ability to realistically render a drawing (Kellogg; 1969, Lindstrom; 1989, Oster & Montgomery; 1996). Shapes and representative forms grow more recognizable over a time of developmental evolution. This is the information that can be useful when appraising a drawing. However, to ignore the social/economic/biological components of the child's life, in conjunction with the assessment of their art work, would be arrogant.

Looking at a client-made art project with a supervisee provides the ideal moment for the supervisor to reinforce the basic qualities of good therapy with the new therapist. Pointing out how to restrain from assuming a power position in the relationship, relying on curiosity and naivete (Dyche & Zayas, 1995), not having to know the answer until the client offers the way to understanding, can be better discussed when there is a concrete object, the art piece, to look at and dialogue about in the supervision session.

Art and Communication

Art therapists have traditionally seen the art product as a method of communication. Some, in this profession, believe that art mainly reveals intrapsychic conflicts, some feel that art is a direct effort by the client to share a world view, and some of us believe that art is a metacommunication that embodies a combination of personal ways to inform the self and the other. I believe that art expression can serve any of these needs, and will reflect the requirements of the child or adult at that particular moment in time. Art expressions are useful; both therapist and client can focus on a product that is creatively rendered by the client. Through this focus they can establish a midway point from which they can mutually contribute to a method of understanding a story, create visible exceptions to the tale, and experiment with new solutions in a risk free atmosphere (White & Epston, 1990).

Summary

Supervisors are obligated to protect the client through their supervision of the supervisees. Therefore, if the client is using art, and children certainly will, it is our responsibility to know the boundaries and the perimeters to which we should go when handling this powerful tool of therapy; client's sharing of themselves, exposing themselves, in their art expressions. Staying with the art, enjoying the enrichment it can bring and taking a walk into another person's world of imagination are all safe and delightful ways of honoring children. Listening to their stories, gaining valuable information through metaphorical communication, will enhance the therapy and is a safe and profitable way for supervisors and therapists to encourage creativity, both in the client and in themselves.

References

Anderson, H. & Goolishian, H. (1988). Human systems as linguistic systems: Preliminary and evolving ideas about the implications for clinical theory. *Family Process, 29,* 157–163.

Bloch, H.S. (1995). *Adolescent developmental, psychopathology, and treatment.* Connecticut: International Universities Press.

Dyche, L. & Zayas, L. *(1995).* The value of curiosity and naivete for the cross-cultural psychotherapist. *Family Process, 34,* 389–399.

Kellogg, R. (1989). *Analyzing children's art.* Palo Alto, CA: National Press Books.

Lindstrom, M. (1989). *Children's art.* University of California Press.

Oster, G.D. & Montgomery, S. S. (1996). *Client's use of drawings.* New Jersey: Jason Aronson

Malchiodi, C. (1990). *Breaking the silence. Art therapy with children from violent homes,* New York: Brunner/Mazel.

Malchiodi, C. & Riley, S. (1996). *Supervision and related issues.* Chicago: Magnolia Street Publishers.

Riley, S. & Malchiodi, C. (1994). *Integrative approaches to family and art therapy.* Chicago: Magnolia Street Publishers.

Tinnin, L. (1990). Biological process in non-verbal communication and their role in making and interpretations of art. *American Journal of Art Therapy,* 29, 9–13.

White, M. & Epston, D. (1990). *Narrative means to therapeutic ends.* Adelaide, South Australia: Dulwich Center.

A Chronicle of Parallel Process: Supervision in Chemical Dependency Treatment

Kate Burns, M.S.

Published in the AAMFT Supervision Bulletin, Vol. 9, No. 3, Winter 1997.

A year and a half ago, I became the clinical supervisor at our free standing chemical dependency hospital holding weekly group and individual supervision sessions with clinical staff. My purpose here is to describe the training process over those twelve months and the parallel processes that were engendered between supervision and supervision-of-supervision.

The supervision training objective was to sharpen the staff's skills and broaden our scope of treatment approaches. The final goal was to diversify chemical dependency treatment to accommodate patients who had not found success with the traditional 12-Step Model and those who required shorter lengths of stay. The former included patients for whom accepting a "higher power" was an obstacle to accessing treatment benefits and also dually-diagnosed patients, whose assessment and treatment required more highly-skilled and sophisticated clinicians.

Previously, group supervision sessions had been structured in a traditional format, with most information coming from the top down. Now the sessions were organized around informal case discussions. Staff members seemed uneasy at first with the collaborative style, but gradually they began talking about their individual desires to improve their knowledge base and their fluency in using interventions from other models. Nurses, on-call counselors and evening program staff began attending. More and more people spoke up, volunteering ideas and experiences, both as providers and as former patients. Learning began to take place across departments and even "from the bottom up." What we previously considered infallible and all encompassing, the 12-Step Model for treating the "disease," we came to see as limited.

Questioning Clinical Assumptions

From the start, our facility had conceptualized treatment for the individual within a systems framework (Valentine, 1994). Most of the counselors were fluent in systemic interventions, and some had begun learning cognitive and strategic methods. At the same time, an unstated belief in the efficacy of the traditional model had gone unchallenged among us: that the patient would, could and should conform to the one-size-fits all 12-Step Model. Now, as doubt seeped in, two opposing realities seemed to be in competition. Personal issues were at stake. In questioning our clinical assumptions we were asked to reflect on our embedded spiritual beliefs and experiences. We had to ask how these latter fit into an expanded clinical view.

The turmoil of transition was my own as well as the group's. I relied heavily on my AAMFT Approved Supervisor, again and again carrying my struggles to her. Each time we returned to a handful of grounding principles that placed value on every members' experience and trust in their integrity; normalized my frustration as well as the group's; and emphasized providing a safe haven for staff to work out the uncertainties that accompany new skills. My supervisor was doing with me what I in turn would do in group supervision, and ultimately what the counselor would do with the patient (three parallel processes).

Meanwhile, as we grappled with the implications of a more integrative model, case discussions continued. The absence of hierarchical structure fostered the free expression of strong emotions and ideas that were often far from orthodox. As group members became aware that the new format lent itself to change within our system, they began to include in their case presentations references to contextual issues such as gender, class and power, all reflective of their own conscious process; and all this, within a medical model.

Validating Staff Efforts

At the next in-service, I took the opportunity, in previewing the upcoming Joint Commission on the Accreditation of Healthcare Organizations (JCAHO) survey, to tie in JCAHO's new emphasis on organizational efficiency and measurable outcomes with our own goals of ensuring staff cohesiveness and providing state-of-the-art treatment. The in-service served it's purpose. It validated the efforts of the staff as they struggled with both managed care's shorter lengths of stay and our own system's fiscal constraints. It allowed for dialogue regarding decreasing resources for both patient and staff, and it promoted a sense of pride and group empowerment.

The soil was now seeded and the time seemed right for a catalyst, perhaps an "outside expert" to legitimize (and add sizzle) to the process. The idea of having a well-known consultant to help move along the change process led to a meeting with the Medical Director and the clinical nurse-manager. This meeting was our first official conversation about the possibility of expanding the program to include treatment modalities which would (1) require a staff fluent in state-of-the-art counseling skills, (2) accommodate a clinical fit to the shrinking length of stay, and (3) recognize the needs of non-believers by offering appropriate treatment for them as well as for those who had previously been unsuccessful with the 12-Step approach. While there was agreement on the first two points, the third caused some anxiety, anxiety that was evident in the weekly supervision group. It would be months before we came to terms with our ambivalence.

As our "outside expert," the administrator and I had singled out Michael Yapko, PhD, my clinical supervisor. An author and a master teacher, Dr. Yapko is fluent in Cognitive and Short-Term Therapy as well as pattern interruption. Opening a day of all-staff training, Dr. Yapko acknowledged the value of the 12-Step Model, then introduced some aspects of Brief, Solution-Focused Therapy. He was able to get agreement on the benefits of a client-specific approach, while at the same time, he avoided setting up a value-based evaluation of one model over another.

Enlarging Our Repertoire of Skills

The afternoon session focused on a current case at our hospital that so far had left the staff feeling like failures. But hearing it approached step-by-step, according to the considerations and strategies of the new model, gave us hope. Dr. Yapko was directing counselors as we would direct patients: he assumed we could learn the new methods; he showed us how to enlarge our repertoire of skills; we practiced them in the context of the current case. Isomorphically, what was happening in the training would happen in the therapy.

We were making progress but we still had a way to go. It was not easy to unequivocally accept a model which de-emphasized history and traditional notions regarding insight. Still it was a good beginning.

Two months later in another training session with Dr. Yapko, we wrestled with a much knottier case, one which had caused the staff to experience considerable negative counter-transference. Dr. Yapko took us through the case, paying little attention to our feelings (process) about the patient, but directing us to find the patient's most critical deficit. Then he charged us with creating an experiential intervention to reduce or, even better, eliminate it. In much the same way, we learned to pay less attention to the patient's history and feelings and instead to direct her to an experience (resource) that would help her to achieve the stated goal.

This instruction provided us with an experiential change. We now had a tool we previously lacked and, isomorphically, we could provide the patient with what she needed to eliminate her deficit. This case was our first test of second order change; through it we came to accept the validity of other treatment approaches.

In summary, we set out over a year ago to train counselors in the use of interventions from a variety of theoretical orientations. It has been an adventuresome undertaking and it is still evolving. As you might guess, we are now known to regularly invite trainers who were previously considered threats to our model, and in this transition, not one member of the staff has left because a failure to agree with how things are going.

The author is indebted to Clark Smith, M.D., Medical Director at Vista Pacifica Hospital, Christie Turner, L.C.S.W., AAMFT Approved Supervisor, Daniel Valentine, Ph.D., Administrator at Vista Pacifica Hospital, and Michael Yapko, Ph.D., Director, the Milton H. Erickson Institute of San Diego.

References

Valetine, D. (1994). Family systems approaches in chemical dependency treatment, *Family Therapy News,* February, p.3–12.

Collaborative Practice Within a Child Protection Agency System

Harlene Anderson, Ph.D. and Harriet Roberts, Ph.D.

Published in the AAMFT Supervision Bulletin, Vol. VI, No. 3, Fall 1993.

Clinical practice within child protection agency systems challenges the best of therapists and supervisors. The larger social context usually entails multiple players representing political, legal, community, cultural, professional and personal realities. A complex system evolves that is ripe for strife among professionals and contention between therapist and client.

The therapist and other professionals involved with these families are the endorsers and conveyors of society's legal and cultural norms. Practice also involves dearly held personal values, morals, and expectations. To further complicate matters, the therapist is often given the dual mandate to assure child safety while providing therapy to the child's family. Agency policies and guidelines designed to operationalize these mandates hold inherent assumptions about human behavior. These assumptions, paradoxically, often trivialize the complexity and reduce the family and its individual members to typology categories, thus risking ignoring their uniqueness and strengths.

Even though agency staff may hold similar cultural values and beliefs, clinical dilemmas can tempt colleagues to judge one another, whether they be peers, supervisors, or supervisees. Although often universal standards of practice, they are broadly interpretable throughout the biases of each individual involved— especially when circumstances and events pull the practitioner to be pragmatic and to act in a timely manner. Clashes in biases can lead to immobilization, treatment failures, and breakdowns in client–therapist, supervisor–supervisee, and team relationships.

Our Biases

Supervisors often limit their efforts, attempting to influence change in either the family in the room or the supervisee, or both. This is not enough to work successfully with complex problems peculiar to child protection agencies. In our experience, maximization of opportunity for movement in supervision, and therefore treatment, that is more successful depends in part on the clinician's ability to operate in complex interactional systems. This requires the clinician to work collaboratively with other professionals who are key players as well as with family members.

By collaborative, we mean "co" in the sense of together. We make a distinction between collaborate and cooperate. In the mental health field, cooperate usually refers to compliance. In collaboration, members of the system are mutually involved in a co-exploration and elaboration of the familiar and a co-developing of the new. Our goal as supervisors is to create an atmosphere that leads to collaboration.* This involves creating a conversational context in which professionals and clients engage in dialogue with self and other. We create a process in which people are able to listen to and talk with one another in a manner that is generative, that leads to expanding, thinking, and creating options. Through such conversations, new descriptions, meanings, and narratives emerge.

A Dangerous Mother

We were engaged by a child protection agency to consult with agency teams on difficult problems. In this setting, we prefer group over individual supervision for several reasons. Meeting with the team offers an opportunity for the members to work together and share cases which can help with the isolation and burden that leads to burnout. Team members can experience collaboration. Finally, the more ideas the better with such difficult cases. However, on occasions, we might want to (or others might want us to) talk with persons (e.g., a case worker, family member, etc.) separately.

Recently, a team supervisor was referred to us by the director. One of her staff was in a struggle with a mother around child visitation, and the mother had threatened the case worker's life. The director suggested the supervisor invite us to meet with her and her team to resolve the issues. We asked the supervisor if she thought we should meet with the whole team or with just her and the staff member. The supervisor and staff member preferred we meet with the whole team. The supervisor added that the director and she felt the team was grieving and questioning their competency because of the recent death of a child in another case. The team, following all the guidelines, recommended a child, who had been in custody, be returned home after her mother had successfully completed a treatment program. Two weeks later the child died of injuries caused by the mother's boyfriend who was baby-sitting while she worked.

When we met with the team, the atmosphere in the room was tense and depressed. We told them what we knew about the recent tragedy and the current case, acknowledged their distress, and asked them to tell us who was involved in this case and what the issues were as they saw them. The cast of characters included the case worker, the supervisor, a previous case worker, the director, the mother, the child, an agency security guard, foster parents, and a judge. Everyone on the team knew about this mother and the current problem.

We then asked the case worker to tell us what *she* thought we needed to know about the situation. She described the mother, an agency client for over two years, as dangerous, paranoid, hostile, and manipulative. The mother's child was in custody and the case worker was responsible for supervised visits held at the agency. The mother was notorious for not showing up at scheduled visitations but periodically appearing at the agency demanding to see her child and threatening the agency, the supervisor, and the case workers. The case worker highlighted that this mother's hostility and threats were not new. This was echoed by some of her colleagues.

The case worker did not want to let this mother get by with bullying her. This current conflict arose when the case worker refused to change the mother's visitation day so she could see her child the week of Christmas. The case worker wanted the mother searched for weapons and accompanied by an agency security guard on all visitations. The case worker believed that she was in danger and deserved the protection of the agency. She legitimized this position with an account of another worker whose house had recently been shot at by a drive-by shooter who the team unanimously agreed was a disgruntled agency client.

We asked the supervisor what *she* thought we needed to know. The supervisor downplayed the drive-by shooting. She talked about the bad press the agency was receiving and how it had increased scrutiny of the agency. Hesitantly, she shared her thoughts about the difference in the race of the caseworker and the mother.

We then asked the other team members what *they* thought we needed to know. They had little to add, mostly wanting to give advice to the case worker. Some were clearly on the therapist's side; others agreed with the supervisor. They talked about feeling under surveillance by their colleagues in the agency and community.

We told them we were curious about a lot of things. For instance: What did they think was going on with this mother? Why would she act like this? All had assumptions about the mother's intentionality and motivation. We were inquisitive about each possibility and asked if each were true, then what position or action would logically follow. What would they expect the mother's reactions to be? Did the mother know the case worker was afraid of her? Had she ever told the mother? Did they imagine the mother experienced the case worker as a person or as a representation of the agency? If the security guard was in the room during the visits, what would the mother do? What if the guard was outside the door? Did the mother get along with anyone in the agency? If so, whom? And how did they understand the relationship? What were the agency's policies concerning staff safety? What was the director's position concerning the media? Had any other team ever experienced a situation like this? If so, how did they handle it?

Our curiosities and their ideas were interspersed with our talking with each other out loud in front of the team. We shared with each other some of the thoughts that their ideas were triggering in us.

We invited the supervisor and case worker to reflect on what they had heard and share what they were now thinking. Following their reflections, we turned and talked with each other, sharing what we thought we had heard the supervisor and case worker saying, weaving in some of what we thought the group had said—leaving ideas, possibilities, and questions in the air for further discussion between the supervisor and the supervisee.

During this intertwining process, all joined with

us in a mutual puzzling about how to better understand this mother and to develop options for working with her. The group began to shift from telling the therapist what she was doing wrong and what she should do. The therapist slowly began to sound less defensive and demanding, and the supervisor visibly relaxed and sat back in her chair. No longer did the case worker feel so alone in her responsibility for the case, as a sense of shared responsibility developed. The case worker felt heard; not only did her supervisor now understand the extent of this problem, but her colleagues did as well. The supervisor said she was feeling more hopeful.

All talked about how their treating this as another "dangerous mother" case not only prevented them from learning new information about the mother, but also excluded their influence in the struggle. Most glaring to all was how the theme of violence and need to control it had blinded them to the emotional and psychological state of the mother and to the possibilities for getting help rather than controlling her. They were still taking the mother's hostility and threats seriously, but were developing alternative ways of understanding the situation. This freed them to work in a less adversarial manner. They concluded that with this mother, much like the mother whose child was killed by her boyfriend, "There's another life out there and we have to find a way to learn about it, a way that lets us help people with it."

Attitudes and Actions that Lead to Collaboration

Through our attitudes and actions, we provided a context and created a process in which the supervisor, the case worker, and their teammates could work collaboratively. The experience served as a springboard for the case worker to work more collaboratively with the mother. The collaborative effort began with an awareness, acknowledgment, and attempt to understand each component of the supervision and treatment in a larger social context. We included ourselves as part of the conversational process—puzzling, questioning, sharing our thoughts, and thinking with them.

We demonstrated an awareness of social contextual components (i.e. community, agency, cultural, legal, ethical, and individual). For example, we asked about the members of the drama, including those not present in the room. We acknowledged the multiplicity and distinctions of each reality—the uniqueness of each role, each definition of the problem, and desired solutions—by making room for and showing an interest in all descriptions and opinions. We respected the expertise of each person and accepted each view as important no matter how opinionated or obtuse. As we began to try to learn and understand by wondering, puzzling, and asking questions, the participants in the consultation were invited into the process. As team members began to try to understand along with us, their language, descriptions, and explanations became less pejorative. Differences began to create curiosity rather than antagonistic positions.

References

*For a further discussion of a "Collaborative Language Systems Approach to Therapy and Supervision," the reader is referred to the following two sources:

Anderson, J., & Goolishian, H. (1988). Human systems as linguistic systems: Evolving ideas about the implications for theory and practice. *Family Process*. 27:371–393.

Anderson, H. (1993). On a rollercoaster: A collaborative language systems approach to therapy. In S. Friedman (Ed.) *The New Language of Change*. New York: Guilford.

Supervision and Business: A Nonreimbursable, Yet Valuable Commodity

Sharon Raggio, M.S.

Published in the AAMFT Supervision Bulletin, Vol. VII, No. 3, Fall 1994.

Traditionally, community mental health centers have been bastions of excellent training, supervision, outside consultation and experience. Often funds were set aside to send employees to conferences and workshops or to hire outside consultants. Supervision was regular and a priority. Therapists were expected to participate in consultation/supervision meetings as part of their employment. Often supervision was live and time was allowed for other staff to watch to enhance their learning. Centers provided a setting where experienced staff "taught" new recruits, all staff freely shared ideas with one another and everyone benefited from the "rich learning environment." Staff viewed this "rich in learning environment" as a perk that helped to offset the lower pay most centers offered.

In my experience, I have seen this "rich in learning environment" begin to change. Colleagues from other centers also confirm that things are changing. Training money is drying up and outside consultation discontinued as it is too expensive and staff time too needed elsewhere. Supervision has become less regular or even provided "only as needed," often accompanied by a change to an exclusive group supervision format. There is a decreasing emphasis on live supervision as it is time intensive. I do not believe these changes are due to a change in thinking about the value and need for supervision. Rather, I believe this change is due to increasing demands and less funding. As supervision is a nonreimbursable item, it is a vulnerable commodity as community mental health centers are competing more and more in the business marketplace, and taking on a "for business" frame. Certainly, not all centers are in this position, and this article confines itself to my experience and conversations with colleagues about the future of supervision in community mental health centers.

In my opinion, there are two main issues. The first is the real life issue of money. Administrative staff tell me that more and more mental health centers will need to compete with private providers for the same insurance dollar. Clinical staff report more demand from clients whose insurance has run out and who seek services at the center because of our sliding scale. There seems to be less and less federal and state monies available. Thus, there is more demand for services and less money available to operate. This pushes centers into making decisions based on a "for business" frame rather than a "most effective services" frame. Centers that already have good billing and collection practices in place will probably have less difficulty with these changes and issues and there will be less fall out effecting areas such as supervision. For those centers, there may be some changes in money available for training or outside consultation, but supervision practices probably will be less vulnerable, even though supervision is a nonreimbursable item. However, centers that do not have good business practices in place will probably experience more fall out effects. They will struggle more with decisions regarding supervision, such as how much of it should be available and how it should be used.

The second issue is an ethical and philosophical one. The ways centers resolve the above financial constraints and increasing demands will impact their traditional role of being an excellent training ground rich in learning opportunities. Historically, community mental health centers have been natural training settings for inexperienced and unlicensed therapists. Will supervision that is provided "only as needed" allow inexperienced therapists to develop professionally? How will changing supervision practices affect the development of new therapists? Will using an exclusively group supervision format be enough for centers to continue the high quality of services and training they traditionally offer? Will more experienced therapists look elsewhere for employment if the centers lack a "rich in learning environment?" If mental health centers are less able to contribute to the profession by providing on the job and professional learning opportunities as they have, who will? These are important questions I have pondered and discussed with colleagues. While I do not know how widespread this issue is, I know it exists in my little corner of the world.

As an Approved Supervisor, I have looked for ways to preserve the quality of supervision offered, while realizing the struggles centers must face economically. It reminds me of working with families who struggle to have a decent quality of life *and* a relationship with their children where the parents teach children their values and hand down traditions. The parents' ultimate goal is to enable their children to be productive members of society. Families often face problems in finding the time and resources to accomplish this goal. Likewise, the ways we, as supervisors and family therapists, address our own "family's" struggle with money, time and responsibility will help to shape the future values and traditions of our profession.

Marketing Your Approved Supervisor Designation to Increase Practice Income

Reo Leslie, Jr., D.Min.

Published in the AAMFT Supervision Bulletin, Spring 2000.

The Approved Supervisor designation has value. Although other professional organizations have supervisory credentials, the AAMFT standards, including instruction in systemic supervision, are the highest in the clinical field. Since competent and sensitive supervision is critical to the development of therapists, how can an Approved Supervisor both contribute to mentoring and teaching the next generation of systemic and relational therapists and increase her or his income?

Several years ago I became an AAMFT Approved Supervisor and, in partnership with my wife and other clinicians, began to build a post-degree institute (PDI). Out of the experience of growing the Family Therapy / Play Therapy Institute and developing a staff of predominantly African-American and women supervisors and supervisors-in-training, many questions surfaced about clinical supervision and supervision-of-supervision. These questions included, but were not limited to:

1. What are the components of competent and culturally sensitive supervision and supervision-of-supervision?

2. What are the ethical, legal, and professional issues inherent in contemporary supervision and supervision-of-supervision?

3. What are ways that supervision and supervision of supervision can generate income for clinicians in private practice and post-degree institutes training clinicians?

In this brief article I will review what my staff and I learned in response to these questions and the larger issue of how to increase income by effective use of the AAMFT Approved Supervisor designation. The discussion will include issues like marketing and business strategies; ethical, legal and professional issues; and collaborative efforts to provide supervisees for supervisors-in-training and clients for supervised therapists. Storm and Todd (1997) challenge Approved Supervisors to address business considerations in supervision and supervision-of- supervision to "prevent us from having a generation of unemployed clinicians" (p. 221) in a professional environment where "these clinicians are in serious danger of remaining unemployed" (p. 221). Although money was not the primary motivation for our entering the psychotherapeutic profession, all of us spent a lot of money earning our clinical and supervisory credentials. Our clinical and supervisory services have great value and we deserve to be properly compensated for the good work we do.

Who Wants to Pay for Supervisory Services?

Both states and professional organizations require clinical supervision for licensure and certification. Supervised clinical experience is essential to the professional development of therapists. Although important in all phases of a psychotherapist's life, it is particularly significant at the beginning stage of a clinician's career. Systemic clinical supervision, as viewed by the AAMFT, involves more than just case review. Teaching, modeling, professional orientation, and gatekeeping are all components of the supervisory system.

First, post-master's and post-doctoral clinicians wanting licensure, professional certification, and the AAMFT Approved Supervisor designation will contract with us for supervisory services. Opportunities for licensure in supervision vary from state to state. A survey of your own state's regulations is necessary. Customers for supervision will include candidates for post-master's and drug and alcohol licensure.

Second, students completing practicums and internships for clinically-based graduate programs require supervision. Many graduate programs will contract with an outside supervisor to supervise interns at a clinical placement site. In other situations, to get an authentic experience of post-master's life, interns must pay for their own supervision. Third, agencies providing clinical services without the benefit of licensed therapists contract with licensed supervisors. Clinical supervision is provided under contract for the staff serving agency clients. Sometimes the contract includes consultation, in-service training, and clinical supervision of graduate interns at the agency.

Where do I Get Supervisees?

Developing a private practice in supervision is a similar process to developing a private practice in psychotherapy. Let your colleagues, universities, clinical agencies, and professional organizations in your locality know your availability for supervision and supervision-of-supervision. Use your state AAMFT and other professional organization newsletters to market your supervisory services. Visit meetings of therapists, post-master's interns, and graduate students in clinical programs.

Identify your areas of expertise as a clinical supervisor. Supervisees will have interests in your particular theoretical orientations, your knowledge of specific client populations, and competence in different aspects of our profession. For example, in some states, like Colorado, a post-master's clinician cannot legally counsel clients unless supervised by a licensed therapist competent in treatment of that client population. Additionally, candidates for LMFT licensure and/or AAMFT Clinical Membership in many instances will be required to have a supervisor with the Approved Supervisor designation. The most effective way to reach your target audience is to put yourself and your supervisory credentials into the marketplace.

Interact with potential supervisees and supervisors in training whenever possible. Face-to-face contact with potential consumers, whether in a classroom, a conference, a chapter meeting, or an interview, is invaluable. Once the customer meets you, he or she will want to contract with you for supervision or supervision-of-supervision.

How do I Integrate Supervision into my Practice?

Supervision is contracted in a similar way to psychotherapy. Contracts for supervision and supervision-of-supervision should include fees, terms, conditions, and legal and ethical issues. The supervisor and supervisee, or supervisor-in-training, should negotiate concerns like the length of supervision, mutual termination, handling disagreements, mode of super-

vision, and anything else relevant. Supervision is handled like any other aspect of a clinician's business practice.

In an institute setting, like ours, the most effective business and marketing strategy is the ability to provide clients for your supervisees and supervisees for your supervisors-in-training. This can be done two ways. Both will involve establishing several levels of training and services that can generate income.

First, the institute can create a clinic to serve clients in the community. Therapy can be offered at a discounted rate or on a sliding-scale basis and the graduate students and/or post-master's licensure/certification candidates can provide the clinical services. The institute's interns can be supervised by the supervisors-in-training, who in turn receive supervision-of-supervision from the Approved Supervisor. The supervisory system is one where everyone gets what they need.

Second, if the institute does not have a clinic, collaborative relationships can be formed to provide a client population to the supervisee. An agency that meets the standards of the institute can serve as a clinical placement site for supervised interns. The Approved Supervisor does the supervision of supervisors-in-training who supervise the interns at the site. Of course, universities negotiate similar arrangements for graduate interns. If the Approved Supervisor can insure, through the practice or the institute, clients for the supervised therapists and consistent supervisees for the supervisors-in-training, then the system will be harmonious and the income will flow.

What are Some or the Legal, Ethical, and Contextual Issues I Need to be Aware of?

Case law in Cohen vs. New York (1975) establishes "supervisory liability for supervisee decisions and actions" (Moline, et al., 1998). Approved Supervisors must protect their practice, institute, licensure, and designation by making sure supervisees do not commit ethical or legal misconduct. Contracting should address all issues like level of competence, duty to warn, duty to protect, representation of credentials, informed consent, boundaries, and multiple relationships. The Approved Supervisor will need to stay current in state licensure law, be well versed in the *AAMFT Code of Ethics*, and be familiar with practice standards for therapists.

If doubts develop in these areas, I recommend

three courses of action for Approved Supervisors. First, consult your own attorney as quickly as possible. Second, consult with the regulatory authorities for psychotherapy in your state. Third, consult with the AAMFT ethics staff. After the consultations, evaluate the feedback and make the necessary supervisory decision.

Marketing the Approved Supervisor Designation

This brief article has suggested ways Approved Supervisors can increase their income by doing supervision-of-supervision with AAMFT supervisors-in-training, supervising graduate students and therapists working toward professional certification and state licensure, developing clinics or collaborative relationships with clinical placement sites, and marketing their supervisory expertise.

References

Storm, C. L., and Todd, T. C. (1997). *The reasonably complete systemic supervisor resource guide*. Allyn and Bacon: Boston.

Moline, N. E., et al. (1998). *Documenting psychotherapy: Essentials for mental health practitioners*. Sage: Thousand Oaks, CA.

Supervising Systems

John VanDeusen and Jay Lappin, MSW

Published in the AAMFT Supervision Bulletin, Vol. VI, No. 3, Fall 1993.

Supervision, like whitewater rafting and other "multiply determined" processes, is influenced by one's personal fitness in the role and ability to adapt to conditions in which it is performed. Today, the conduct of family therapy is increasingly embedded within a myriad of larger systems—educational, legal, medical, social, economic—forcing supervisors to reexamine their focus, format, and impact of their work. While individual supervision of the single therapist, one family at a time, will continue as a basic approach, many innovations are likely to emerge in the future, as we learn to use systems to supervise systems.

One key to survival in this new milieu is understanding the many sorts of "tensions" that occur routinely at the macrosystemic level. Most of us are by now familiar (if not yet comfortable) with the notion that gender, racial, and generational differences "make a difference." Beyond these, there are numerous dimensions of professional diversity, for instance, professional discipline, job function, rank, seniority, and service philosophy. At a more global level, the formal cultures of most organizations (manifest in organization charts and policy manuals) are sharply offset by their "shadows" (implicit in restroom graffiti and coffee-break conversations).

These sorts of tensions are configured into the day-to-day life of every organization, as undercurrents to stress and conflict. While at times their impact can be dramatic, their influence is far more likely to be oblique and difficult to pinpoint.

In order to manage their relations with these larger systems effectively, supervisors and therapists need to become fluent in applying systemic tools with organizations and networks. In our own work, we find that four such tools—scanning, joining, improvising, and reflecting—are becoming increasingly valuable.

Scanning is the ability to track complex patterns of expression and behavior (including one's own), and thereby gain awareness of boundaries, alignments, and power bases in organizational systems. Two-dimensional modelling of social networks via ecomaps is a useful starting point for this, and, fortunately, a growing number of therapists use this technique routinely. Scanning of interactional processes requires more direct methods, however, including live supervision (Montalvo, 1973).

Scanning should commence when contracting with a new supervisee. It is important to get a clear view of who in the larger system your supervision will impact, and how. Conversely, it is equally important to identify the various ways in which all of the members of the larger system may impact your supervision. "Locating" the supervisory relationship in this manner is not meant to fix the operations in a static sense, but rather it is the beginning of an ongoing, recursive process. It allows a subsequent assessment of the goodness of fit between the therapist and a particular organizational milieu.

We offer as an example the Phillips family. We learned about this family through a local police officer, who sought our help to untangle what he called a difficult case. The officer led a task force of representatives from 12 different governmental agencies, all of whom had encountered the Phillips, a family of 35 persons living together in a single house. Eviction notices, arrests, warnings from the local child protective services—all had been unsuccessful in getting this family to change. This story was too rich with detail to follow, so we asked the officer to draw a genogram of the family and ecomap of its relationship with the task force. This exercise made it plain that despite the drama involved, the two systems were only marginally connected with one another. We proposed that the officer convene the entire network in a single meeting, to establish a more direct linkage.

Joining is the ability to build effective partnerships, that is, how a supervisor relates to each member of the larger system and how she manages her therapist's joining. Mastery of this skill at the organizational level is strongly linked to one's tolerance for ambiguity and comfort with "both–and" situations. A supervisor is always in the position of speaking simultaneously for the "guild" of family therapy, for the supervisory contract, and for himself, individually.

Supervisors can help therapists find ways of eliciting tensions among members of the client system, and to weather the ensuing discomfort long enough to establish stable ties with all of the warring factions. In our work with public sector systems, for instance, we nearly always encounter a tension between child safety and family empowerment as primary values. Hence, we search for strategies capable of spanning both paradigms.

As members of the Phillips family entered the room for the initial macrosystem meeting, the entire task force was already seated, filling all but a few chairs. This was a formidable challenge. As the family seemed to be on the verge of retreating, we quietly asked them if this seating arrangement was comfortable. No, it was not. So, we asked what change might make things more comfortable. "One big circle," a family member said "It's more friendly." The task force took this cue without hesitation. In less than thirty seconds we were all joined in one big circle.

Improvisation is the supervisor's ability to improvise strategy and tactics, and to do so at least one step ahead of the therapist. In organizations, as in families, there is an unending struggle between feeling good and getting chores done. Improvisation is the craft through which these contrasting needs are kept in balance, by finding new uses for things that might otherwise obstruct or distract the therapist from his task. The most effective improvisers are like bricoleurs, masters at taking whatever is at hand—words, actions, tangible resources—and adapting these to their own needs. Supervisors can help therapists learn to scan the background for messages and media worth incorporating into clinical strategies. The "props" for such improvisation are bountiful at the macrosystemic level.

Early on in our meeting with the Phillips family, we learned that one obstacle to their securing better housing for several siblings and their children was the lack of furniture and housewares. As this was said, every official in the room was listening, heads nodding emphatically. We grabbed a sheet of paper, wrote "donations" across the top and started passing it around the circle. By the time it came back around, the sheet was full. Everyone had something to offer.

Reflection is the supervisor's ability to take stock (empathically and objectively) of what has and has not been achieved in her work with the therapist; to plot and steer a new course; and to move ahead. We find that reflection is weakest when performed alone or only with the supervisee. It gains strength as additional elements in the system get actively involved, and is probably optimal when the supervisor invites a fellow supervisor to look over her shoulder as she engages the entire system in a reflective discussion. When the right people are assembled, reflection occurs almost spontaneously—as a collaborative catching of breath.

After achieving an initial breakthrough in our first meeting with the APARC team and the Phillips family, the system quickly "refroze" when we inquired about holding a second follow-up meeting. As we all sat waiting for someone to make a decision it began to dawn on everyone that the room we were meeting in was not very comfortable—did we really want to come back here? The point of critical mass was reached when one of the family members said, "We could meet at our church!" Needless to say, we did—and it was better.

Chapter 7

Ethical and Legal Issues

Professional Boundaries and Ethics: Ongoing Considerations

Dorothy S. Becvar, Ph.D.

Published in the AAMFT Supervision Bulletin, Vol. 11, No. 1, Summer 1998.

Applicants for the Approved Supervisor designation are required to include in their Supervision Case Study a description of their "efforts to maintain clear and appropriate professional boundaries and ethical behavior" (AAMFT, 1997, p. 16). As Approved Supervisors (ASs), perhaps the greatest service we can provide not only to our supervisors in training (SITs) but also to clients and to the profession is to heighten the awareness of SITs about the need for constant attention in this domain. And having included discussions about boundary and other ethical issues throughout the supervision of supervision process, addressing this dimension and dealing with it in an appropriately thorough manner in the written materials will become a natural and simple matter.

Contracting for Supervision of Supervision

Attention to boundary and ethical issues is a process that begins with the first meeting between AS and SIT. Indeed, providing clinical supervision is complicated by challenging dilemmas and heavy legal responsibilities. While the goal of supervision of supervision is to develop the abilities of the supervisor and supervisee, as well as to facilitate the therapy process, it is important to address the fact that the supervisor is, in fact, legally responsible for the supervisee's behavior, and thus close attention must be paid to ethical and legal issues at all levels of the AS/SIT/supervisee/client system. Under the legal principle of *respondent superior,* supervisors can be charged with the negligence of their supervisees even though the supervisor played no part in unethical action, has done nothing to aid or encourage it, and has done everything possible to prevent it.

The creation of a supervision contract begins the process of clarifying professional roles and responsibilities as well as articulating boundary and ethical considerations. An important dimension to be included in this document, a model of which is provided below,

are specifications regarding the ways in which therapeutic emergencies are to be handled. For example, what are the issues (e.g., suicide threat, legal violations) regarding which the AS expects to be contacted immediately? What is the appropriate procedure to be followed should hospitalization become necessary?

Also to be addressed are the requirements for maintaining confidentiality appropriately. What are the policies of the agencies involved? Who may have access to what records and under what circumstances? How will clients be informed about the limits of confidentiality? Attestation regarding knowledgeable willingness by all parties to abide by the appropriate professional code of ethics is another important contractual issue. Do all parties have copies of and knowledge about the code of ethics? Do all parties involved have copies of and knowledge about state/provincial regulations? What are the requirements for inclusion of ethical issues in the supervisory process? Further, outlining supervisory responsibilities and discussing the ways in which personal issues will be handled alerts everyone involved about the limits of supervision and the potential for referral should the need for therapy for a therapist or supervisee arise.

Model Supervision Contract

This is an agreement between [*name of supervisor*] and [*name of supervisee*] for supervision which is to take place at [*site of supervision*] from [*date*] to [*date*].

A. Service Requirements
  1. Work Schedule
  2. Case Load
  3. Administrative Responsibilities
  4. Consideration/Fee
B. Supervision Requirements
  1. Time and length of supervision
  2. Delimitation of supervisory responsibilities
  3. Handling of therapeutic emergencies
  4. Out-of-office client or referral contacts
  5. Confidentiality

6. Preparation for supervision
7. Knowledgeable willingness to abide by code of ethics
8. Content of supervision
9. Modalities of supervision/theoretical orientation
10. Review of progress and evaluation of supervision
11. Grievance procedures
12. Timely response - supervision documentation, letters of recommendation
13. How personal issues will be handled
14. Supervisor's credentials
15. Supervisee's credentials and insurance verification

I understand and agree to abide by each of the preceding obligations of the supervision contract.

Date _____
Supervisor's Signature _____

Date _____
Supervisee's Signature _____

(Adapted from Haber, 1997)

Providing Supervision of Supervision

Having negotiated the contract in a manner that addresses boundary and ethical issues, and having specified requirements for attention in this area, the next step is to make sure that they are included in each session. A simple question on the part of the AS such as, "Were you aware of any potential conflicts in the realm of ethics while you were working with your supervisee?" may be all that is necessary. Or, if the SIT and supervisee are students in the same program, or work in the same agency, a question might be posed regarding dual relationships and how they will be managed. What is important is that awareness of boundary and ethical issues be uppermost in the minds of both AS and SIT. When they are not, the potential to avoid problems may be missed.

To illustrate, in a recent live supervision of supervision session, the therapist presented a videotape of a session with a family to the SIT and to myself as a guest AS. All appropriate permissions had been obtained from the clients. The family was introduced using a genogram and some general background in-

formation was provided. Following the videotape, the therapist gave a brief overview of progress to date, described proposed plans for future sessions, and asked for assistance regarding a feeling of stuckness. During the course of the presentation, and almost as an aside, the therapist mentioned that one of the children in the family had talked about suicide but that was no longer a concern to the parents. The SIT responded to the therapist by validating the work that had been done and by asking more in-depth questions about the therapist's feelings of stuckness. There then ensued a dialogue in which the therapist was encouraged by the SIT to expand the conceptual framework being used and to evolve some new ways in which to work with the family. When the SIT then turned and asked me, as an AS, for feedback or suggestions, I also validated the work but said that my immediate question was, "Are you comfortable with the way the suicide issue has been handled?" The SIT immediately returned to the therapist and asked for further clarification. With more information, it became apparent that it would be important for the therapist to do more thorough follow-up with the parents and others involved with the child. The SIT and the therapist made a verbal contract, agreeing upon what steps were to be taken and how and when the SIT was to be informed. A personal communication to me from the SIT several days later confirmed that the situation was well under control. There was also an expression of gratitude for bringing attention to this issue. And I suspect that such heightened awareness will not soon decrease.

Preparing the Supervision Case Study

According to Storm and Haug (1997, p. 37), "supervisors are more than passive conveyors of ethical information. They assume a proactive stance to help their supervisees and themselves develop ethical awareness and to make decisions consistent with ethical values, both internal and external..." If, consistent with this position, boundary and other ethical issues have been addressed and have been ongoing considerations throughout the course of supervision of supervision, the SIT will be hard-pressed to avoid attending to them when preparing the application materials. That is, when the SIT sits down to write a supervision case study, these considerations will naturally emerge as part of the description of what transpired and how the SIT thought about the process of supervision. Thus, as we Approved Supervisors remain ever-attentive in this domain, the principle of isomorphism once again is operative and all involved are better served.

References

AAMFT. (1997). *Approved Supervisor designation: Standards and responsibilities handbook*. Washington, DC: Author.

Haber, R. (1997). *Dimensions of psychotherapy supervision: Maps and means*. New York: W. W. Norton.

Storm, C. L., & Haug, I. E. (1997). Ethical issues: Where do you draw the line? In T. Todd, & C. Storm, (Eds.), *The complete systemic supervisor: Context, philosophy, and pragmatics*, pp. 26–40. Boston, MA: Allyn & Bacon.

MFT Supervision: Evaluating and Managing Critical Issues

Charles Huber, Ph.D. and Colleen M. Peterson, Ph.D.

Published in the AAMFT Supervision Bulletin, Vol. IX, No. 1, Winter 1996.

Ethical and legal issues pertaining to marriage and family therapy supervision, particularly section 4 of the *AAMFT Code of Ethics,* are the focus of this article. Both the broad ethical and legal responsibilities for MFT supervisors and dual relationships will be considered. Material relevant to managing such relationships in MFT supervision was drawn from the second author's dissertation.

It is important that issues of morality, legality, and ethics intertwine and that virtue and principle ethics play out in the decisions that supervisors make. Virtue ethics pertain to a subjective focus on the qualities, traits, and habits of the person making a choice and subsequently carrying out an action. Principle ethics pertain to an objective focus on rational standards, rules, and universal codes.

An issue that is related to supervisor ethics for practice is supervisor liability. That is, supervisors are held accountable through two types of liability: direct, and vicarious. A brief summary of each liability as it pertains to the supervisory relationship follows.

Direct Liability

In relation to <u>supervisees</u>, supervisors are responsible for:

1. informing supervisees about their roles, expectations, goals, and criteria for evaluation at the beginning of supervision;

2. monitoring and assessing supervisees' performance consistently and carefully; and

3. providing periodic feedback and evaluation to supervisees, preferably in written form.

In relation to <u>supervisee's clients</u>, supervisors have direct liability when the client is injured and the supervisor:

1. gave the supervisee inappropriate advice about treatment and the supervisee carried it out;

2. failed to listen carefully to a supervisee's comments about a client and therefore failed to comprehend that client's needs;

3. failed to carry out agreed upon supervisory duties; and/or

4. assigned a supervisee a task that the supervisor knew, or should have known, was beyond the supervisee's training to execute.

Vicarious Liability

Supervisors are responsible for the acts of their supervisees. Risk management for this type of liability involves a four-step process whereby supervisors:

a) Identify potential risk areas;

b) Evaluate whether the risk area is serious enough to merit further attention;

c) Treat an area worth consideration with some method of risk control or prevention; and

d) Review practices and procedures periodically to ascertain their appropriateness and continuing effectiveness. The primary risk areas tend to be: abandonment, marked departure from established therapeutic methods, failure to obtain informed consent, unhealthy transference relationships, practicing beyond the scope of competency, sexual intimacy with a client, misdiagnosis, and failure to control a dangerous client. The standard of care for MFT supervision requires that the MFT supervisor:

1. Select supervisees with due care.

2. Define the scope of their responsibilities so that they are performing only functions for which they are competent.

3. Monitor supervisee performance

4. Be sure that clients are fully informed about the qualifications/status of supervisees and the implications of the supervision process for therapy

Relative to dual relationships we would refer the reader to Humphrey's 1994 summary of the changes in the *AAMFT Code of Ethics* and principle 1.2 of the current *Code of Ethics.* A brief summary of seminal writings in the area dealing with theoretical rationales for avoiding dual relationships includes (Shopland & VandeCreek, 1991), what makes dual role relationships problematic (Kitchener, 1988), boundary violations (Peterson, 1992), and the inevitability of dual relationships in academic settings (Ryder & Hepworth, 1990).

According to Peterson (1992), the positive aspects of dual relationships may include such things as professional socialization, humanness of supervisors, affirmation, and learning, whereas negative aspects of dual relationships may include hurt, being taken advantage of, and distrust. In Peterson's study participants were asked to list the criteria that they use in determining whether a dual relationship would be harmful or successful. The following themes that emerged from these questions are:

Harmful Criteria

1. Impaired Judgment
2. Jeopardized Client Welfare
3. Contrary to Professional Standards
4. Power Differential/Imbalance
5. Potential Misuse of Power
6. Unclear Boundaries
7. Discomfort/Confusion
8. Concealing Information from Peers
9. Compromised Supervisory Relationship
10. Sexual Involvement
11. All Dual Relationships are Harmful/Do Not Enter Any

Successful Criteria

1. Clear Boundaries
2. Open Communication/Discussion
3. Outstanding Personal Attributes
4. Equality
5. Attention to Ethical Guidelines/Practices
6. Oversight by Disinterested Third Party/Procedures
7. Avoid All Dual Relationships

Inasmuch as the *Code of Ethics* states that in those circumstances in which dual relationships cannot be avoided, "appropriate professional precautions" should be taken. The questionnaire used in Peterson's study included a question soliciting participant recommendations to avoid impaired judgment or exploi-

tation. The summary of participant recommendations are as follows:

1. Discuss/Consult with Colleagues
2. Supervision (of supervision/group/peer)
3. Discussion by Both Parties Involved
4. Clear Supervision Contract
5. Set Limits/Boundaries
6. No Sex
7. Follow Accepted Ethical Standards/Practices
8. Get Therapy
9. Don't Do It (Dual Relationships)

Editor's note: Principle 4 of the 1991 AAMFT Code of Ethics states, "Marriage and family therapists do not exploit the trust and dependency of students,employees, and supervisees." Principle 1.2 states, "Marriage and family therapists are aware of their influential position with respect to clients, and they avoid exploiting the trust and dependendy of such persons. Therapists, therefore, make every effort to avoid dual relationships with clients that could impair professional judgment or increase the risk of exploitation. When a dual relationship cannot be avoided, therapists take appropriate professional precautions to ensure judgment is not impaired and no exploitation occurs. Examples of such dual relationships include, but are not limited to, business or close personal relationships with clients. Sexual intimacy with clients is prohibited. Sexual intimacy with former clients for two years following the termination of therapy is prohibited."

References

Humphrey, F. (1994). Dual relations. In G. Brock (Ed.) *AAMFT Ethics Casebook.* Washington, DC: American Association for Marriage and Family Therapy.

Kitchener, K. S. (1988). Dual role relationships: What makes them so problematic? *Journal of Counseling and Development,* 67, 217–221.

Peterson, M. (1992). *At Personal Risk: Boundary violations in Professional-client Relationships.* New York: W. W. Norton.

Ryder, R., & Hepworth, J. (1990). AAMFT ethical code: "dual relationships." *Journal of Marital and Family Therapy,* 16(2), 127–132.

Shopland, S. N., & VandeCreek, L. (1991). Sex with ex-clients: Theoretical rationales for prohibition. *Ethics and Behavior* 1(1), 35–44.

Legal Liability in Supervision: An Interview with AAMFT Legal Counsel

Interview conducted by Anthony Heath, AAMFT Supervision Bulletin editor, with Steven Engelberg, AAMFT's legal counsel

Published in the AAMFT Supervision Bulletin, Vol. III, No. 2, June 1990.

Heath: *Steve, from your experience with the AAMFT Legal Consultation Plan, what kinds of situations give rise to legal liability for family therapy supervisors?*

Engelberg: Generally speaking, supervisors are accountable to provide appropriate supervision to their supervisees. So when a supervisee is negligent or does something clearly inappropriate, the supervisor could become liable. Having said that, I want to stress that liability cases involving therapists are not very common and liability cases involving supervisors are even less common. But the risk is there.

By the way, obviously supervisors sometimes act unethically or illegally. They have been known to take money and not perform services and to fraudulently sign insurance forms. But here I'm talking about liability for the actions of the supervisee.

There are three major areas of malpractice liability for supervisors. The first is encountered when a therapist has sex of any form or inappropriate intimacy with a client. It's very difficult to hold a supervisor accountable when a therapist engages in this form of dual relationship, though. Very few therapists ask their supervisors, "Is it all right for me to sleep with my clients?"

The second situation of liability arises when therapists work with dangerous clients. Liability is most commonly incurred when there's a risk of someone being hurt or killed, either though suicide or murder. When supervisors don't properly advise therapists in these situations, and the therapists fail to fulfill their legal duty to protect life, both run the risk of ending up in court. In my opinion, these "duty to warn" and suicidal cases are most likely to end up in litigation.

The third situation of liability involves breaches of therapist-client confidentiality. For example, if a supervisee released case records without a client's permission, the client could have grounds to sue both the therapist and the supervisor. Again, supervisors can be held responsible for failing to educate and direct their supervisees.

Interestingly, it's very rare for family therapists to be sued for providing ineffective therapy. These cases are usually too difficult to prove. But if a therapist was engaged in some bizarre form of therapy which harmed a person, the supervisor could be liable for failing to provide appropriate guidance.

Heath: *In general, there are more malpractice suits when someone is injured, is that right? And isn't it important that the injury be provable?*

Engelberg: Generally speaking, Tony, you're quite right; there has to be some fairly ascertainable harm to the client or a third party before there's going to be a successful liability case. Of course, a case that never gets to court can be traumatic and expensive, even for innocent therapists and supervisors.

Heath: *When you met with the Commission in April, we talked about the standard of care in supervision. Will you explain the concept of standard of care as it might apply to family therapy supervision?*

Engelberg: Generally speaking, to win a professional liability or malpractice case the plaintiff has to establish that there was a standard of care and that the defendant failed to meet this standard. Usually the standard of care is established through expert testimony, provided in this case by another therapist or another supervisor.

In my recent discussion of the standard of care in supervision with the Commission, we used a hypothetical example. A supervisor, working in a private practice, regularly focused the supervisory session on two or three cases selected by the supervisee. Now, if an ongoing client of the supervisee went out and killed someone, but the supervisor had no knowledge of the case because it had never been presented to him, could the supervisor be held liable? The critical question here is whether the supervisor's professional behavior met the standard of care in supervision.

If I were representing a family of the victim in this hypothetical situation, I would be fairly confident. Assuming that the therapist knew about the threat to the victim and that the therapist failed to fulfill his duty to warn the victim, I'd sue the therapist and I'd haul in the supervisor. No doubt, the supervisor would attempt to use the old "hear no evil, see no evil" defense. "I wasn't told about it, so it wasn't my responsibility," he'd say. "All supervisors do supervision this way," he'd argue.

I believe I could shatter that defense by bringing on a highly qualified AAMFT Approved Supervisor who, when I asked the right questions, would say that the supervisor had a duty to do more than inquire about three cases. The standard of care for supervision, we'd insist, would suggest that supervisors normally oversee all of their supervisees' cases, at least where dangerous cases are concerned.

Of course, this is only my theory. But I don't think you could establish as a standard of care that the supervisor is only responsible for the three cases. If the supervisor is representing himself as an expert who, for a fee, helps less-experienced therapists improve and learn, certainly he is responsible to see that the basic legal duties of a therapist, such as the duty to warn, are fulfilled. It's the supervisor's duty, in other words, to be sure that serious problems in the therapist's caseload are discussed even if it's outside the usual three cases.

There are no cases I can point to that say this is the standard of care for supervision, but when I turned this question to the Commission, I had the impression that most of the members agreed with me that it probably was unacceptable to restrict your attention to three cases. But even if only 50 percent of the Commission agreed with me, that means I could find a lot of Approved Supervisors who would say "Yeah, that's what a good supervisor would do."

Heath: *Steve, it almost sounds like supervisors are legally responsible for things way outside of their control.*

Engelberg: I don't think so. Supervisors can't be expected to insure good treatment. If a supervisor learned of a case in which there was a duty to warn problem and talked it through with the supervisee and said "I think you have a duty to warn, but to be sure you should talk to a lawyer" and "I recommend that you do so immediately" and the supervisee went out

and didn't do anything and the client subsequently killed his ex-girlfriend, I don't think the supervisor would have any liability.

Heath: *In my opinion, it probably is standard practice for supervisors—at least those in private practice—to focus on the cases that the therapists bring to them. I bet they don't generally cast a wider net.*

Engelberg: Yes, but again, if I'm right, the goal of supervision is to help supervisees become better therapists. Focusing on three cases is a teaching method that supervisors use. The role of the supervisor is to help the therapist improve as a therapist not just in those three cases. That's why I assume that trying to claim that you're only responsible for the three cases ultimately would not wash.

Heath: *It sounds like you're suggesting that supervisors enlighten their supervisees on legal issues in therapy.*

Engelberg: Well, if supervisors are supposed to be the highest trained therapists, I think they need to know how to spot legal issues and what to do about them. They should at least know the questions, even if they don't know the answers. In my opinion, Approved Supervisors should not be ostrich-like with regard to legal problems.

I think supervisors could begin by saying something like, "Look, I'm no legal expert, but I know that these are issues that all therapists have to be aware of," and start ticking them off: "duty to warn, suicidal patients, confidentiality, how to fill out insurance forms," etc.

Then supervisors could say, "I don't know that I can solve these problems, but you need to be alert to these issues. So if you get anything in these general areas, bring it to my attention so I can advise you. I won't know all the answers, and sometimes one or both of us may have to go to a lawyer."

Heath: *So maybe at the beginning of each supervision session, supervisors should ask their supervisees if they have any cases in which there are legal concerns.*

Engelberg: That's a good point, Tony. But it has to be even more refined than that. Asking whether there are any legal concerns is too broad. I'd ask if they had any suicidal or otherwise dangerous clients. I'd ask if they had any questions about potentially dual relationships or about maintaining client confidentiality.

Heath: *Then supervisors should take notes on what advice they gave in each session?*

Engelberg: Yes, absolutely. And if supervisors have questions about what is the right advice, they should talk to lawyers, too.

Heath: *And then part of the defense that supervisors could use if they were ever accused of malpractice would be to point to the notes and say "Here's what I advised—"*

Engelberg: Right. Document as best as you can.

Heath: *It might also be a good idea to follow up with the therapist in a phone call after a risky situation is discussed.*

Engelberg: Right. Especially if it's a really dangerous one.

Heath: *So, in summary, what precautions would you advise supervisors to take to limit legal liability?*

Engelberg: First, I think supervisors have to be reasonably sophisticated about legal liability in therapy and supervision. They have to have the knowledge base to know what questions to ask. And if a supervisor says "I don't have the foggiest idea about this stuff," I think the supervisor has to acknowledge that there's a deficit in his or her own training.

Second, supervisors—no matter what is their method of supervision (including review of three cases)—must be able to cast a wider net, as we've talked about. Once you know the issues, casting the net is not very difficult. You could simply ask a few questions at the beginning of the supervision session, then get to the three cases. And let's face it, the majority of cases will not contain serious legal problems, so this won't take a lot of time. And of course supervisors should continue to educate supervisees that they must keep themselves informed.

Third, once a problem presents itself, supervisors should give the right advice, which may mean involving a lawyer, depending on the complexity of the problem. When in doubt, consult a lawyer, maybe with the supervisee.

Fourth, supervisors should thoroughly document what happened in their supervision notes. And finally, supervisors should follow up, as you suggested.

Supervising Defensively: Advice from Legal Counsel

Interview conducted by Cheryl Storm, AAMFT Supervision Bulletin editor, with Steven Engelberg, AAMFT's legal counsel

Published in the AAMFT Supervision Bulletin, Vol. IV, No. 3, October 1991.

Storm: *Previously, you stated the standard of care for supervision suggests that supervisors normally oversee all of their supervisee's cases even if only a few are actually talked about in supervision. In response, several supervisors have asked how this applies to a therapist in private practice who contracts with an MFT institute to receive training and supervision. The training program and therapist agree that supervision will be provided on a limited number of cases. The therapist continues to practice with his other cases from an individual perspective and the supervisor assumes she is not liable for those cases not in the original agreement. Is this an erroneous assumption?*

Engelberg: This is an uncharted legal area. Assume that one of your supervisees was sued on a case that was outside your agreement. The client was a depressed man who committed suicide and there were obvious warning signs the therapist did not heed. As the supervisor of record, you are also named in the suit. Your attorney argues that this case was outside your expertise based on your agreement of providing supervision to a limited number of cases from an MFT point of view. This particular case was treated from an individual point of view outside your expertise. This argument is plausible because it is not that you didn't want to help the supervisee, but that you did not have the expertise to do so. Some judges may accept this argument. However, the attorney on the other side could very well counter by asking: Do marriage and family therapists treat depression? Of course, they do. Does the standard of care for marriage and family therapists require action if a client is in danger? Again, the answer is yes. Essentially, the legal issues in handling the suicidal case are the same regardless of the model of therapy used. Thus, it is prudent to go through the drill I outlined in my last interview for a supervisee's entire caseload. The idea is to force the supervisee to reveal information about serious cases and for the supervisor to attempt to spot problems and take responsible action. Remember, legal issues do not usually arise around bad therapy. Rather, they arise in regard to whether the therapist provided therapy consistent with the standard of care in the field or acted unethically. In the above case, all well-trained therapists should react in a similar way in a crunch.

Storm: *This situation also may occur when therapists seek supervision for their private caseloads, but also work for an agency in which they receive non-MFT therapy supervision. Is your answer any different in this situation?*

Engelberg: This is a variation on the same theme. Can you pretend to not be responsible? In a murky situation, you could be held responsible. I am not saying you will be, but there is a question. Clearly, the best course of action is to talk in general ways about your supervisee's caseload to make sure there is not a problem lurking somewhere. Exceeding the standard of care is always the safest course of action. Additionally, since you are hired to help the supervisee, I believe supervisors should go beyond their technical duty in providing supervision.

Storm: *Some have proposed that a formal written contract may help a supervisor practice "defensively." Do contracts, in fact, protect supervisors?*

Engelberg: A contract can be useful and it certainly doesn't hurt. If a problem arose, a written contract could strengthen the supervisor's case if the contract limited supervision in a legitimate way. But a written contract does not necessarily shield a supervisor from legal liability. A principle of law is that you cannot limit certain types of liability by a contract. Another reason to develop formal written contracts with supervisees quite apart from liability is because it makes good business sense to clarify the supervisor–supervisee relationship.

Storm: *If a therapist cancels regularly sched-*

uled supervision and practices for a period of time without contact with his supervisor, I am assuming the supervisor is still legally liable since she is the supervisor of record? Is this true?

Engelberg: Depends. Let's assume you've reviewed the supervisee's caseload in your last supervision session and there were no legal bombshells. The supervisee cancels the next three supervision sessions.

In the meantime, the supervisee mishandles a case that he never contacted you about. This does not mean you are negligent. You are not in the shoes of the therapist. In my opinion, supervision has essentially been suspended. This does not mean that when supervision resumes you don't have the responsibility to inquire about what has happened during the interim. It may not be a bad idea to put in your contract a statement saying that if supervisees don't keep appointments you can't ward off problems.

Storm: *Many times a therapist will contract with a supervisor for consultation. Usually this is a short-term contact, often for one session. The therapist is requesting the supervisor's opinion.*

Is there any legal liability in providing consultation?

Engelberg: If the consultation is clearly defined as a one-shot contact for a specific one or two cases, I think the consultant doesn't have the same degree of responsibility as a supervisor. If, however, the consultation is an ongoing arrangement, I think you enter a gray area because it begins to resemble supervision.

Storm: *So then you are back to the checklist, acting on certain issues, and following through.*

Engelberg: Yes. The real legal question always is: Are you acting as a responsible supervisor?

Storm: *What is the responsibility of the supervisor in insuring that supervisees follow through with their recommendations?*

Engelberg: Again, the question is: As a supervisor, did you act responsibly? You are not responsible for supervisees' actions, but you are accountable for taking responsibility for providing supervision that is helpful for the supervisee and for spotting problems.

Supervision as an Ethical Gym

Russell Haber, Ph.D.

Published in the AAMFT Supervision Bulletin, Vol.. 10, No. 1, Summer 1997.

Emotional demands of divisive and contentious family systems challenge even highly experienced family therapists' ability to make decisions that promote the rights and welfare of each client and significant other. It is no wonder that supervisees have difficulty with on-the-spot reactions in emotionally charged situations.

Most supervisees receive adequate preparation about the nature and guidelines of ethical and legal issues by the time they enter the clinical and supervisory arena. Hopefully, they feel safe enough to bring novel, complex, or fuzzy ethical dilemmas to their supervisor. Some of the questions that I have recently encountered are: "Should I report a mother who hit her child on the arm to Child and Protection Services?" "Can I go to lunch with my clients for my termination interview?" "Should I call the personnel office on behalf of my client who was sexually harassed by her supervisor?" "Can I see a family in therapy that I know peripherally from my church?" "How should I handle my dreams about my clients?"

Sometimes these and other questions are well formulated and clearly articulated while others are cloaked behind vague references such as: "The parents may be too punitive with their children." "This family is very special to me." Supervisors need to teach supervisees how to formulate and address ethical questions while reinforcing the integrity of their inquiry as they expose confusion about managing appropriate boundaries or procedures. If they feel safe and trust the guidance in the ethical gym, then questions and concerns will be more forthcoming. Ethical dangers lie in unasked questions and unstated concerns. Since professional ethics are the moral lighthouse that direct the practitioner to consider and advance the rights and welfare of clients' systems, what better place to strengthen moral fortitude, aptitude, and decision-making than in the supervisory milieu?

However, the practice of ethical inquiry in supervision need not be limited to concerns about murky boundaries, legal issues, and clarification of ethical codes. The supervisory meta-setting provides increased emotional distance that can reflect on Socratic questions about overlooked or underdeveloped moral decisions. Just imagine how easy it would be to market a magic wand that would allow family therapists to pause or stop sessions during difficult moments and provide adequate time to review and preview therapeutic decisions. Fortunately, the equipment room in the supervisory arena usually contains video playback with remote controls.

During a videotaped supervisory session of a blended family that included mother's son, father's daughter, and the two parents, my supervisee accepted and reused the label, "mentally ill," as a descriptor of a thirteen year-old girl's absent, biological mother. My intuitive negative reaction to the label was further supported upon review of the session. The girl, who initially cried when the session addressed her mother, increasingly looked defeated and utterly alone as the session progressed. Meanwhile her step-mother became more adamant in her determination to control her step-daughter so that she would not replicate behavioral problems of her mother. All the while, the girl's father passively supported the step-mother's vigilance. The therapist handled the daughter-father-stepmother triangle by positively reframing the step-mother's authoritarianism as "protective" of her step-daughter. In addition, most of the session focused on the step-mother's cut-off with her own mother in an attempt to lower the reactivity of the stepmother. The session avoided discussion of the actual abilities of the biological mother as well as the effect of the maternal cut-off on the daughter. The girl left the session looking sullen and withdrawn.

Although there are dozens of directions and issues to consider in handling this case, for the purposes of this essay I wish to emphasize questions to the supervisee that centered upon the rights and welfare of the biological mother. "How do you think the girl felt when she heard you confirm the parent's diagnosis that her mother was mentally ill?" "How does she deal with her longing for her mother?" "What do you actually know about the level of mother's impairment?" "What about the biological mother's extended family?" "What values guided your decision to focus the session on the step-mother as opposed to the father, daughter or biological mother?" "Do you think the step-mother is doing father's bidding by fostering distance between the biological mother and daughter." "What can you do to help the daughter voice her concerns and needs related to her mother?"

These questions broach the issue of who, actually, is the client. Furthermore, if the therapist accepts the familial definition, should the supervisor supervise along these parameters? Is this a matter of theoretical discretion or one guided by ethical judgment? When a therapist's action or inaction affects the rights and welfare of a significant member such as a non-custodial parent, then this is an ethical issue that deserves supervisory attention. Otherwise, therapists would become like adversarial lawyers who advocate for the rights and welfare of family members who retain them rather than consider the rights and welfare of the members of the entire family system.

Maintaining a dialectical balance between the needs of each individual and the system requires attention to the quieter or inaudible voices in the therapy room. Since there are natural tendencies to attend to the loudest and most emotionally insistent voices, supervisors can offer supervisees a broader view by considering unintrusive and absent ones. The needs of the individual and the system do not present an inherent contradiction. The individual and the system need to thrive in a process of coevolution. Supervisory input that flexibly considers the impact and relevance of the larger system can offer increased options to our supervisees and consequently to their clients. Therefore, supervision can indeed provide an ethical challenge by advancing a multi-directional view of essential rights and welfare of the relevant members of client systems. Supervisees usually welcome such good-natured workouts because they feel stronger and more flexible with therapeutic positions that consider ethical concerns of all family members.

In the same vein that Virginia Goldner (1988) stated that there is no such thing as a "gender" or "generational" case, there is no need to constrict an "ethics case" to one fraught with code or legal violations. Hopefully, supervisors can train supervisees to develop ethical reflexes and questions by internalizing the supervisor's watchful attention to ethical decisions.

References

Goldner, V. (1988). Gender and generation: Normative and covert hierarchies. *Family Process, 27, 17-31.*

Covert Agendas in Supervision: Identifying the Real Culprit

Marilyn Peterson, M.S.W.

Published in the AAMFT Supervision Bulletin, Vol. VI, No.1, Winter 1993.

Rethinking dual relationships grows out of a compelling need by supervisors to identify and remedy those situations that cause harm to vulnerable supervisees. Victim-survivors report, however, that their injuries are not the result of dual relationships, but are caused by a dual agenda in which one of the agendas is duplicitous and kept covert. Since supervisees cannot see clearly what is happening, they cannot use their perceptions to monitor their safety in the relationship. While dual relationships undoubtedly increase the prospects for a dual agenda, we have erroneously focused on the structure of the relationship as the answer to the problem. This convenient remedy is highly problematic.

Dual relationships abound in supervisory relationships, rural communities, minority populations and bounded social groups. They cannot be regulated out of existence. Making the structure the enemy and the point of redemption can unnecessarily and unjustifiably impose a judgmental prison around whole peoples, some of whom are already discriminated against by society.

The following excerpt from *At Personal Risk: Boundary Violations in Professional-Client Relationships* flushes out what can happen to supervisees if a dual agenda exists in which supervisors put their needs ahead of those of the supervisees. The generic term "client" refers to clients, supervisees, students, parishioners and other consumers who receive service from members of the professions discussed here.

Two Realities

With a boundary violation comes two realities. The first and official relationship between professional and client already exists. It establishes the formal and legitimate reality built around the client's need. A boundary violation, however, twists the relationship and establishes a second and duplicitous reality, one that is covertly built around the professional's needs.

Clients' inability to gain clarity stems from living with these two realities. They are left swimming in a murky pool of ambiguity. Indeed, the spawning of the second, conflicting reality is one of the worst consequences of boundary violations because clients are held captive in a confused state where they cannot decide what is real and what they should believe.

The covert reality arises from a reversal of roles and a mixed agenda. The victim of a boundary violation is already a client of the professional. However, when the professional uses the client to fulfill his or her needs, the client is forced into the role of caretaker. This lowers the client's status, which adversely affects identity and feelings of self-worth. For example, clients given special treatment may initially feel powerful. Unfortunately, as they become aware of what has happened, they may also feel diminished. Caught in the middle of a paradox, they cannot assess reality, their relative power, or who they are in the relationship. An art student who was courted and harassed by her professor expressed her confusion about having received a scholarship: "I'll never know if I was chosen because of my talent or because the teacher wanted to score with me."

While the official agenda, or intent, of the relationship is to take care of the client's needs, another agenda emerges when the professional uses the relationship to fulfill his or her own needs. The professional's intent is often disguised, however, under a cloak of concern for the client.

Even as clients become aware of the second agenda imposed by the professional, they are handicapped in their search for clarification by the fact that they cannot tell which agenda is primary. Since both are going on simultaneously and are interwoven with each other, clients cannot accurately sort out the implications of the situations or the meaning of events. They cannot figure out how to respond. They can only speculate about the professional's motive and frequently have to base their conclusions on inference.

Confusion in Decision-Making

Faced with two realities, clients cannot see safe options about how they should proceed. Since the truth eludes them, they feel unsure about what they are seeing and experiencing. They therefore have no solid foundation from which to make their decisions. Indeed, they find that each solution jeopardizes something else they value. A client who was uncertain about whether or not her attorney was being seductive expressed it this way: "Maybe I am doing something to lead him on, but if I change the rules and become more rigid, he may take it as rejection and not work as hard on my case. If I say something to him, he may be insulted. If I do nothing, it may get worse. I don't even know if my perceptions are accurate."

In their decision-making, clients also struggle with the unfairness of having to pay an additional price to protect themselves from the person or the institution entrusted to be their caretaker.

Dual roles and mixed agendas keep the boundary of the relationship ill-defined. The resulting confusion keeps clients paralyzed. Being held in a state of limbo magnifies their vulnerability. A client compared her difficulty in seeing reality with having an eye examination: "When the optometrist tries out different lenses and rotates them for clarity, I always feel sick to my stomach. There's that point when I have double or even triple vision for a second before the lines come together."

Because the coexistence of two realities distorts and filters what they can see, clients mentally reenact their history with the professional in an attempt to explain away their confusion. Without a perceptual map that allows synthesis of discrepant facts, however, clients cannot assess their power in the relationship, the meaning of the professional's behavior, or the priorities and possible options. Their lack of success compels them to search even harder. Rather than finding a way out, they are often bound tighter to an endless and unrewarding pursuit.

The above excerpt describes the perceptual damage that can block the supervisee's ability to gain clarity. Since supervisees are dependent on us for recognition, evaluations, pay raises, grades, the meeting of licensure requirements, and recommendations, we cannot expect them to monitor our behavior. We can, however, guard against the possibility of creating duplicitous and covert agendas if we acknowledge the size of who we are and how we can hide what we need from ourselves.

Reference

Peterson, M. (1992). *At Personal Risk: Boundary violations in professional-client relationships.* New York: W.W. Norton.

Defining Supervision and Therapy: A Fuzzy Boundary

Karl Tomm, M.D.

Published in the AAMFT Supervision Bulletin, Vol. VI, No. 1, Winter 1993.

As a young supervisor, I was taught that supervision could be, and should be, clearly separated from therapy. Thus, my work in supervision during the 1970s and early 1980s was limited to giving "constructive" feedback about a trainee's skills. My clinical work was problem-oriented then and isomorphically my supervision tended to be deficit-focused. Trainees were expected to acquire what they did not have. For instance, a trainee's failure to respond to strong emotion or to provide needed confrontation would be pointed out for attention and correction. To help trainees identify precisely what they needed to learn, Wright and I outlined a comprehensive set of family therapy skills (Tomm and Wright, 1979). I assumed that clinical competence was developed by internalizing the skills and techniques of more seasoned practitioners, i.e., from the "outside." If supervisees had any prior "internal" issues that interfered with their learning or clinical work, they were referred elsewhere.

As my clinical work became more resource-oriented in the late 1980s, I began to focus on trainees' personal resources as well. Maturana's (1984) assumption of structure determinism helped me realize that "instructive interaction is possible." It was, however, possible to contribute to the conditions in which learning could take place. For instance, White's (1988) method of attending to "unique outcomes" was one such condition that was resource-oriented. I began to look for and honor the enormous amount of interpersonal knowledge and skill that trainees already had by virtue of their prior experience. As a supervisor, I tried to draw upon these resources so that they could become available in the context of doing therapy. This led me to pay more and more attention to the person of the therapist in the course of my training activities. I began to regard the values, attitudes, and assumptions of trainees as a more important basis for clinical competence and ethical practice than specific skills and techniques. As a result, the presumed boundary between supervision and therapy became rather fuzzy. I found myself doing things with trainees that were similar to what I did with clients. When trainees expressed an interest in some personal therapy with me, I usually welcomed the opportunity to extend my work with them.

Thus, my teaching style evolved and became more varied. I found myself becoming less authoritarian, less impositional, more caring, more facilitative, and more authentic as a person. These continuing changes were valued, not only by me, but by others around me. Then, about three years ago, I realized that the "dual relationships" I was sometimes developing with trainees were considered unethical. Had my evolution as a supervisor betrayed me? Or could it be that there was a problem with the existing *Code of Ethics?* Similar changes towards dual involvements had occurred in my work with clients and research subjects as well (Tomm, 1992). I was in a dilemma. Should I revert to earlier, more narrow, patterns of professional practice or should I try to change the *Code?* While my direction of change entailed greater complexity and called for more attentiveness towards the experiences of trainees, it intuitively felt sound. I spoke with various respected colleagues, many of whom agreed with my impression that the *Code* was unduly restrictive. Upon further reflection it became evident that the ethical prohibition of therapy for supervisees presupposes an ideological separation between supervision and therapy and privileges a particular orientation to training and supervision. It gives priority to disembodied skills and techniques over the holistic integrity and authenticity of the therapist as a person. It also promotes silence, deviousness, and dishonesty among those supervisors who want to be seen as ethical but who are committed to the personal development of their trainees as a basis for developing their clinical competence.

References

Maturana, H. (1984). *Bringing forth of reality*. Presentation at Construction of Therapeutic Realities Conference, Family Therapy Program, University of Calgary, Canada.

Tomm, K., and Wright, L. (1979). Training in family therapy: Perceptual, conceptual, and executive skills, *Family Process* 28(3), 227–250.

Tomm, K. (1992). The ethics of dual relationships. *The Calgary Participator, 1, 11–15*.

White, M. (1988). The process of questioning: A therapy of literary merit? *Dulwich Centre Newsletter.*

Dual Aspects of Dual Relationships

Max Hines, Ph.D.

Published in the AAMFT Supervision Bulletin, Vol. VI, No. 1, Winter 1993.

Dual relationships are to be avoided by marriage and family therapy (MFT) supervisors. As dual relationships are commonly conceptualized, this means it is unwise and ethically questionable for a supervisor to provide supervision to his or her brother-in-law who is an up-and-coming marriage and family therapist. Doing so could place the supervisor's brother-in-law in a situation involving potential confusion, stress or more severe consequences. Metaphorically switching hats, supervisors in dual role situations usually cannot differentiate between the two roles. Hat-switching is sometimes possible when dual role refers to socially defined roles. If the supervisor and the brother-in-law are well differentiated and have a favorable family relationship, they may be able to effectively switch hats. It is clearly advisable for the brother-in-law to look elsewhere for supervision. There seems to be agreement in the field regarding dual relationships where two or more socially defined roles are involved. This might be called an external dual role phenomenon since the roles are externally defined.

I suggest another perspective involving an internal dual role phenomenon. Dual roles result from discrepancies in a supervisor's internal perception of his or her role and the socially defined role of supervisor. For example, a male supervisor may believe that power and hierarchies are negative and antithetical to beliefs in egalitarian relationships. Depending on how big a torch the supervisor carries for the cause of egalitarian relationships, he may deny the power differential inherent at the beginning in the senior supervisor/novice supervisee relationships. If so, a novice supervisee may well attend all the more to the power differential, intuitively picking up on the supervisor's considerable power, since it is inherent in the socially defined role of supervisor. If the senior supervisor minimized the power accompanying his advanced expertise, the novice supervisee's position of vulnerability may increase. This could be very confusing for the supervisee because of the simultaneity of the dual roles. This can sometimes be much more difficult for supervisees than a situation, for example, in which a supervisor is also the supervisee's aunt or uncle. In the latter situation, it may be possible for the supervisor and the supervisee to switch hats, separating the dual roles and shifting from one into the other.

Such role differentiation may not be possible in situations involving the internal dual role phenomenon if the more powerful supervisor is denying the power which accompanies his role as senior supervisor in relationship to the novice supervisee. There may be no way out of the double bind for the novice supervisee.

MFT has been criticized for ignoring the internal uniqueness of each individual, the so-called black box theory of personality. In supervision, perhaps the internal dual role phenomenon needs as much attention as the external dual role phenomenon has received. The internal mindset of a supervisor is very important. Perhaps MFT supervisors need to give more consideration to the dual aspects of dual relationships.

Provision of Therapy to Supervisees

Published in the AAMFT Supervision Bulletin, Vol. VI, No. 1 & 2, Summer 1993.

Questions

Dual relationships occur when supervisors engage in therapy with their supervisees. Yet most supervisors focus, albeit to varying degrees, on the person of the therapist and/or the influence of significant family relationships on supervisees' work. The Supervision Committee is interested in your opinion. Please reply to the following questions:

1. How and when do you decide to include family of origin/person of the therapist issues in your supervision?

2. How is family of origin/person of the therapist work integrated into discussion of clinical cases?

3. Describe how you use your knowledge of the supervisee's family of origin/personal issues in your supervision of that person.

4. Recognizing that all supervisees are different, approximately what percent of your supervision time would typically be spent on family of origin/person of the therapist?

5. Regardless of the extent to which you include family of origin/person of the therapist work, under what circumstances would you believe that this type of work would conflict with the dual relationship problem in the AAMFT Code of Ethics that prohibits supervisors from providing therapy?

-Cheryl L. Storm, AAMFT Supervision Bulletin Editor

Responses

Below are representative responses from the many letters to the questions posed on supervisory dual relationships in the last issue. My apologies if the meaning changed because an excerpt was selected. Overall, responses acknowledged the prevalence of supervisory dual relationships, described ways of managing the complexities and supported the spirit of prohibiting becoming a therapist to one's supervisees.

-Cheryl L. Storm, AAMFT Supervision Bulletin Editor

I am always listening for person-of-the-therapist issues, but I don't advertise that in every response to supervisees. I'll be listening to a tape of therapy, thinking on several channels at once:

• What is the client saying and doing at the time?

• How adequate is the supervisee's response to the client's need?

• What are the supervisee's learning needs as reflected in this chunk of tape?

• How are those learning needs a reflection of the fullness or lack of fullness of the student's personal repertoire? The actual time that supervisees know that we are working on personal issues is 10%–29%. However, I'd like to think that I am always listening for these issues.

Brian Grant, Ph.D.

Most of us do our personal "work" as our issues get in the way of our performing our life tasks, and specifically our work as therapists. We don't "do therapy" and then never have to touch these issues again. As we grow clinically, we touch areas that were not previously apparent. It often seems logical to supervisees that to avail themselves of the supervisors' special knowledge and do a "piece of work" would be more efficient than to begin anew with a stranger who is ignorant of their issues. As supervisors, we have sought to determine with the trainee if that is the safest way for them to do their work. (Safest always being defined in terms of the supervisees/

clients.) If we all agree, the personal work may begin at the end of the training year. We always continue to evaluate that decision during the process of treatment... Does it always work? No. Does it work well more often than not? Yes. Does this mean that we can have one simple rule that will work for everyone? No. It means that if we are ethical therapists and supervisors committed to the process of creating safe environments for our supervisees, our clients, and ourselves, we will struggle with whatever we are confronted with.

Zona G. Scheiner, Ph.D.

Faculty working as a mutual consultation team is probably the best insurance that knowledge of supervisees vulnerabilities are not used to their disadvantage, and that inevitable dual relationships are not misused. Because instances of supervisors' concerns with supervisees are discussed routinely among faculty, faculty have an opportunity to receive collegial feedback regarding their interaction with or evaluation of supervisees. For example, it is not unusual for supervisors to comment in faculty meetings, "This is the concern. What is your view about how I handled it?"

Syracuse University faculty

I personally agree with defining any dual relationship that imparts the therapeutic process as a violation of the ethical code. However, this has been broadly interpreted by some to mean that *any* relationship is automatically a dual relationship. Such an interpretation may work in large metropolitan centers where society is organized as *gesellschaft society* (based on secondary contacts). It becomes very awkward in the smaller communities and rural areas in America where social organization is based on *gemeinschaft* (primary-face to face) relationships. In these communities supervisees are often acquainted with supervisors before a supervision contract and after the termination of supervision. These are persons seen at church, the grocery, or drug store, and in various recreational activities.

John Curtis, Ph.D.

My response to reactions that my supervision is indistinguishable from therapy is that the experience the student has in the two situations is probably very similar. The difference, and it is a significant one, is that path to that experience; in supervision, is through the student's cases, and in therapy, through the student's own family.

Tom Schur, M.S.W.

A couple of guidelines are useful in assessing whether isomorphic issues are consuming too much supervisory time. One has to do with frequency. Isomorphic issues infringe upon supervision when the student is not able to adjust his or her clinical service following one or two examinations of an invasive isomorphic process. A second guideline has to do with repetitive and nonproductive examination of family of origin and person-of-therapist issues. From our perspective, a problem that requires an outside-the-system intervention exists whenever a student or supervisor repetitively and unproductively focuses upon the same subject matter. Isomorphic issues may be safely, responsibly, and justifiably addressed until one of these guidelines is breached.

University of Winnepeg faculty

Supervisors which focus on the family of origin of supervisees should be notified that they have special responsibility to protect student confidences and that they should not require personal revelations to complete requirements. While the practice, in my opinion, is not in itself unethical, I believe it is a risk-filled teaching style which must he carefully monitored.

Tom Conran, Ph.D.

When Supervision is Mandated: Education or Punishment?

Originally published in the AAMFT Supervision Bulletin, Vol. V, No. 1, February 1992.

Mandated supervision is one of the sanctions that can be imposed by our Ethics Committee when a member is found in violation of our Code of Ethics and/or state regulatory boards. Below, an Approved Supervisor, who was found in violation of our Code of Ethics and required to seek supervision to maintain his membership, and his supervisor, reflect on the process of mandated supervision.

Special thanks to both for sharing how to turn mandated supervision into "education rather than punishment."

-Cheryl L. Storm, AAMFT Supervision Bulletin editor

The Supervisor's Perspective

Anonymous

I feel good about my supervision experience with Jim (a pseudonym), largely because he used our time together so well I respect him for that. It was not easy for Jim, whose pride got him into trouble in the first place.

Jim has an excellent reputation as a therapist. However, what started out as good therapy with one female client turned into a symmetrical battle and a lot of hard feelings. There was no sexual involvement between Jim and his client, and no intended malevolence on his part.

The ethical principles Jim violated included discussing his case with someone else without a release and not arranging for an appropriate therapy referral. However, what led up to these violations and fueled his client's increasing antagonism involved his own area of personal vulnerability: his competitiveness. For example, as the perceived manipulation of his client increased, Jim used strategic directives in what he now recognizes as a way of "winning." (Several Haleyesque ordeals thoroughly irritated his client.) The Ethics Committee mandated two years of supervision for Jim, focusing on appropriate case management, "therapy within a congregational context, dual relationships, and psychiatric diagnosis and treatment of severe mental disorders." I approached my supervision contract with Jim the same way I approach court-ordered therapy. That is, "we are in this now—how can we make the best of it?" We worked together to develop a contract around what we could accomplish within the broad mandate set by the Ethics Committee. I tried to be supportive and empowering, but not to lose touch with why we were there. Foreground for Jim was the case that led to the ethics complaint. He talked about it in detail, first with anger, then with despair and shame, and finally with reflection and insight. We discussed what he had learned, what he would do differently, and how he could curb his competitiveness in the future.

As our sessions progressed, I suggested certain readings and audiotapes on case management and ethical and legal issues. We discussed these in several of our sessions. Jim and I also read and discussed sections of the DSM-III manual, as well as appropriate treatment and referral. We also replayed certain common ethical dilemmas. Jim and I contracted to develop written professional disclosure statements applicable to private practice. In Jim's disclosure statement, he informed his clients of his qualifications, scope of therapy, and policies related to billing, emergencies, testifying in court, and so forth. Jim subsequently used this disclosure statement in his private practice. Finally, we talked about his pride, his shame, his hopes, and how he was making sense out of all that led up to our sessions.

Jim grew to be a friend. He also grew in his understanding of himself and became a more responsible, ethically sound practitioner. I am not sure everyone could have made such good use of mandated supervision. Jim was clearly motivated, at first to keep his AAMFT membership, and later to learn from his ethics violation. He paid me my individual therapy fee for every session, drove three hours for every appointment, and never cancelled. Because of Jim's progress, I suggested to the Ethics Committee that they waive his second year of supervision with me, which they did. From my point of view, the system worked, and Jim and AAMFT benefited in the process.

The Supervisee's Perspective

Anonymous

It was a nightmare. Never in my wildest dreams did I envision myself being censured by a professional ethics committee. A tremendous blow to my self-esteem as a person, and my self-confidence as a therapist and supervisor of other therapists, I felt the shame to be incredible. I likewise felt an immense amount of anger toward myself and others.

I was a humiliated and an enraged person— certainly not the kind of supervisee which I would want to work with. But, mandated supervision was a requirement.

Before I selected a supervisor, I spent time discussing my situation with my spouse and several close friends. They all gave me the same wise counsel— cooperate completely and do my utmost to treat this as an opportunity for learning. As I reflect back on my supervision, I think that was a determinative initial decision which my supervisor affirmed from our first meeting. In keeping my desire to make this a redemptive experience, I selected a supervisor whom I knew was respected in the profession, I felt was very competent, and I myself could respect. I wanted someone who would be emphathic but would also stick to the agenda outlined by the AAMFT Ethics Committee. I wanted someone with whom I could feel safe, who would stretch me, and who would not delight in my plight or exploit me as a colleague in a vulnerable position. I chose someone with whom I was acquainted, but who had not been a close personal friend.

My supervisor did an excellent job in joining with me from our very first meeting— giving him the authority to do what was to come later. He let me tell my story. He was willing to listen to my "broken record" as I repeated some things over and over again. At appropriate times he challenged some of my perceptions while affirming some others. I believe my supervisor enabled me to drain off a lot of my angry and bitter feelings, while facilitating me in taking a look at the case that resulted in a complaint being made against me. I believe together we gleaned a lot of learnings from that case.

During this process it was essential that I reframe this experience as education rather than punishment. This was not easy. I discovered it had to be done numerous times because events would arise causing the waves of pain and anger and self-pity to come back again. During these times my supervisor, as well as my loved ones, listened to me compassionately, but then firmly and gently encouraged me out of such self-destructive behavior. I found myself really tempted at several points to make excuses for what had led to my difficulties. It was simply much easier to blame AAMFT or the complaintant or my circumstances than it was to accept personal responsibility for what had happened. I read that one definition of a coward is simply "someone who makes a lot of excuses." The last thing I wanted to be in this whole process was a coward. My supervisor did his part in helping me not to be one.

I think I would be a different person if I had not been found in violation of the *Code of Ethics*. My mandated supervision was the most intense and memorable course in family therapy I have ever had. Although I would not want to repeat some of my experiences and feelings prior to and during that supervision, I believe I have profited greatly from it both personally and professionally. My most memorable quotation which I clung to with some amusement during this whole process comes from Friedrich Nietzsche: "That which doesn't kill me probably makes me stronger."

Chapter 8

Contextual Variables

Explicitly Recognizing Contextual Influence Broadens Our Scope of Inquiry

M. Laurie Leitch, Ph.D.

Published in the AAMFT Supervision Bulletin, Vol. V, No. 3, November 1992.

To use context in supervision means to explicitly recognize that such factors as gender, race, age, SES and sexual orientation shape the experiences of our supervisees, clients and, of course, ourselves. Learning about and utilizing the multiple contexts that construct and shape our relationships deepens and expands the scope of our inquiry as we guide the supervisory process. The sociopolitical realities of our lives that flow from race, gender, etc. often result in collective experiences which can be used as points of reference in broadening the supervisory process beyond the psychological. In supervision, whether of a supervisor-in-training or of a therapist, the incorporation of "context" into the assessment and intervention process broadens the scope of the investigation. Drawing upon contextual elements helps the supervisor to avoid or at least minimize one of the most common pitfalls of family systems thinking, reliance on the idea of contingent behavior (i.e., what we see in the room is only a product of that particular relationship or that individual's "self").

In a recent supervisory group of hospital-based social workers a case was brought up for discussion which was generating heated discussion on the unit. An African-American teen was dropped off by her mother at the Emergency Room door while she was in the early stages of miscarriage. During the course of her hospitalization the mother seldom visited. The staff felt angry that the mother was so neglectful of this frightened teen. Pressure was being put on the social worker by the primary care physician to confront the mother. The staff had organized themselves around the proposition of a "neglectful mother." This way of thinking not only pathologized the mother but also put the staff in an adversarial relationship with her; a dynamic which could only limit the possibilities for constructive change. The supervision group consisted of eleven white women and one American-American woman; all professional, middle class. I, too, am a white, middle-class woman.

Four ways of working with the contextual dimensions of this case are discussed below. Each one focuses on how the use of context enhances the supervisory process.

Using Context to Create and Deepen Attachments

The supervisory relationship, like the therapeutic relationship, is one which models a boundaried and caring connection. One way this occurs is when supervisors and/or therapists demonstrate a wisdom or a "knowing" of supervisees or clients. Learning about and utilizing the multiple contexts which are a part of our daily experience enables supervisors to draw from certain "universals" or collective experiences. Of course, not all of us have the same experiences as members of an ethnic group or gender, but an understanding of the collective experience can serve as points of reference in building familiarity as well as in maintaining a respectful stance throughout our work with people. I began our case discussion in the above example with questions about ways the group members could begin to think about this "neglectful mother" in terms of their own life experiences. For example, some group members were single parents. They had struggled with the competing demands of work and children. Our discussion helped expand my own understanding of each supervisee and her understanding of herself in relation to others. It also began to connect the members of the group to the client because as they talked the mother became increasingly familiar to them. In this way the group is helped to recognize that the life experiences of each member has relevance to their professional knowledge. This realization is particularly important to workers in institutional settings which tend to depersonalize people.

Using Context to Promote and Enhance Competency

Competency-based supervision and therapy has two components, support and challenge. The supportive component comes more easily to most of us, since it involves giving positive feedback and reinforcement. The challenge component, however, requires more of us as supervisors and therapists. By "challenge" I mean intervening in supervisees' way of thinking in such a way as to expand supervisees' beliefs about themselves and/or their clients. Using challenge in supervision expands the supervisors' role from one of an enhancer of technique or facilitator of skill-building to one which promotes new ways of thinking. The supervisory challenge in the case example was to expand the group's thinking beyond the "neglectful mother" proposition by developing a line of inquiry about what the mother's life was likely to be like as an American-American, single parent working in a low-paying job where she had no autonomy. What would happen to her job is she left work for many hours? What would happen to her ability to provide for her daughter if she lost her job? Where would they live? A new narrative began to emerge...one about a woman struggling against many forces to keep body and soul together. Perhaps she was, in fact, a "responsible mother" who when confronted with the terrible decision of whether to remain with her daughter at the hospital or lose her job, chose the option of keeping a roof over their heads and food on the table. Certainly this group of middle-class women could recognize that these survival issues were not a part of their own fortunate lives. The hypotheses the group generated about alternative explanations for the mother's actions created a sense of expanded possibilities for intervention; and helped the worker to experience a more benign stance toward this woman.

Using Context to Enhance Manageability

One of the main factors which overloads supervisees is collecting too much of the "wrong" (in the sense of competency-diminishing) information. Many clinical settings actually promote the overload because of various requirements for information which must be collected from clients. It is easy for supervisees to forget that they know much more about the clients than merely what they have been told. Using contextual elements in supervision helps to remind us that there are collective experience shared by people of the same race, ethnicity, gender, age, etc. During supervision these universals can guide the construction of a new narrative and open avenues of intervention which promote manageability.

Using Context as Process

In the example above, as the discussion progressed the African-American worker remained almost silent. I became concerned about how to engage her in the discussion. I imagined that she might want to avoid being put in a position of spokesperson for her race, yet I also knew that she brought a valuable point of view as an African-American woman. As supervisors we impose a constraint on ourselves by not utilizing the potential of each group member. Although my initial feeling was to avoid putting the supervisee on the spot I decided this was a disrespectful stance to take. We needed her help, not as a spokesperson for her race but as an informer of our clinical discussion. I structured by question to her in a way that helped her to focus on a particular dimension by first sharing my own thinking and then asking for her opinion. "My guess about this case is that the mother may have more of a support system in terms of extended family than we might expect in a white family. What is your sense about that?" In this way I hoped to create a focused opening that would be centered on competency of the supervisee and the mother, and would enhance the group's thinking about this case.

The uses described above are only a few of the ways in which the incorporation of contextual elements into supervision can enrich the process.

The author wishes to thank Marianne Walters for her helpful comments.

Contextual Supervision Involves Continuous Dialogue with Supervisees

Harriet Roberts, Ph.D.

Published in the AAMFT Supervision Bulletin, Vol. V, No. 3, November 1992.

Anyone who undertakes the task of providing marriage and family therapy (MFT) supervision takes on a complex and multidimensional responsibility. There are no easy answers about how to address in supervisory relationships, the same sociocultural contextual issues we struggle with in society at large. Unless there is a continuous effort to dialogue and to understand the issues such as race, ethnicity, culture, gender, socioeconomic levels etc. in every aspect of the treatment system, we encourage or allow for incompetence in our work. As supervisors, one of our primary goals is to help supervisees develop a systems-oriented approach to resolving human problems in ways that are sensitive to these contextual issues.

The supervisory context is as important in the outcome of treatment as is the therapist's-client's context and the client's context. Supervisees and supervisors represent multiple levels of experiences, multiple racial, ethnic and sociopolitical groups as well as clinical ideas. Von Foerster (1984) suggested that observers in a system participates in defining (drawing distinctions about) what they observe. In other words, as supervisors, our conceptualization of problem formation and problem resolution are indicative of who we are.

Observations about any situation are observer dependent, not observer independent; observers are therefore a part of the treatment system and not separate from it. Each component of the system brings a world view. Our world view limits or allows us to maximize ways of addressing or solving problems.

Although systems (supervisors-supervisees; therapists-clients) may be inherently hierarchical, the role of supervisors is to create a context that facilitates learning and change. In a collaborative, nonjudgemental and nonperjorative context the realities and experiences of supervisors and supervisees are utilized. A willingness to listen, and to understand like or conflicting views allows open dialogue about subjects such as race, gender or cultural differences. It is difficult to conceptualize how clinicians could declare themselves systems-oriented therapists or supervisors and fall to take these influences into account as a part of the total context. If our conversations relative to these issues are not maximized, we tend to hamper the flow of information, risk continuing the lack of understanding and comply with stereotypical assumptions and ideas. When supervisor-supervisee relationships are based on mutual respect, understanding, and a willingness to listen and to test out one's opinions, values, beliefs, biases and prejudices, clients as well as all others in these systems become beneficiaries.

The process begins with supervisors' awareness of themselves as an integral part of the treatment process. The goals of supervision in MFT are as varied as are treatment models and approaches. A pattern that connects the systems-oriented approaches to supervision and treatment is the recognition of the need to examine problems and relationships in context. Common goals of supervision must include increased awareness and understanding of contextual issues that influence our conceptualization of supervision as well as the treatment process. A starting point is a careful examination of how your supervision contributes to stereotypical assumptions about race, culture, socioeconomic conditions, gender, etc.

Supervisors must be willing to respond to cultures, attitudes, ethnicity, ideas, or behaviors that are consistent with stereotypical roles as they become apparent in supervisory relationships.

An open conversational context allows supervisors and supervisees to risk sharing the need to know more. When there is a need to examine and to learn more, the chances of holding on to stereotypes and myths are minimized. Misinformation or stereotypes in any context are constraining in that they do not allow us to see the uniqueness of each individual. We therefore attempt to apply solutions that do not work. Again, supervision must embrace a context that will allow learning and change to occur.

References

Von Foerster, (1984). On Constructing a Reality. In P. Waltzlawick (Ed.), *The Invented Reality*, New York: W. W. Norton.

Males Supervising Females: The Risk of Gender-Power Blindness

Jean Turner, Ph.D.

Published in the AAMFT Supervision Bulletin, Vol. VI, No. 1, Winter 1993.

When men find themselves supervising women, and women find themselves being supervised by men, the potential for problematic outcomes is considerable. Discussion on this has focused to an overwhelming degree on the dangers of sexual intimacy. In my opinion, this is too limited. Duality can present substantial dilemmas and challenges even in instances where there is no sexual intimacy. The dilemmas are gender-role specific; they occur when men and women are on either side of a supervisory relationship. However, the risks for misunderstanding, confusion and sense of betrayal are particularly high where women are supervised by men.

Power shifts Affect Supervisors

This particular male-female relationship combination is at the nexus of two important power shifts taking place in contemporary history. The first is one of gender role change in which women are gaining power in new domains and having a more equal voice. The second is one of paradigm transformation in which the exclusive privileging of "expert," objective knowledge and power is giving way to approaches where there is greater recognition of the subjective knowledges of all participants in a relationship, including those who wield little power. We can expect to experience complications, misreadings and confusions because we are currently in a transitional stage in the overall changing of gender and expert power toward a new pattern.

The intersection of shifting gendered and expert power is further complicated in the area of supervisee-supervisor relationships when there are additional roles. The multifaceted structure of contemporary social relations has created a world of duality. It is a world where professional training is often spread out intermittently between periods of professional work. Lateral teamwork relationships are becoming more common in the workplace, people are developing friendships with colleagues who are their peers and individuals may be working contractually in diverse roles at several institutions concurrently. As a result, friendships, collegial, training, and business relationships tend to be dynamically interconnected; double or triple roles within one relationship are not uncommon.

When these multiple roles occur in supervision, the individuals involved must sort out the attendant queries regarding whether their roles as supervisors or supervisees are or will be in any way compromised by the other roles, even when sexual intimacy is not an issue. In close-knit communities of the past there was less burden upon the individuals to ensure that their work together was hazard-free. As Foucault (1977) noted, the "normalizing gaze" provided by observers has the effect of increasing control and security. The lack of a close audience for today's supervisors and supervisees leads contenders on one side of the heated debate about dual relationships to suggest that they be avoided entirely. However, Ryder and Hepworth (1990) believe we cannot banish duality, we can only seek to minimize risks and maximize its benefits

If multiple relationships are an almost inevitable feature of our post-modern world and they tend to entail dilemmas, then those which involve gendered power are probably the most troublesome. The area of highest risk is defined by the cross-roads of three dimensions of the relationship. The first is the expert power dimension: supervisor-supervisee. The second is the gendered power dimension: male-female. The third is the additional role dimension: friend, colleague, business-partner, etc. People are entering one of the most risk-prone zones in this three dimensional space when a male supervisor combines some other relationship with a female supervisee. There is the likelihood that the relationship will fail with respect to supervisory goals and lead to feelings of confusion and betrayal.

Gender power Blindness

What leads well intentioned and often well-informed male supervisors and female supervisees into trouble? Our society and profession are moving slowly toward greater gender equality but some legacy of patriarchy still remains. This incomplete transition from male dominance to greater equality between the sexes leaves men and women at risk for gendered power "blindness." Egalitarian men may be "blind" to the power they continue to hold. Males with authority do not necessarily experience themselves as powerful in their relationships with women, even at the moment when they are exercising considerable power. For example, when men who have been coached in patriarchal habits begin to support the transition toward gender equality, they may do this by taking leadership on behalf of women. In so doing, these well-meaning but "blind" men paradoxically silence the voices of those whose self-empowerment they are trying to nurture. Women may be "blind" to opportunities for power which they can safely access. Failing to see these, they may unintentionally fall into habits learned for survival in an earlier, more patriarchal context even when their goal is equality and a stronger voice in relationships with men. Specifically, women may restrict themselves from speaking out, not recognizing that their fear of doing so is no longer warranted. Or, they may find themselves reflexively (due to cultural conditioning) asking for more assistance from men than they actually need. In either case, they later resent the men for their complicity in this complex struggle to move through an ideological and practical transformation. When these gendered-power blindnesses are operating, the outcome for both men and women is a sense of betrayal and resentment.

Consider the case of a male supervisor who responds favorably to a request for marital therapy from a female supervisee. She has turned to her male supervisor precisely because she perceives him to be sensitive to issues of gender equality. As the therapy with the couple progresses, the therapist/supervisor begins to insist on the husband making changes and his interventions are effective. In so doing, he creates a paradoxical situation: as the female supervisee gains voice at home, she experiences a loss of voice and a sense of confusion in relation to her supervisor

in professional matters. He has now begun to speak for her in one important dimension of her life, and this has spill-over effects.

Consider also the case of two colleagues who decide to add a supervisory relationship to their lives. If the supervisor is a man and the supervisee a woman, the hidden linkages between gender and expert power may create special problems for their dual relationship. The problem is that they are moving from an egalitarian "friendship" relationship into a hybrid "friendship/supervisory" relationship. As the man begins to give advice along the "expert" power dimension, her experience of gender power in relation to him is transformed. Before, as colleagues she felt free to talk to him about many personal issues, and to work out conflicts with him in an open egalitarian way. Now, as supervisee, she begins to experience him for the first time, not only as a powerful professional supervisor, but also a powerful man. Without intending to, she finds herself holding back information, feeling somewhat fearful and acquiescing to his ideas across all fronts. Not surprisingly, she feels defensive, he becomes confused and they both experience a sense of betrayal.

Opening Our Eyes

What guidelines may be proposed to avoid these unhappy outcomes? The blindnesses to power are partial; they only restrict or narrow vision. More importantly the blindnesses for men and women are operating in different fields of vision. Therefore, dialogue between supervisor and supervisee is a likely path to new, more encompassing shared systems of meaning. As Doherty, (1991) believes it is the "cross-gender dialogue" which will eventually provide freedom for everyone from the surviving traces of patriarchy. Male supervisors and their female supervisees are advised to talk about how incomplete gendered-power shifts, expert authority-personal authority issues and probable duality dilemmas may affect their work. This dialogue would best commence as part of the initial supervisory contracting discussion and continue to periodically be brought into their conversations over the length of the relationship.

Those encumbered with partial blindness to gender-power can also invite observers who have a different vantage point. Tomm (1991) argues that the supervisor should join with the supervisee to find a mutually agreed upon third party. For the particular constellation of male supervisor-female supervisee, I recommend the third party observer be: 1. a supervisor in order that their knowledge include the experience of being supervised and of being a supervisor, 2. a person who the supervisor and supervisee perceive to be sensitive to gendered-power issues in order to prevent "the even more blind leading the particularly blind" and 3. someone who is contacted at the onset of the supervision and agrees to be available over its course.

The goal here is certainly not to supervise the male supervisor. Rather the third party person is a consultant responding to periodic requests made by the supervisor-supervisee pair. Her/his role is to cast a proximate "nurturing gaze" on the male supervisor-female supervisee relationship which would be in addition to the distant "standardizing gaze and judgement" cast by the AAMFT Supervision Committee.

The issues raised above cover only specific topics in a broad and complex field. There are many other versions of gendered-power blindness which should be pointed out. For example, I am aware that my personal history as a woman growing up in a highly patriarchal context restricts my vision when I work with male supervisees. I may not always experience the power related to my supervisory role, even at the moment when I am exercising it. All supervisors and supervisees in relationships where there are added roles and power dilemmas might usefully reflect upon their probable blindnesses and seek out practices which diminish the risks.

References

Doherty, W.J. (1991). Defining men's realities: An upcoming struggle between men and feminists? *AFTA Newsletter*, Fall.

Foucault, M. (1997). *Discipline and punish: The birth of the prison.* New York: Random House.

Tomm, K. (1991). The ethics of dual relationships. *The Calgary Participator*, 1, 11–15.

Locating Self in Relation to "Other": Supervision and White Privilege

Kyle D. Killian, Ph.D.

Published in the AAMFT Supervision Bulletin, Fall 2000.

If we are always arriving and departing, it is also true that we are eternally anchored. One's destination is never a place but rather a new way of looking at things.

-Henry Miller

The vast majority of AAMFT Approved Supervisors and family therapists are white men and women from the US (Killian and Hardy, 1998), and most of their families have been in the US for several generations. It is all too easy in a country that places considerable stock in the "melting pot" paradigm of mass assimilation to become accustomed to occupying a normative, non-prefixed social location as a culturally generic "white" person. The more implicit one's sense of normativity and accompanying privilege, the easier it is to reap the benefits of white privilege unconsciously, in the sociopolitical sense. However, whiteness as a racial and ethnic category has become the subject of academic study, and key components to the constitution of white privilege and identity have been examined (Frankenberg, 1993; Hooks, 1990; Hurtado, 1999). Interestingly, there is considerable overlap between core aspects of whiteness and the culture of psychotherapy and counseling (see Sue & Sue, 1999). Part and parcel of these two cultures are rugged individualism, dichotomous thinking, and a belief in a competitive economic system where status is measured in the accumulation of material. Because white people, therapists, and supervisors from the US have been socialized into and informed by these basic tenets of white culture and psychotherapy all their lives, the identification of and sensitization to these beliefs and values can be quite difficult. Therapists and trainers who operate from this framework may inappropriately impose these values and assumptions without a regard for the legitimacy of other views (e.g., collectivism, dialectics, cooperative economics) (Sue & Sue, 1999). But while the effects of this form of cultural oppression have been explored and documented (Fine, Weis, Powell & Wong, 1997), "we have yet to chronicle how those who oppress make sense of their power in relationship to those they have injured" (Hurtado, 1999, p. 226). As the opening quotation suggests, it is important for us as supervisors to anchor or locate ourselves ecosystemically in terms of our privilege and power, and lack thereof, so that we can more fully understand how that social location informs what happens in supervision with a culturally different supervisee. This reflective piece critically engages power issues as they are linked with race and culture.

The Philosophy of Individualism and MFT Supervision

Realizing what it means to be a white, US citizen is crucial in supervision and training contexts. One of its major tenets is individualism. The core philosophy of individualism translates into the following two beliefs about the self and society: (1) I am okay, and have control over myself, and (2) society is okay, and I can make it in the system (Sue & Sue, 1999). The mere recognition and acknowledgment of individualistic assumptions of white, US society works to make their "rightness" or "goodness" contestable, and the benefits to complying and cooperating with the sociopolitical and economic system versus the consequences that can come from critiquing it and trying to change it begin to become visible as well. This individualistic philosophy seems to contradict our professed goals and way of thinking as MFTs: systemic understandings and transformations of families and society. If we believe in principles of interdependence, circular causality, and second order cybernetics, why do we reduce this more complex way of seeing ourselves and relationships by using the lens of individualism? Are we truly systemic or ecosystemic thinkers (and doers) if we see ourselves changing lives one individual at a time, and, like the proverbial light bulb, only if they really want to change? And if we subscribe to this reductive lens, and see society as "okay," how can we then act as agents of social change and transformation?

Critical Incident: Individualizing Power

A 58 year old, white female supervisor recalled an incident in her supervision group: [1] I had three young, white women who had taken feminist therapy and had found their voice, and three non-white women, one African-American, one Vietnamese, and one Japanese. I paired them up originally across cultures so that they could support each other and learn from each other. The first thing that happened was one of the white women said, "I don't want to work with her; I want to work with my friend here," who was also a young, white woman, "because we have a lot to learn from each other." I said, "Well, maybe next time, but we are going to start out like this." I made the Anglo group be quiet while we sat for thirty seconds, and I would ask the Vietnamese student, "What do you think about this?", and I would use my hands to be sure no one else took the floor, while we waited the minute it took for her to start to respond. She would say wonderful things, and after I'd modeled it five or six times, I said, "You see? There's a cultural difference here. These guys aren't going to participate at all in the supervision group unless we make a space for them. We have a lot to learn from them. Why don't we work on this?" And the answer was: "No. We just got our voice. We're going to use it. If they want their turn, they can take the floor." So, the Anglo side refused to accommodate people from other cultures because their culture was right. And they'd just taken feminist family therapy and that proved it (laugh).

Having "found their voice," and resonating with a newly discovered sense of feminist empowerment, the three white women refused to relinquish the floor to their fellow supervisees of color in the group "because their culture was right." In this particular case, the axis of gender acts as an entry point of empowerment, but renders invisible the axes of power of race and culture. In the name of gender equity, they use their whiteness and US nationality as the sites of privilege and power and silence other "cultures." Thus, the logic of individualism enables them to collapse their race and class positions by viewing the world through the single, individual lens of gender (Agathangelou, 2000). This display of white privilege demonstrates unspoken rules of power, and Hurtado

(1999) articulates some of these rules in the following quotation:

If I am not the central actor in the drama, I will not listen to you, I will not acknowledge your presence... my ability not to see you is my power... I claim my right to be central to all action by claiming my special needs as a... (white) woman with special demands that supersede the needs of anybody else involved in the situation. If you claim your own needs, I will proceed as if I did not hear you and reassert my initial claim... Unless I want you to exist, you do not (pp. 228, 229).

The three white women ignored the needs of their culturally different peers even after the white female supervisor explicitly advocated for them. As the supervisor related, "The willingness to consider [culture] wasn't there." A liberal discourse of individual responsibility and their inalienable right to their own voice seemed to inform their marginalization of their racially and culturally diverse fellow supervisees. Clearly, a supervisor's or supervisee's awareness and sensitivity to gender as an ecosystemic axis of power is crucial to sustaining a contextually informed perspective in supervision and therapy. However, the reduction of social relations and the privileging of one axis of power over all others does not sustain the complexity of various ecosystems' tensions and contradictions with one another in the clinical, supervision, and larger social contexts and can lead to the systematic marginalization of other crucial processes which are ongoing but undetectable when using a single lens.

A 45 year old, Jewish female supervisor from the US shared the following: "As trainers, we want to be sensitive to gender, ethnicity, race, culture, class, but we tend to see one of these more clearly than the others, possibly because it's been experienced as crucial to our own sense of being, possibly because we tend to look at only one thing at a time." This supervisor speaks to difficulties of sustaining the complexity of identity, social location, and social relations because as people, therapists, and supervisors, we tend to resonate with, or privilege, a particular ecosystemic axis of power more than others. Nevertheless, it is the intersections of our locations on various axes of power that inform our social relations in and out of training contexts and organize who does and does not speak, what is and is not spoken about, and whose beliefs, values, and expectations are deemed normative and granted a privileged, implicitly superior, status in the room. Though difficult to attain and sustain, an awareness and sensitivity to white privilege is integral to a contextually sensitive approach to therapy and training and calls for creative and recursive interventions by those holding power to make its various forms and uses explicit.

Transforming Supervision By Locating Self and Other Ecosystemically

According to Breunlin, Schwartz, and Kune-Karrer (1992), multiculturally skilled therapists are aware of and sensitive to their own racial/cultural heritage and understand how it affects psychological processes and definitions of health and normality. Cultural awareness and sensitivity is important for the "person of the supervisor" who hopes to facilitate the development of these skills and knowledge in his or her trainees (Watson, 1993). With these multicultural competencies in mind, I offer by way of conclusion seven sets of sensitizing questions for supervisors and supervisors-in-training to reflect upon to help them assess their cultural competence and potential effectiveness in working with culturally diverse supervisees:

• To what extent do you possess cultural knowledge of groups other than your own in terms of race, nationality, ethnicity, and sexual orientation? What groups would you feel most and least competent to supervise, and why?

• To what extent are you familiar with current literature (journals, books, and conference proceedings in the past 5 years) on multicultural therapy and contextual issues in supervision?

• How do you respond, emotionally and verbally, when you find yourself having difficulty understanding the words or ideas of a cross-cultural supervisee of a different race, nationality, ethnicity, and sexual orientation?

• Would you expect a favorable supervisory relationship with a supervisee from: Russia, Japan, Kenya, Germany, India, Mexico, China, etc.? Why or why not?

• What feelings do you have toward other races, ethnicities, and classes? What do you think other races, ethnicities, and classes feel towards your race, ethnicity, and class?

• Reflect on an interaction with an upper class person. What were your feelings during it? How did the interaction affect how you felt about yourself? If such feelings were elicited by a higher class supervisee during supervision, how might your work be affected?

• Reflect on an interaction with a person from a working class background. What were your feelings during it? How did that interaction affect how you felt about yourself? If such feelings were elicited by a working class supervisee, how might your work be affected?

---

[1] For a qualitative study examining the impact of culture of origin on supervisory relationships, see Killian, K.D. (2000). Differences making a difference: Cross-cultural interactions in supervisory relationships. *Journal of Feminist Family Therapy*, 12 (1-4).

References

Agathangelou, A. M. (2000). Nationalist narratives and (dis) appearing women: State-sanctioned sexual violence. *Canadian Woman Studies/les cahiers de la femme, 19*, 12-21.

Breunlin, D. C., Schwartz, R. C., & Kune-Karrer, B. M. (1992). *Metaframeworks: Transcending the models of family therapy*. San Francisco: Jossey-Bass.

Fine, M., Weis, L. Powell, L. C., & Wong, M. (Eds.). (1997). *Off white: Readings on race, power, and society*. New York: Routledge.

Frankenberg, R. (1993). *White women, race matters: The social construction of whiteness*. Minneapolis: University of Minnesota Press.

Hooks, B. (1990). *Yearning: Race, gender, and cultural politics*. Boston: South End.

Hurtado, A. (1999). The trickster's play: Whiteness in the subordination and liberation process. In R. D. Torres, L. F. Miron, & J. X. Inda (Eds.), *Race identity, and citizenship: A reader* (pp. 225-243). Malden, MA: Blackwell Publishers.

Killian, K. D., & Hardy, K. V. (1998). Commitment to minority inclusion: A study of AAMFT conference program content and members' perceptions. *Journal of Marital and Family Therapy, 24*, 207-223.

Sue, D. W., & Sue, D. (1999). *Counseling the culturally different: Theory and practice*. 3rd ed. New York: Wiley.

Watson, M. F. (1993). Supervising the person of the therapist: Issues, challenges and dilemmas. *Contemporary Family Therapy, 15*, 21-31.

Spirituality and Therapy: Supervising at the Intersection

Loren Townsend, Ph.D.

Published in the AAMFT Supervision Bulletin, Spring 2000.

At least weekly (or so it seems) I recycle several brochures advertising workshops in spirituality and psychotherapy. Polls continue to show that clients expect therapists to address their religious and spiritual needs. As a clinician, supervisor and theological educator, I should welcome such explosive interest in spirit and healing. Certainly, human communities knew of a connection between spirituality and health five thousand years before the advent of modern therapy. I believe it is important to reclaim some of what was lost to the hegemony of post-enlightenment rationalism and logical positivism. So, why am I uncomfortable now that so many colleagues dance to this now-popular tune? On one hand I celebrate the "recovery" of spirit in marriage and family therapy. On the other hand, my discomfort erupts when:

- spiritual concerns in therapy are represented primarily as unexamined, intuitive celebrations of human transcendence;
- when parochial religious language and psychotherapeutic process become indistinguishable;
- when clinicians naively or uncritically respond to spiritual and religious impulses in clinical contexts.

All of these concerns revolve around a common hub—where does the creative intersection of spirituality and therapy find accountability in some grounding context?

Marriage and family therapists find anchors for practice in a body of knowledge and generally accepted clinical skills. As supervisors, we teach these to students and endorse those who learn them to certification. However, the intersection of spirituality and clinical practice is most often left up to students' intuition or individual faith stands. When these are not carefully examined, students are allowed to fly by the seat of their pants in ways we would never tolerate with clinical concepts or skills.

Responding to spiritual concerns demands the same rigor we would expect in any other dimension of the therapeutic process. Without it, spirituality is reduced to naive heartfelt self-disclosure, emotionally blurred boundaries between therapist and client, or a recapitulation of the therapists religious beliefs defined as part of therapy. My own method for grounding this spiritual-therapeutic tension begins with four basic assumptions and results in a conceptual model which guides reflective integrity

Basic Assumptions

First, it is impossible to escape moral and religious dimensions in the practice of psychotherapy (Browning, 1987). Any action that helps persons or families organize their priorities passes necessarily into a traditionally religious and spiritual domain. We need not attend so much to whether we are in spiritual territory, but how we are.

Second, psychological studies of religion affirm across time and culture that healthy religiosity and spiritual experiences will include three elements: 1) attachment to a community of shared language and belief, 2) a belief system that is "morally useful" to organize life, and 3) self-transcendent awareness that enhances a sense of connection to life and well-being in the world.

Third, conversation at the spiritual/therapeutic intersection must affirm both rational and analogical ways of knowing and be grounded in interpretive communities of creative and recalling discourse. In other words, work at this intersection does not happen in a therapeutic vacuum. It is part of a larger meaning-making conversation about being human and spiritual in a complex and diverse world. This requires therapist sensitivity to multiple spiritual languages and the variety of ways people will make sense of their spiritual lives.

Finally, when conversation moves toward the spiritual, therapy enters what most religious traditions consider holy space. This space is open to guidance by priests, shamans, or ministers who interpret and articulate the community's shared values and beliefs. It is a place of great power both for client and therapist. A therapist who moves into this space must do so critically—that is, with careful judgment, increasing levels of integrity, and consciously reflective awareness of the place of both self and other.

A Critically Grounded Method

The model of critical reflection I teach (Townsend, 1996; in press) is phenomenological. It begins in experience and seeks to make sense of that experience as it is grounded retrospectively and prospectively in communities of meaning. It is also dialogical. It presses reflection about spiritual experience beyond individual sentiment and into a context-sensitive process of mutual interpretation and meaning-making. As a training tool, it takes the form of a case consultation and provides a model for how critical processes can take place in session. Presented here in outline form, the consultation includes six basic steps.

Step One: Perception. Student therapists are asked to ground their own observations of clients in meditative and reflective awareness. Case conference begins as one member shares some meditative resource that has recently quickened their own spirit. The point of this exercise is to spark right-brained, analogical openness which encourages the group to perceive complex experiential totalities which transcend rational sense. From this position, the "other's" experience can be received in a way that "jars" our sensibilities because we "see" it in a more complete form than can be observed objectively.

Step Two: Unknowing. Apprehending and sharing this spirit-laden event is often an ending point for therapists. However, it is a beginning for critical reflection Our analogical awareness presses us to know that our understanding is inadequate. It also points out our own need for newness in perceiving another's experience. In the group, students learn simultaneously to move back toward sources of their own self-understanding and toward the client with informed respect.

Step Three: Returning to Sources. New questions turn us to creative dialogue with our primary sources of religious and spiritual meaning-making. Integrity at the spirit-therapy intersection requires careful understanding of how our own beliefs, traditions and values create a matrix of interpretation for the client's experience. In supervision, the group takes new questions raised by therapy to an inquiring conversation with the religious and spiritual traditions which inform them. "Who are the client and therapist in this religious and spiritual context?" guides conversation. In my seminary setting, therapist-client experience turns to creative dialogue with Christian religious metaphor, theological theme, and biblical story. This reflective conversation helps clarify therapeutic self-awareness and challenges the adequacy of the religious sources themselves. The group's agenda is to explore equally what spiritual sources offer the therapist and how experience in therapy renews our understanding of these same sources.

Step Four: The Scope Broadens. Rooted in therapist-client experience, the supervised group is constructively "writing" new theology. This critical conversation broadens the therapist's understanding of self in relationship with the client at the spiritual-therapeutic intersection. Careful decisions are made in the group about how new understandings about self and client might be cultivated back into therapeutic conversations with integrity. How has the therapist's sense of self and client relationship changed through critical reflection? How can he or she access this spiritually informed self and other awareness in coming sessions with integrity? What are possible agendas for exploring the client's spirituality and religious health in coming sessions? How will this affect therapy or the client's own spiritual quest? The point of this phase is to generate questions with the therapist which anchor careful judgment about crucial spiritual issues and broaden the scope of therapeutic conversation.

Step Five: Integrating Conversations. This step takes the therapist back to dialogue with the client. Important spiritual issues can now be raised by therapists who's own values and commitments are clear and who are accountable to a community of critical reflection for respecting the integrity of the client's spiritual life. From this position, therapists can provide a crucible for spiritual questioning and help clients to process, evaluate, and discover spiritual values and experience. At the same time, clients will be pressed toward dialogue with their own communities of belief by the therapeutic process.

Step Six: Recursion. Critical reflection is an ongoing process. As therapeutic conversations create new realities at a spiritual intersection, the therapist's ongoing reflective process in a community of accountability will face new questions brought about by the first five steps.

This method gives supervisors one way to help students move toward critically reflective responses to spiritual issues. It grounds reflection in indigenous communities of shared belief. At the same time, it keeps a dialogical tension between historic tradition and new experience; between self-transcendence in engagement with another and deepened self awareness. Like all methods, it is a schematic which points us to exploration and experimentation within boundaries of accountability. As the bare diagram of reflection takes form in the rich textures of clinical encounter, "steps" cease to be bland conceptual categories and become living encounters within the group itself and with the client. Participation in a critically grounded method becomes a process of formation for student therapists at the intersection of spirituality and clinical practice.

References

Browning, D. S. (1987). *Religion and the modern psychologies*. Minneapolis, MN: Fortress.

Townsend, L. L. (1996). Creative theological imagining: A method for pastoral counseling. *The Journal of Pastoral Care*, 50, (4), 349-364.

Townsend, L. L. (In Press). A *walk in the wilderness without compass or map*. St. Louis, MO: Chalice Press.

Latina/os, Latino/a Families, Therapy and Supervision

Andres Nazario, Jr., Ph.D.

Published in the AAMFT Supervision Bulletin, Vol. 9, No. 2, Fall 1996.

The Latino/a population in the United States is fast growing and there is a need for adequate and effective mental health approaches for working with this population. This article attempts to present a brief description of the Latina/o population in the United States, some observations about Latina/os and their families in general, and some ideas about therapy and supervision with Latino/a families.

The Latino/a population in the US grew 53 percent from 1980 to 1990, compared to seven percent for non-Latino/as. Latino/as are expected to grow into the largest minority group early in the 21st century. The Census Bureau counted 22.4 million Hispanics in 1992 and it projects that figure to double by the year 2020 (U.S. Bureau of the Census, 1993).

The Federal government and many other "naming" bodies utilize the term Hispanic to classify those of us with roots in Latin America. I prefer the term Latino/a, considering it to be more inclusive of all the people of Latin American origin. The term Latino/a embraces the African heritage in many Latin countries as well as the indigenous population. The term Hispanic excludes people from Latin-America whose origins are not related to the Spaniards and/or whose skin color is not white. It is important to recognize that the term Latino/as is useful to politically coalesce an often disenfranchised and marginalized group of people in the United States. Yet, there is danger in assuming that we are a homogenous group.

Latin America is a mosaic of different peoples, cultures, customs and even languages. Despite similar colonial experiences, diversity rather than uniformity characterizes the region that runs from Mexico to Tierra del Fuego and includes some Caribbean Islands. Each nation has been shaped by specific historical experiences following their independence and each has a particular cultural richness. Spanish is the official language for all of the region with the exception of Brazil, the largest and most populated nation of Latin America, where Portuguese is the official language; and Haiti the poorest of the Latin countries, where Haitian Creole is spoken. Yet, most of these nations have one or more indigenous people with their own languages (Nazario, in press)

Within the United States there are more than thirty Latino/a groups. Describing all the between-group differences and/or many possible ways of grouping Latina/os in the U.S.A. is beyond the scope of this article. For the purpose of this discussion, a few key observations will be helpful:

• There is wide diversity among Latino/as in the United States.
• 58.8 percent of them were born in the United States.
• They live in each and every state.
• They have come from every Latin-American country.
• They left their homelands for different reasons ranging from the search for better economic and professional opportunities to the escape from wars.
• As a whole, regardless of similarities and differences, Latino/as represent a marginalized segment of our society.

Latina/o families in the United States do not form a homogenous group. Their level of adaptation and acculturation as well as language and fluency may vary across families and even within a single family. As with any other oppressed people, there is danger of stereotyping in describing the characteristics of a group. However, there are some shared characteristics applicable to most Latina/o families that can serve "as the basis for informed inquiry" (Vasquez, 1994p. 114). The concepts of *respeto* (respect), *personalisom* (personalism), *familismo* (familism), *machismo* and *marianismo* have been described as applicable to most Latina/o families (For a discussion of these concepts see: Stevens, 1973; Bemal, 1988; Falicov, 1988; Garcia-Petro, 1988; Boyd-Franklin &

Garcia-Petro, 1994; Chin, 1994; Vasquez, 1994).

Therapy may not be the first choice for seeking solutions when difficulties arise, since Latino/as usually do not like "to air our dirty linen in public." Seeking advice from the family physician, church, *curandera,* folk healer, *santero, espiritista* or other forms of healing more indigenous to the Latina/o cultures may take precedence. Yet, Latino/a individuals may seek therapy for a variety of difficulties such as anxiety, depression, substance abuse, adaptation to school, coming out of the closet, eating disorders, HIV and AIDS, as well as a variety of court referred problems. Latina/o families often present difficulties such as parent-child conflicts, domestic violence, infidelity, separation and divorce, substance abuse, marital difficulties, depression, illness in the family and death and dying. Therefore, presenting problems for Latino/a individuals and/or Latina/o families are not different from those presented by members of the dominant culture. It is the context in which these difficulties occur that require additional expertise, cultural awareness and cultural sensitivity. The impact of racism, sexism, heterosexism, classism, ethnocentrism and other forms of oppression need to be explored when working with Latino/as and Latina/o families.

The diversity of Latino/a individuals and Latina/o families makes it difficult to suggest a specific strategy as the "appropriate one" for working with this population. The variety of presenting problems and concerns that Latino/as and Latina/o families bring to the family therapist requires, as with other populations, adequate training, understanding of the culture, understanding of the larger systems in the context of the client(s) and a willingness to challenge one's own biases and prejudices. Bernal and Flores-Oritz (1982) suggest the contextual approach developed by Boszormenyi-Nagi as the most helpful in the evaluation and treatment of Latino/as. In my opinion, any approach that takes into consideration the larger system influences and the context of the individual within the family may be helpful in working with Latina/o families, as long as therapists and supervisors avoid "negative and inappropriate stereotypes, and prevent the replication of the experience of discrimination in the therapeutic experience" (Vasquez, 1994 p. 135).

At the Gainesville Family Institute we have been developing a therapeutic approach for working with a variety of presenting problems and diverse populations. We consider race, gender, class, culture, ethnicity, age, sexual orientation, spirituality and physical and mental ability as sociopolitical organizing principles of existential meaning. These organizing principles influence our perceptions, attitudes and behaviors in our society. They structure how our society operates and makes decisions. These principles impact the therapeutic and supervisory process in) family therapy. They influence the attitudes, perceptions and behaviors of clients, therapists, supervisors, agencies and institutions and other larger systems. These organizing principles of existential meaning form the cornerstone of the approach utilized for training and supervision in the COAMFTE accredited post-degree program at the Gainesville Family Institute. The approach, which we call Oppression-Sensitive (Early, Nazario & Steier, 1994), is primarily, but not solely, influenced by the feminist critique of family therapy (e.g., Hare-Mustin, 1978; Avis, 1985; Ault-Riche, 1986, Goodrich, et al. 1988), the postmodernism and narrative therapies of New Zealand and Australia (e.g., White & Epston, 1990; White, 1989; Epston, 1989; Waldegrave & Tamasese, 1994), and is inspired by the work of Kenneth V. Hardy (e.g., Saba, Karrer & Hardy, 1990; Hardy, 1992). The approach has been successfully employed in working with Latina/o families. Oppression-Sensitive therapy is health oriented, gender-sensitive and supports and affirms diversity in terms of ethnicity, race, cultural background, sexual orientation, age, ability and lifestyles (Early, Nazario & Steier, 1994). The Oppression-Sensitive approach provides a broad umbrella of social justice under which many therapeutic techniques may be utilized.

Psychotherapy and supervision of psychotherapy from an Oppression-Sensitive frame builds upon a philosophy of inclusion and collaboration. Therapists and supervisors are committed to an open context promoting equality, social acceptance and the embracing of multiple views. Oppression-Sensitive therapy requires the creation of an environment wherein the client-family system, therapist and supervisor work together in a collaborative manner, resulting in empowerment. This process takes place when we build upon the strengths of the client/family in therapy, and of the supervisee in supervision; when we recognize the inherent power differential that exists between client/family and therapist, and between therapist and supervisors; and when we do not distance ourselves from the client/family and or supervisee as if we knew what is best for them.

The job of the Oppression-Sensitive therapist working with a Latino/a family is to develop "an atmosphere of curiosity, openness and respect" (Griffith & Griffith, 1992 p. 11), in which discussions of the client/family's difficulties are nestled within the context of the social and political struggles of the family *vis a vis* the dominant culture. The ultimate goal in working with Latino/as, as with all marginalized groups, is to develop a therapeutic process that is transparent, in which the client/family, therapist and supervisor work collaboratively towards liberation from the oppressive nature of the presenting problem. This approach places different demands on the therapist/supervisor according to his/her own placement on a privileged-oppressed continuum (Early, Nazario, Steier, 1994). This continuum is based on the organizing principles of existential meaning. For example, a white middle-class, male, heterosexual, young, able and Christian supervisor would fall at one end of the continuum, while an older, poor, black Latina, physically challenged, Muslim, lesbian therapist would fall at the other end.

In addition, according to the Oppressive-Sensitive approach, when engaging Latina/o families it is important to engage with the entire person and/or persons interviewed rather than with their presenting problem. Thus, learning to pronounce their names, finding out about their history, both in terms of their roots in the Latin country of origin as well as their history in the United States, is essential. If they are immigrants it is important to learn the reasons for their departure and the difficulties of adaptation they have encountered in the United States: "Although most people have access to their culture, for some reason their sense of belonging has been destroyed by war, political oppression, migration, or whatever" (Waldegrave & Tamasese, 1994p. 98). If they are U.S. born we suggest exploring what they know of their family heritage. Regardless of the presenting problem, immigration status or country of birth, family therapists are encouraged to open space for the discussion of the impact of racism, sexism and other forms of oppression in their lives.

References

Ault-Riche, M. (1986) (Ed.). *Women and Family Therapy*. Rockville, MD: Aspen Systems Coorporation.

Avis, J.M. *(1985).* The politics of functional family therapy: A feminist critique. *The Journal of Marital and Family Therapy,* vol. ll., p. 127–138.

Bernal, G. (1982). Cuban Families. In M. McGoldrick, J. K. Pearce & J. Giordano, (Eds.). *Ethnicity and family therapy.* New York: Guilford.

Bernal, G. & Flores-Oritz, Y. (1982). Latino families in therapy: Engagement and evaluation. *Journal of Marital and Family Therapy,* vol. 8, p.357–365.

Boyd-Franklin, N. & Garcia Petro, N. (1994). Family therapy: The cases of African American and Hispanic women. In L. Comas-Diaz & B. Greene, (Eds.). *Women of color: Integrating ethnic and gender identity in psychotherapy.* New York: Guilford.

Chin, J. L. (1994). Psychdynamic approaches. In L. Comas-Diaz & B. Greene., (Eds.). *Women of color: Integrating ethnic and gender identity in psychotherapy.* New York: Guilford.

Early, G., Nazario, A. & Steier, H. (1994). Oppression Sensitive Family Therapy: A health affirming model. American Orthopsychiatric Association. Washington, DC. April 29.

Epston, D. (1989). *Selected papers.* Adelaide, South Australia: Dulwich Center Publications.

Fialcov, C. (1982). Mexican families. In M. McGoldrick, J. K. Pearce, & J. Giordano, (Eds.). *Ethnicity and family therapy.* New York: The Guilford Press.

Garcia-Preto, N. (1982). Puerto Rican families. IR M. McGoldrick, J. K. Pearce, & J. Giordano, (Eds.). *Ethnicity and family therapy.* New York: Guilford.

Goodrich, T. J., Rampage, C., Ellman, B. & Haistead, K. (1988). *Feminist family therapy: A casebook.* New York: W. W. Norton.

Griffith & Griffith, (1992). Owning one's epistemological stance in therapy. *Dulwich Centre Newsletter,* vol.1, p. 5–11.

Hardy, K. V. (1992). Race, class and culture. AAMFT 50th Annual Conference. Miami Beach, Florida. October 17.

Hare-Mustin, R. (1978). A Feminist Approach to Family Therapy. *Family Process,* vol. 17, p.181–194.

Nazano, Jr., A. (in Press). Counseling Latina/o families. In W. M. Parker. *Consciousness raising: A primer for multicultural counseling.* New York: Charles C. Thomas Publishers

Saba, G. W., Karrer, B. M. & Hardy, K. V. (1990) (Eds.). *Minorities and family therapy.* New York: Haworth.

Stevens, E. (1973). Marianismo: The other face of machismo. In A. Pescatello (Ed.) *Female and male in Latin America.* Pittsburgh: University of Pittsburgh Press.

U.S. Bureau of the Census. (1993). *Hispanic Americans today.* Washington, D.C.: U.S. Govemment Printing Office.

Vasquez, M. J. T. (1994). Latinas. In L. Comas-Diaz & B. Greene, (Eds.). *Women of color: Integrating ethnic and gender identity in psychotherapy.* New York: Guilford.

Waldegrave, C. (1990). Just therapy. *Dulwich Centre Newsletter,* vol. l, p. 5–46.

Waldegrave, C. & Tamasese, K. (1994). Some central ideas in the "Just Therapy" approach. *The Family Journal.' Counseling and Therapy for Couples and Families,* vol.2, p. 94–103.

White, M. (1989). *Selected papers.* Adelaide, South Australia: Dulwich Centre Publications.

White, M. & Epston, D. (1990). *Narrative means to therapeutic ends.* New York: W. W. Norton.

Entering Into Different Worlds: Ethnographic Participatory Supervision for Bilingual Clinicians

Shi-Jiuan Wu, Ph.D. & Arlene Katz, Ed.D.

Published in the AAMFT Supervision Bulletin, Vol. 11, No. 2, Winter 1998.

Discourse lives, as it were, on the boundary between its own context and another, alien context. (Bakhtin, 1981, p. 284)

In order to write of my childhood I have to translate. It is as if I am writing about someone else. As a boy, I lived in French; now I live in English. The words don't fit, because languages are not equivalent to one another.. ..It's not that the boy couldn't understand these phrases. It is that in order to do so, he would have to translate, and that would mean engaging an electrical circuit in his brain, bypassing his heart. (Sante, 1997, p.99)

I suppose I am never completely present in any given moment, since different aspects of myself are contained in different rooms of language, and a complicated apparatus of airlocks prevents the doors from being flung open all at once. (Sante, 1997, p.111)

An Invitation

This article is written to introduce a way of supervision for bilingual clinicians who are practicing therapy in their local language and necessarily are having to navigate between their local language and English. For one of us (SJW), a Chinese clinician practicing therapy in an English dominant discourse environment, fitting-in with the developed theories, journal articles, presentations of well-organized workshops and conferences had always been the priority in her professional development. However she was aware that something about herself as a person was still missing. She did not at first realize what it was. But as she began to work with her supervisor (AK), she was able to articulate these concerns in ways which

made sense to her. From SJW's perspective, the overall concern of bilingual trainees is that if they are supervised solely through the dominant supervision discourse (such as various supervision theory models) without receiving much curiosity about what might be the unknown, they are not often invited to speak about their cultural experiences and how such experiences inform them as a person and therapist in a moment to moment kind of practice. How bilingual practitioners travel between their native language and English is rarely addressed in supervision. Consequently, their voice is not fully present; only the voice that fits into the mainstream can be present.

In supervision with AK, SJW experienced many moments of being invited to speak in her own, indigenous, native voice. It created in her not only a sense of access to her own language and culture, but a new sense of resourcefulness. Together, we felt that in the local world we were building together. We could draw on both the Chinese and the Western worlds (Katz & Shotter, 1996; Shotter & Katz, 1996). Each of us could be, and were "struck by" events which raised possibilities for navigating between the world of Western professional language and culture, and SJW's own Chinese language and culture.

Ethnographic Participatory Supervision

To give it a name, we can call this different kind of supervision, Ethnographic Participatory Supervision. Although it resonates with and builds on some of the ideas of collaborative language system (Anderson & Goolishian, 1988) and reflecting process (Andersen, 1991) approaches, it elaborates on them in perhaps unexpected ways. We share with them an emphasis on relational meaning as co-constructed through reciprocal conversations and constant co-reflection on a moment to moment, ongoing basis. Central to our stance, however is the crucial role we attach to events which we feel signal the making of significant differences in the client's world. We focus on events, on poetic moments, which arouse in us the most curiosity and wondering. A poetic stance of this kind invites and addresses multiple potential possibilities instead of a single kind of truth (Katz & Shotter 1996; Shotter & Katz, 1996).

Joint Creative Engagement in Ethnographic Participatory Supervision

In order to understand SJW's local and practice experiences of working with Chinese clients, we tracked the process of supervision in our "local worlds." SJW kept a journal, recording' in it events which illustrated the differences between her Chinese and Western sensitive practices in the following manner:

1) Conversations with clients were documented and reflected on before her ethnographically sensitive supervision with AMK.

2) These reflecting notes were brought to supervision and co-reflected with AMK.

3) Then we documented this conversation.

4) And then we began the process again —SJW talked with clients, documented, reflected and brought the writings again back to supervision.

This ongoing documentation of reflections and co-reflections allows us to collect data and to reflect on the data as we move along. Such a self-articulating, self-elaborating process allowed SJW to begin to describe her own practice from within it, both to herself (in her own inner dialogues) and to others (including AK) (Katz, Siegel, & Rappo, 1997). It encouraged her to articulate what she was doing from within her "doing" of it in such a way that she could grasp how to carry it across from one situation into another.

For SJW, crucial in doing this, were certain "ways of speaking," certain words of AK which drew her attention to issues which otherwise would have passed by unnoticed. AK, so to speak, "entered into" SJW's world to remind her of the "something" she had felt early to be missing from her psychotherapeutic experiences: what is at stake for each of us in our lived experience, for clients, supervisees, and supervisors alike. Psychotherapy became no longer only a cognitive process for SJW. She began to sense "from the inside," so to speak, why her Chinese experiences mattered.

Multi-Cultural Episodes

For SJW, the turn to a more multi-cultural stance began with the following questions and response:

AK: "Would you like to bring your Chinese case notes to our next meeting? So we can talk about your client's experiences in her own words?"

SJW: "I have never thought about that I can do this with my Chinese client in English-speaking supervision. What a wonderful idea! Yes! I definitely want to give it a try after so many years of losing my usage of my mother language in supervision."

Later co-reflections

SJW: "I was totally shocked when my supervisor asked me to bring my Chinese case notes to supervision. I could not believe what I heard but felt so welcomed in bringing in the client's own language and my native language. My heart was pounding fast and I felt more openings would come. I could not wait. It's just a wonderful moment. Later I thought about what does this mean to me. It means my memories from being a Chinese finally gets invited in my own language, not just primarily in English. This is very special for me."

AK: "I was struck by Shi-Jiuan's embodied sense of herself and others, and how an immediate sense of what matters and what is meaningful can get invited. There is a difference between a position of having to translate and work out what matters through a professional framework and reclaiming a sensibility from her own language and the nuances of her world - an immediate and spontaneous sense from Chinese."

SJW: "I was given significance and voice - rather than felt differences being silenced, colonized. I feel I can be more who I am and this can help me enter my world with others and appreciate words differently."

But why was SJW so moved by such a simple invitation? The risk to the bilingual clinician—the loss, in practicing therapy and having supervision solely in a dominant language setting—is that all the nuances, sounds, local phrases, sensations from the local language are put aside if not openly welcomed. The bilingual clinician is not able to access her local resources through her mother-tongue language. Sometimes this is of crucial importance. We offer below what could appear as a "typical" referral of a client who is depressed. Yet we soon realize that we can't automatically translate "depression" from Chinese to English. A whole world opens up for us as we enter into her Chinese words and her world - what matters to her. We begin with her own words (as translated by SJW):

Client: "Because my husband does not have job, I let him cook. But I also become lazier. I used to live with my mother-in-law in Taiwan. At that time, I was under more pressure but it's easier to kill the time. Now my business does not go well, it's much harder to kill the time."

In Supervision

AK: I am interested in the words and meaning of 'killing the time'.

SJW: In Chinese, it is pronounced da fa. Da means beat up, fa means releasing. Fa is how you use your time. Oftentimes it means one may not have to plan how to spend the time. This client wanted to be able to use her time well but did not know how to use her time in a good way.

AK: So 'killing the time' is more how she can manage her time positively. It's not like she did not want to do things.

SJW: Exactly. What word would people use for this meaning here?

AK: Probably, passing the time, going with the flow.

In other words, what could easily have been a misunderstanding here—that by "killing the time" the woman meant "wasting time," "getting through it somehow," rather than "being fully engaged," or "captivated" by her tasks—was brought to light. It would have been easy for a supervisor to see the Chinese woman, and her relations to her husband, in a completely wrong light.

Later Co-Reflections

SJW: I was struck by how Arlene approached the translated words. She did not assume she knew the meaning of "killing the time." Instead, she asked curious questions to invite me to reflect on what does it mean and shift thinking in between Chinese and English. It's so easy to think from our point of view and risk pathologizing our client. This is a powerful

lesson for me and I need to sense words even with more humility and curiosity because it allows me to better enter into my client's world and help my client based on her world view, not upon mine.

AK: We notice how a short phrase can be striking—fa—it invites a whole world of meaning—fa—and we want to know what that world is. For this client a sign of wanting to feel better would be that she could 'kill the time'—she would then be able to 'go with the flow,' let things happen, go along with her energies. By entering into the words and "worlds" themselves, I was afforded an opportunity to learn of the different aspects of words and phrases in Chinese from the characters that form them, a kind of invitation to enter into spaces of possibility, a sense of wonder in learning the subtle nuances of words that can too often be taken for granted. In navigating these different worlds, we 'make visible' what we can learn from each other; and become aware of what matters most for each of us. It asks us to become aware of another world, point of view, culture—a particular kind of answer ability that makes us aware of what is at stake for each of us in this emerging 'local moral world' (Kliman, 1995) between us and with our clients.

And SJW not only became my guide, but she went on to become aware of aspects of her own language that she herself had taken for granted. As she said, "If you were a Chinese speaker these questions may not be asked."' And she then went on to be struck by seeing what had been a "familiar" word in a new way. This space of engagement is not just about Chinese and English, or professional discourse and lived experience, but about the richness of daring to enter into very different worlds with another person. What is at stake for clinicians in training whose first language is not English, whose lived experience is divided between (at least) two different cultural worlds? A whole world of experience can be kept in the background, in learning a professional practice. Not only listening to their voices—but what is at stake for them as they navigate between very different 'worlds,' the professional world and their own local cultures, their own languages."

Conclusion

We write this paper as an invitation to dialogue and exchange on what we have found to be critical issues in the process of multicultural supervision. We have experienced the process of Ethnographic Participatory Supervision as one way in which to conduct bilingual supervision. For SJW, a bilingual clinician, the process has been striking and has brought out more of herself as a Chinese clinician who wants to share her personal and professional experiences with the readers. As AK commented: "It's like two languages, two cultures play and mingle with each other." The question now is how we can invite bilingual clinicians to bring forward more of who they are, of their world, thus to enrich our knowledge in the field of supervision from native and local points of view; how can we play some more with each other? For SJW, this collaborative and generative process has been transformatory; something that she has not experienced from the textbooks. Even now she is still touched by it and believes it will stay with her throughout her life.

References

Andersen, T. (1991). *The reflecting team.* New York: W. W. Norton.

Anderson, H., & Goolishian, H. (1988). Human systems as linguistic systems: Evolving ideas about the implications for theory and practice. *Family Process, 27,* 371-393.

Bakhtin, M. M. (1981). *The dialogic imagination.* In M. Holquist, (Ed.), Translated by C. Emerson & M. Holquist. Austin, TX: University of Texas Press.

Katz A. M., & Shotter, J. (1996). Hearing the patient's voice: Toward a social poetics in diagnostic interviews. *Social Science and Medicine, 43(6)919-931.*

Katz, A. M., Siegel, B. S., & Rappo, P. (1997). Reflections from a collaborative pediatric mentorship program: Building a community of resources. *Ambulatory Child Health, 3,* 101-112.

Kliman, A. (1995). *Writing at the Margins: Discourse between anthropology and medicine.* Berkeley, CA: University of California Press.

Sante, L. (1997). Lingua Franca. *Granta,* 59, 99-111.

Shotter, J., & Katz, A. M. (1996). Living moments in dialogical exchanges. In V. Hansen (Ed.), *Dialog og Refleksjon: Festchrift for Professor Tom Andersen's 60th birthday.*

Supervising in an Urban Multi-Cultural Agency

Janet Anderson, Ed.D.

Published in the AAMFT Supervision Bulletin, Vol. VII, No. 1, Winter 1994.

In urban, multi-cultural agencies, contextual variables shape the process of supervision. And supervision is most effective when the supervisory relationship creates a context in which differences can truly be examined. To act "as if" context and diverse cultural/ethnic beliefs are irrelevant, or of minimal importance to supervision, is a disservice to our supervisees and clients. We run the risk of being unaware of the influence of our own belief systems and that of our supervisees. To counter this danger, supervision must challenge supervisors/practitioners to know and understand their own cultural values and biases. We cannot supervise responsibly if we remain unaware. In fact, I believe working with context and "multiple versions of reality" (Kantor & Neal, 1985) to be essential to the effectiveness of work in a multicultural setting.

Contextual Variables and Related Constraints

The setting is a comprehensive health care and human services center. The mix of clients, staff and trainees is approximately: 75% African heritage, 10% Caucasian, 12% Hispanic/ Latino, 3% Asian heritage and other. Presently, the overall approach to treatment which we expect supervisees to learn is an ecostructural (Aponte & Van Deusen, 1981), culture-based competency model (Brisbane, 1990).

This setting presents two significant training constraints: financial and soci-cultural. Since the program operates out of a resource poor urban health center, the technology and time available to us is limited. Practices of confidentiality are particularly critical. The community is composed mostly of people of African-heritage people, who are poor, who have a long history of insensitive and disrespectful treatment, where boundaries between staff and clients are often thin, coupled with a cultural value which states: "We don't air our dirty laundry outside of our family." Consequently, while we use a one-way mirror, all of the family members meet all of the team members. If a team member is known to a family member they do not participate in sessions. My responsibility as a supervisor is ultimately to respect and protect the rights and situation for supervisees and clients. (i.e., the context shapes the process).

Steps to Honoring Diversity

The issues of power, gender and culture are critical in negotiating and establishing a working supervisory relationship. As a white, Swedish American woman working in a predominantly black community, at an "African American" agency, I am supervising a wide variety of therapists-in-training including staff of the health center, respected community leaders and graduate school interns from various ethnic and cultural backgrounds. Because the potential for shaming and the functioning of internalized oppression/racism are part of this context, they need to be made overt and repeatedly checked. The question then becomes: can I, as supervisor, create a context within the supervisory relationship that is safe and supportive enough to risk new behaviors?

There are several steps I take to address this question. First, I do my homework of becoming experienced and knowledgeable of the process of developing cultural competency and understanding diversity in this community. I listen to the beliefs of my supervisees and clients and am responsible to deepen my knowledge of cultural practices and beliefs. For example, what are the effects of immigrating to the U.S.? What are the myths and stereotypes regarding particular cultural groups? How have these affected the telling of their history? What are Afro-centric values? What are the soci- political forces in the U.S. which have effected the life of African, Asian, Latin and European heritage people in this culture? Then, if I am able to demonstrate in words and actions, a competency to move within the African American and Latino cultural practices of our community, and to know the differences between these and my own, a context is created in which I am most likely to honor and be sensitive to those I supervise. This is a dynamic process. It is not done once (like a graduate degree) and completed. To remain responsible requires creation of an intentional practice among colleagues who value diversity (our team is multi-racial, multi-cultural) and with whom we can voice differences, call each other on our biases, name them as they are seen, sort out personality style from family from ethnic from agency belief systems.

Second, I assume the potential for change and the presence of strength, search it out, acknowledge it and encourage the expansion of these strengths to facilitate change. Third, I practice a method of supervision in which I view myself as part of a team. We work to create a context for growth and learning in which critique and examination of assumptions are to go in both directions. Difference is honored, not pathologized or negated. Simultaneously, a greater responsibility always lies with the supervisor to the supervisee and the supervisee to the client to provide leadership and support in creating a safe context for learning new practices (Tyler, Brome & Williams, 1991).

Recognizing and acknowledging the significant cross-currents in this model, between an eco-structural approach, a more collaborative, horizontal hierarchy of the supervising team, and the growing body of work on the practice of cultural competency; the overarching component of this model remains an attention to identifying the multiple versions of reality or diverse belief systems that are operative between client and therapist and between therapist and supervisor.

To supervise within a framework that truly values diversity, I believe that the context of supervision must facilitate examination of these differences. This practice goes beyond the eco-structural framework to explicitly include the person of the supervisee and that of the supervisor as critical determinants in the creation of the context for change.

References

Aponte, H. (1974). Psychotherapy for the poor: An eco-structural approach to treatment, *Delaware Medical Journal*, 46, 432-448.

Aponte, H. & VanDeusen, J. (1981). Structural Family Therapy. In A. Gurman & D. Kniskern (Eds.), *Handbook of Family Therapy*, vol. 1, (pp. 310-360). NY: Brunner Mazel.

Asante, M. (1990). *Afrocentricity,* Trenton, NJ: Africa World Press.

Brisbane, F. (1990). *Working with African Americans: The professional's handbook.* Needham Heights, MA: Ginn Press.

Kantor, D. & Neal, J. (1985). Intergrative shifts for the theory and practice of family systems therapy, *Family Process*, 24, 13-30.

Tyler, F. & Brome, D. & Williams, J. (1991). *Ethnic validity and psychotherapy.* NY: Plenum.

Are Supervisors Still in the Dark? Supervision of Gay/Lesbian/Bisexual Clients

Janie Long, Ph.D.

Published in the AAMFT Supervision Bulletin, Vol. VII, No. 1, Winter 1994.

Supervisees approach gay/lesbian/bisexual clients with varying levels of comfort, knowledge and bias. Supervisors also approach supervision of gay/lesbian/bisexual clients with the same range of responses. Supervisors can work with supervisees who hold different values and opinions than their own in a way that is respectful and growth-enhancing and at the same time advance the welfare of gay/lesbian/bisexual individuals and families.

Ethical Responsibilities to Clients

Marriage and family therapists are required to advance the welfare of families and individuals and to respect the rights of those seeking their help (AAMFT Code of Ethics, 1991). The *Code of Ethics* states that therapists do not discriminate against or refuse professional service to anyone on the basis of sexual orientation. Supervisors may encounter, however, supervisees who believe that gays/lesbians/bisexuals engage in immoral acts and who may refuse (overtly or covertly) to work with these clients. Therapists are also charged by the ethical code not to use their professional relationships with clients to further their own interests or to exploit the trust or dependency of clients. Some supervisees may work towards conversion of same-sex couples to their own heterosexual view of the world. They may attempt to convince gay/lesbian/bisexual clients that homosexuality is a symptom to cure. They may also encourage someone who is bisexual to only enter into heterosexual relationships.

When do supervisors request or allow supervisees to refrain from seeing clients who are nonheterosexual? The Ethical Code does allow for therapists who are unable or unwilling "for appropriate reasons," to provide therapy to assist clients in obtaining other services. But, what is meant by "for appropri-ate reasons?" Refusing to work with gays/lesbians/bisexuals because of lack of knowledge and skill is a very different issue than refusing to work with them because one believes that their orientation is a choice and thus their lifestyle is immoral. Supervisors in each of these instances must consider clients *and* supervisees. What do supervisors need to do to assure clients who are gay/lesbian/bisexual receive the best possible service? What do supervisors need to do to assure that therapists are encouraged to broaden and examine their own beliefs, skills and knowledge?

While supervisors may believe that exposure to persons who are gay/lesbian/bisexual would be a good training experience for supervisees who condemn non-heterosexual orientations, they must first consider the client's welfare. In recent interviews, I asked persons who were gay/bisexual/lesbian if they would consider receiving services from a therapist who did not condone their lifestyle (Long, 1994). Their response was a resounding "NO." Supervisors can find other avenues for supervisees to gain exposures to persons who are not heterosexual in other arenas besides the therapy room.

The Supervisory Challenge

Whether supervisees have refused to see non-heterosexual clients due to aversion, lack of knowledge or fear of doing harm, a problematic area has been uncovered that supervisees should be invited to examine and pursue. The challenge for supervisors is to provide a safe and informed context in which such exploration can happen.

The necessary initial step in creating a context that protects both clients and supervisees is for supervisors to first examine their own heterosexual bias, i.e. the belief in the superiority of heterosexuality over homosexuality (Lapierre, 1990). Because all of us grew up in a predominantly heterosexual society, most have some degree of heterosexual bias and exhibit some degree of homophobia (Hetrick, 1984). Heterosexual bias is present in much of the foundational family systems theory and in many of the traditional approaches to family therapy (Ault-Riche, 1986; Goodrich, Rampage, Ellman & Hllstead, 1988). Homophobia can be exhibited in many ways: Outright prejudice or discrimination; ignorance of the special issues of gays/lesbians/bisexuals; stereotypical thought processes; and insensitivity. Once supervisors have examined their own level of bias, they can more honestly invite supervisees to do likewise.

Then supervisors must ensure supervisees have adequate knowledge and skills to work with lesbian/gay/bisexual clients Supervisees who acquaint themselves with the growing body of literature on therapy with gays/lesbians/bisexuals and their families avoid over-looking potential problems and solutions in therapy. Supervisees can also learn by observing therapy sessions involving non-heterosexuals from behind the mirror or on videotape. However, the best way to increase supervisees knowledge about gays/lesbians/bisexuals is for them to seek out personal and professional relationships with members of these groups. Supervisees' understanding of the special issues of lesbians/bisexuals/gays greatly increases when they engage in relationships with persons who struggle with these issues on a daily basis.

During the supervision there are several way supervisors can increase learning about bisexuals/lesbians/gays. Use examples in supervision that include gays/lesbians/bisexuals, being careful not to present them and their families as dysfunctional. When working with heterosexual couples, ask supervisees how they would work with the cases if the clients were same-sex couples. Help supervisees be aware of bias in language (i.e. use of the term "partner" versus mate, husband or wife).

The process of becoming a therapist exposes supervisees' vulnerability and challenges supervisors to examine their own personal themes (Satir, 1987). These themes arise from one's own personal history including one's sexual orientation. The supervisory role is not to dictate supervisees' beliefs but rather to provide a safe environment for supervisees to explore their beliefs. Gays/bisexuals/lesbians are indeed out of the closet. May it no longer be suggested that therapists (or supervisors) are still in the dark (Simon, 1991).

References

American Association for Marriage and Family Therapy. (1991). AAMFT Code of Ethics.

Ault-Riche, M. (1986). A feminist critique of family therapy. In Ault-Riche (Ed.), *Women and family therapy.* Aspen: Rockville, MD (pp.1-15).

Goodrich, T. J., Rampage, C., Eliman, B. & Haistead, K. (1988). *Feminist family therapy: A casebook.* NY: W. W. Norton.

Hetrick, E. S. *(1984). Psychotherapy with homosexuals.* Washington, DC: American Psychiatric Press.

Lapierre, R. J. (1990). Homophobia and its consequences for gay and lesbian clients. In R. J. Kus, (Ed.) *Keys to caring: Assisting your gay and lesbian clients.* Boston: Alyson Publications. (pp. 90-98).

Long, J. K. *(1994). Examining the heterosexual bias of the supervisor.* Manuscript submitted for publication.

Satir, V. (1987). The therapist's story. In M. Baldwin & V. Satir (Eds.) *The use of self in therapy.* NY: Haworth. (pp. 17-25).

Simon, R. (Ed). (1991). Gays and lesbians are out of the closet: Are therapists still in the dark? *The Family Therapy Networker, 15, 1.*

Don't Ask, Don't Tell: Supervision and Sexual Identity

Linda Stone Fish, Ph.D., Rebecca Harvey, M.A. & Sheila Addison, M.A.

Published in the AAMFT Supervision Bulletin, Spring 2000.

The number of persons or institutions by whom the existence of gay people - never mind the existence of more gay people - is treated as a precious desideratum, a needed condition of life, is small, even compared to those who may wish for the dignified treatment of any gay people who happen already to exist.

- Sedgwick, (1990) p. 42

As the field of marriage and family therapy becomes sensitive to sexual minority clients, the need to address sexual identity at all levels of training grows evident. Although the field is beginning to address therapy with lesbian and gay couples, there is a well-documented gap in the field's knowledge base about sexual identity and clients who are sexual minorities (Green 1996, Long 1996, Markowitz 1991, & Clark & Serovich, 1997). There is even less written that helps trainers teach about sexual identity issues or that helps supervisors deal with sexual identity issues in supervision (Long, 1996). Green (1996) outlines the need for "supervised clinical experience" on sexual identity issues before student therapists can achieve competency. Since Syracuse University's MFT Program is probably the first in the country to teach a family therapy course on sexual identity, most supervisors have not taken a course that prepares them for focusing on these issues. How can we provide supervision that will support therapists to achieve competency in areas for which the supervisors in our field have not been adequately trained?

Informed by queer theory, we understand sexual identity to be a powerful, complex and necessary component of *all* therapeutic relationships. Therefore, we are hoping to broaden discussion of sexual identity beyond political correctness, to include an increasing awareness (and concern) about how as a field we are in our own developmental infancy with regard to our ability at tapping into the potency of sexuality in supervision and therapy.

Assumptions

All supervisory relationships are embedded in a homophobic, heterosexist culture. All individuals in those relationships, then, regardless of their own sexual orientation, maintain some homophobic and heterosexist assumptions. These assumptions handicap our therapy and supervision because they blind us to possibilities and inhibit discussion and growth.

One such assumption is that everyone is heterosexual unless they blatantly identify otherwise. Sexual minority supervisees frequently fear rejection or punishment if they do not hide their orientation from supervisors; frequently, even in the absence of evidence of homophobia, authority figures are assumed to be "unsafe", because the negative cultural message is so overwhelming. Queer people have learned the hard way that it is better to be safe than sorry. It is crucial that supervisors understand the complex web of personal, professional, and social messages, which discourage disclosure by sexual-minority supervisees as well as clients.

Two closely related assumptions are 1) that heterosexual people do not have a sexual identity and so 2) sexual identity is only relevant in cases which are dealing directly with sexual issues. However, even if both supervisor and supervisee identify as heterosexual, sexual identity informs the supervisory and therapeutic relationships in a variety of ways. For example, it is almost inevitable that every therapist will at some point have a gay, lesbian, bisexual, or transgendered person on his or her caseload, whether clients are open about their identity or not (Green & Bobele, 1994). Supervision must allow for the possibility that not all clients are heterosexual by challenging supervisees on their heterosexist assumptions (such as automatically asking a single woman about "boyfriends") and assisting them in understanding how living in a homophobic, heterosexist culture may affect the issues brought in by openly-identified clients.

Similarly, it would be easy for a heterosexual supervisor and supervisee to conclude that sexual identity is a non-issue for openly heterosexual clients, since they experience their own sexuality as a non-issue in a culture which views heterosexuality as unremarkable (Jagose, 1996) and usually unrelated to family therapy. Misled by these assumptions therapists routinely miss the opportunity to discover 1) in what ways people feel constrained by their view of heterosexuality and 2) learn new knowledges about the variety of ways they can be heterosexuals.

Another damaging assumption is that discussing sexual identity issues in supervision will be alienating to supervisees who have strong religious or moral convictions against homosexuality. However, it is not necessary to advocate or abandon any religious or moral belief in order to understand the effects of heterosexism and homophobia. Supervision should be providing socially conservative therapists with the opportunity to practice and be supported in staying grounded and connected to their spiritual beliefs while simultaneously being challenged by what families bring to therapy. Moreover, limiting supervisory conversations to only those topics that are comfortable for the supervisee is ultimately damaging to the supervision process. The supervisee who is not challenged on his or her "isms" is denied the opportunity to become a more empathetic and effective therapist.

Finally, supervisors may assume that their identity is not relevant to the supervision process. On the contrary, sexual identity is always present in the supervisory relationship even if it is not named. The question is whether we will begin to challenge ourselves to learn how to use sexuality, and the way it informs even the minutia of our life, as a therapeutic tool.

Supervisors may not be addressing sexual identity issues in the supervisory relationship because they do not know how. Using Sophie's (1985-1986) model of lesbian and gay identity development, we have developed a model for introducing sexual identity into the supervisory relationship.

1. First Awareness

In Sophie's [1] model, this beginning stage marks the period when individuals experience feeling different from others. They may be able to recognize that this difference has to do with being attracted to same sex partners or they may simply feel that, for some reason, the dominant world as they understand it does not fit for them. There is often a sense of alienation from self and from others. Relationships with family, peers, and teachers are often strained under the burden of secrecy.

In the supervisory relationship, this is the stage when the supervisor becomes aware that there is some discomfort in the supervisory relationship. The discomfort may be generated by material generated in therapy that is brought to supervision or from within the supervisory relationship itself. It may be manifested as a sense of distance or strain between supervisor and supervisee, or the supervisee may become "stuck" more frequently in therapy with little help from the supervision process.

Ideally, sexual identity has been addressed from the beginning of supervision, establishing a framework so supervisors can address issues more directly as they become aware of some discomfort in the supervisory relationship. When the supervisor experiences the discomfort, s/he may be ready to be open to the possibility that sexual identity issues may be apart of the tension in the relationship. The supervisor then must create space in the supervisory relationship for a dialogue to take place about sexual identity issues. This can only occur when the supervisor is knowledgeable about sexual orientation and comfortable enough with his/her own sexual identity development to leave space for differing experiences.

2. Test and Exploration

In Sophie's model, this stage represents the feelings of ambivalence that precede an individual's acceptance of his/her own homosexuality. Often there are feelings of alienation from the dominant heterosexual community and there may be beginning contact with individuals and communities that define themselves as homosexual.

In the supervisory relationship, this is the stage when supervisors are challenged to look at their own sexual identity development, their own heterosexist ideologies, and their own homophobic interjects. This is difficult work that requires energy and courage, and therefore is easy to avoid. To help supervisees deal with themselves and with clients around the development of sexual identity, supervisors must be open to their own development. Supervisors may find it helpful to map their burgeoning understanding of their own development, in childhood, in adolescence, and at present, and to use the Klein Sexual Orientation

Grid (1993) to help them experience the complexity of the issue. Just as the individual in Sophie's model begins to seek out information about sexual identity and perhaps contact with non-heterosexuals, the supervisor in this stage can begin to research the history of the GLBT movement, and social and familial issues commonly experienced by sexual minority individuals. Seeking supervision of supervision, and contact with peers who are more knowledgeable about sexual identity issues may also be helpful.

During this stage, the ways in which heterosexist assumptions are limiting become visible. If we look at how heterosexism defines us, we must question our constructions around gender identity, the institution of marriage, commitment, and the MFT field. For many, questioning these assumptions is frightening. If we really deconstruct the fragile bond of our sacred institutions we fear chaos. It may be easier to maintain the status quo and perpetuate heterosexism. It is difficult, however, to continue to perpetuate heterosexism once we experience (some of us for the first time, others re-experience) the horrific effects of homophobia. Once we become open to our own experiences and the experiences of sexual minority supervisees and clients, we must face the ways in which we are oppressive. When we do not leave enough space in our supervision for sexual identity discussion, we risk not only losing the opportunity for enriching our lives and the lives of our supervisees, but also being neglectful and even hurtful to ourselves, our supervisees, and their clients. Owning our role in perpetuating heterosexism and homophobia is a task crucial to moving into the next stage.

3. Identity acceptance

In Sophie's model, this stage leads toward positive identity. A sense of community may have developed and there may be disclosure of one's sexual identity to some, although not necessarily all, parts of the heterosexual world. There is increasing comfort with belonging to a sexual minority community, and a preference for social interaction with other gays and lesbians. Applying this model to the supervisory context, supervisors at this point are comfortable enough with their own journey around sexual identity, heterosexism, and homophobia to leave room for and talk openly about sexual identity in the supervision relationship. Supervisors will challenge supervisees to explore these issues, challenge supervisees to leave

space for clients to explore these issues, and continue to challenge themselves to be open to and respectful of differing life choices.

Identity acceptance is also the stage when one's own sexual orientation may be clarified. If the supervisor is heterosexual, chances are s/he has not explored her/his sexual identity. While the privilege of not having your identity questioned, pathologized, challenged, and attacked remains, those whose sexual identity is in the majority have not had the privilege of making the difficult journey towards a clearer self-knowledge that is part of the coming-out process for so many sexual minority individuals. On the other hand, the GLBT supervisor may find a renewed sense of pride in her or his identity, and acceptance of the risk and effort involved in working with heterosexual colleagues, supervisees, and students.

The supervisor in this stage may begin to prefer to work with colleagues and students who are open to the process of challenging heterosexism and homophobia. H/she may also begin to disclose to heterosexual colleagues, friends, or family members about the experience of struggling with sexual identity in supervision even if it is not clear whether these people will "get it" or not. Negative feelings about the difficulties encountered in dealing with the issue of identity may be giving way to positive feelings at this point.

4. Identity integration

Sophie's model defines this last stage as a stage in which individuals take pride in their sexual orientation, feel stable in their identity, and come out more publicly to others. Social prejudice frequently creates a sense of activism and agency around one's place in the heterosexual culture. In supervision, this is the stage when sexual identity is taken as a given, necessary part of all therapeutic processes. The harmful effects of heterosexism are challenged and both supervisor and supervisee work to prevent and mitigate the effects of homophobia for themselves and their clients. Conflicts first experienced in Stage 2 about accepting one's role in perpetuating oppression and one's own internalized homophobia no longer seem so threatening to individual identity or to the supervisory and therapeutic relationships. But more than this, a paradigm shift is taking place. By providing alternative experiences, where we explore our own and others sexual identity development, we find what queer theorists have been writing about for some time. Namely, that contrary to our culture and language there are a range of ways to be heterosexual and a range of ways to be homosexual (Halley, 1993, Kosofsky Sedgwick, 1993) and all of these are precious and crucial.

As a field, we are aware of how our theories about 'normal development', our assumptions about sexuality, and our blindness about the connection between sexuality, gender, sex roles, and marriages and families all constrain us. We are beginning to explore the gaps. That would put us at Stage 2 of Sophie's model. We suggest that queer theory and queer people have a great deal to teach the field of marriage and family therapy about the power, creativity, and sacredness of sexuality as a life force, as well as a therapeutic tool. We hope this article begins a long overdue discussion in our field about the use of supervision in this process.

---

[1] Although Sophie's model references only lesbians and gay men, we want to make clear that when we talk about sexual minorities, we are including bisexuals, transgendered and intersexed people, and others whose sexual/gender identities do not fit the binary, heterosexist norm.

References

Green, R.J., (1996). Why Ask, Why Tell? teaching and learning about lesbians and gays in family therapy. *Family Process, 35,* 389-395.

Green, S.K. & Bobele, M., (1994). Family Therapists' response to AIDS: An examination of attitudes, knowledge, and contact. *Journal of Marital and Family Therapy, 20,* 349-367.

Jagose, A., (1996). *Queer Theory: an introduction,* New York: New York University Press.

Klein, F. (1993). *The bisexual option* (2nd Ed.) New York: Harrington Park Press.

Long, J.K. (1997). Sexual Orientation: Implications for the supervisory process (pp 59-71). In Todd, T. & Storm C (eds.), *The Complete Systemic Supervisor.* Needham Heights MA: Allyn & Bacon.

Long, J.K. (1996). Working with lesbians, gays, and bisexuals: Addressing heterosexism in supervision. *Family Process, 35,* 377-388.

Sedgwick, E. K. (1990). The epistomology of the closet. Berkeley, CA: University of California Press.

Sophie, J. (1985-1986). A critical examination of stage theories of lesbian identity development. *Journal of Homosexuality*, 12, 39-51.

Spargo, T. (1999). Foucault and queer theory. New York: Totem Books.

Homosexual Supervisors or Supervisees

Published in the AAMFT Supervision Bulletin,
Vol. VII, No. 1, Summer 1998.

What If They Ask Me If I'm Married?: A Supervisee's View
Karen Gautney, M.S.

I remember the first day of our MFT practicum. It was finally time to practice and we were pretty nervous. My classmate asked one of those practical questions every therapist thinks about at some point, "What if they ask if I'm married?" For her and many other students, it was a matter of credibility. "Will they respect me if they think I'm too young or if I don't have children?"

For me, the question of whether I was married held a different meaning. As a lesbian, I had thought extensively about how to answer the question from friends, colleagues, anyone. Now, I could expect to hear it from a client. Technically, I could not be legally married to my life partner, but a flat out "no" did not acknowledge that I was in along term relationship like many of my married clients. If I completely acknowledged my relational status, how would clients react? Would this self disclosure inflict my own agenda on clients? On the other hand, if I did not disclose that I was in a lesbian relationship, would my silence give the message that homosexuality is something to hide and be ashamed of?

As I began to see clients, I confronted several other challenging situations around the issue of sexual orientation. As I had expected, I found that many of my clients did not have a positive image of gays/ lesbians. One client, as we were constructing a genogram, announced in a matter-of-fact voice that his brother was a "faggot." A female, accused by her husband of having an affair with a woman, defended herself by proclaiming that she could never do something so gross. A father expressed his fear that his wife was turning their son into a "queer" by making him do household chores. Should I confront these prejudices? Then, there were the times when I suspected that a client was gay or lesbian. Should I bring it up?

I am sure any supervisor reading this article could provide helpful answers, or at least entertain a dis-cussion, about the questions I had as a trainee. Unfortunately, my supervisors did not know I had questions about how to address my sexual orientation with clients or clients' views about homosexuality—unless they guessed—and nothing they said in supervision led me to believe they did. Oh, I was "out" to the faculty and my fellow students; that was not the problem. The problem, in retrospect, was that our attempts to demonstrate that my homosexuality was not an issue led us into a conspiracy of silence.

My motivation to remain silent was very real to me then, although I now wish I had trusted my supervisors more. I had many people ask why a lesbian would want to be a marriage and family therapist, and I wondered if I would be welcome in the field. There was little in the MFT publications to indicate there were many others like me and I felt a responsibility to be a positive example. I was determined to be open about my sexuality, and equally determined to prove that it was not a problem for me and it would not be a problem for my clients. I was afraid that, if I raised these issues, it would be seen as a weakness. As a student, my primary objective was to be seen as competent.

My supervisors had a different reason for not anticipating or discussing my questions. I was the first openly lesbian student in the program, and they wanted me to feel comfortable. They did not want to use me as a guinea pig for their learning, and did not want to presume that my sexuality would present problems. They also did not want it to appear that they had a problem with it, so they waited for me to bring it up. I didn't.

In the profession, we seem to have given ourselves permission to discuss some differences (racial and gender in particular) at length in supervision. I sense, and this is confirmed by my discussions with others, that sexual orientation is still rarely talked about. Sexual orientation is one of those "invisible" differences, or at least some people think it is. Most homosexuals are attuned to the signals others give about their sexual orientation, such as talk of children (not by itself definitive), photos on the desk, wedding rings, references to "him" or "her," etc. Homosexuals see these "blatant" signs, yet we learn to be careful about when and how we send our own. We learn to consider not only our own comfort level in any revelation, but the comfort of others as well. Heterosexuals, trying to be "politically correct" and also respect others' privacy, are all too willing to avoid the topic.

The advice I am about to give is strictly from the perspective of a lesbian supervisee to supervisors: Bring it up. Talk about it. Whether your supervisee or her clients are heterosexual or homosexual, sexual orientation is a relevant issue that may be avoided unless you attend to it. Take the responsibility, because you probably have less to risk than your supervisees. And if your supervisee is gay or lesbian, believe me, they are already thinking about it.

Disclosing Homosexuality: A Supervisor's View
Keith Schrag, M.Div.

As an openly gay supervisor, I believe it is important that I disclose my sexual orientation to my supervisees. Although some people consider this a "private" matter, I wholeheartedly disagree. It is not a personal statement as much as it is a professional and political statement.

In our culture heterosexuality is the accepted and approved way of life. It is supported by religions, common practice and society's laws. Homosexuality is outlawed in many state/provinces and is railed against by most religions. Most of us gay/lesbian/bisexual persons still suffer ongoing emotional and spiritual abuse from homophobic and heterosexist persons. Many of us experience withdrawal of basic human rights—firings, evictions from property, non-promotions—merely because of our orientation. Too many of us across the land are still physically assaulted, even killed, often without full access to police protection.

Although 1973 (when homosexuality was no longer considered a mental disorder by the American Psychiatric Association) is two decades past, many trained therapists are not personally or professionally ready to work with gay/lesbian/bisexual clients in a constructive manner. Their religious, personal or other biases often interfere with their giving homosexuals proper therapeutic service. In my opinion, marriage and family therapists must be both willing to understand bisexual clients and their families and their experience, AND be willing to work for broader societal understanding and healing. Therefore, as a supervisor, I believe it is my duty to inform my supervisees of my orientation. Through my own disclosure and their reactions to it, I help them prepare to deal with the personal and professional issues that such a disclosure by their clients raises. They do not have to agree with me or my beliefs. But they must be prepared to provide the services our Code of Ethics indicates—specifically, not allowing their own biases to interfere with providing services clients need. As a supervisor, I am responsible to assure that my supervisees meet this, as well as all the other, ethical requirements.

My disclosure can serve as rich training ground in itself. It calls for an ethical and appropriate response by supervisees. By self-disclosing to my supervisees I can provide a model of openness and self-acceptance for them which is vital in our heterosexist culture.

Those supervisees who are gay/lesbian/bisexual themselves have access to a good resource for further dealing with their unique issues as therapists/supervisors-in-training. The silence referred to in Karen Gautney's piece does not occur as the questions she raised are central to the supervision I provide. I can offer an opportunity for all my supervisees to deal with their own sexuality issues—be they of gender, orientation or other diversity concerns.

Furthermore, my openness models a method of moving from shame to self empowerment, from abuse to compassion, and from secrecy to taking care of myself. These are pivotal skills for all therapists to acquire. Because of my own journey I offer modeling and professional resources for my colleagues-in-training with me. This is a powerful and empowering privilege both for them and for me.

Dear Supervision Committee: Contextual Issues Protest

Edwin Friedman, M.A.

Published in the AAMFT Supervision Bulletin, Vol. VII, No. 2, Spring 1994.

I wish to register a protest against the Supervision Committee's (SC) decision to make contextual issues a necessary part of supervision. Not only can I not do that and be honest with my own convictions and theoretical framework, I have to question the SC's right to insist on that approach. That decision has all the characteristics of a test of faith and will have the effect of excommunicating those who disagree, forcing them to either pretend to go along by putting a few words in that satisfy the inquisitors or making them leave the faith entirely.

Certainly emphasis on contextual factors is a viable, honest approach to family therapy but it is not the only approach with solid theoretical credentials. Other viewpoints must be honored if the AAMFT is not to become monolithic in its thinking or subservient to specific political interests. Indeed this effort to bring all supervisory practice under one perspective runs the risk of turning the AAMFT into exactly the kind of poorly differentiated family we are always trying to help.

Almost no one trained by the late Dr. Murray Bowen or who would follow his theories would consider context— by which I assume you mean gender, cultural or ethnic issues— to be crucial. The crucial part of "context" for Bowen trained therapists is the emotional system as judged by anxiety and differentiation from a multigenerational perspective, and these phrased in ways that transcend culture and natural systems viewpoint is designed specifically not to be reduced to the categories of the social sciences. In fact, I have written to that specific point on several major occasions. And I dare say that these writings are well known throughout the United States and the ideas have been accepted and incorporated into the approach and philosophy of many therapists and counselors.

• In chapter two of *Generation to Generation* (1985), I go out of my way to demonstrate ten laws of family process that have nothing to do with sociological categories such as culture, ethnicity and gender.

• In my essay in Monica McGoldrick's *Ethnicity and Family Therapy* (1982) entitled "Myth of the Shiksa" I suggested that family emotional process expressed itself in the garb of, rather than was determined by, conventional social science categories, and I suggested that the relationship between culture and family process was that culture (or context for that matter) was the medium through which family process works its art. In fact, I suggested that when families invoke the context not only is that not important information to jot down, quite the contrary, it is denial of responsibility for destiny and being.

• I wrote similarly about Murray Bowen's concept of differentiation in my essay on Bowen Theory in the *Handbook of Marriage and Family Therapy* (1991).

• I made the same points in my keynote address at the 50th anniversary celebration of the AAMFT in Miami.

Any readings of Dr. Bowen's writings or of his successor Dr. Michael Kerr would clearly establish that what is meant by context in Bowen Theory has very little to do with gender and ethnicity.

Lastly, I am in the process of a new book which will contain ideas even more opposed to the SC's decision. I have presented these ideas all over America the past two years with accepting responses everywhere. Principally, I have been saying that not only are social science categories not the stuff of emotional process, focus on data in those categories, specifically, culture, race and gender, rather than being helpful, actually obfuscates seeing the forces that are most powerful.

For someone trained in Bowen therapy the issue of context is not simply one of philosophy. It is also one of method. From the point of view of Bowen theory to engage families and therapists in issues of gender and ethnicity is to support the anxiety in society that helps people avoid taking responsibility for their own emotional being and destiny.

I am not out to prove that my viewpoint is right but to show that there is another viewpoint. The issue I am addressing is whether or not opposing view points are to be treated equally. (It is my guess that there are other experienced, non-Bowenian theoreticians in the field that would agree with me).

It is one thing to insist on standards that involve the importance of solid theoretical knowledge, working one's own counter-transference issues and logging clinical experience. It is quite another to impose one theoretical view or method over another. What scares me is that in the insistence of making the contextual view triumph over others it suggests that the SC has confused models with reality, and has just assumed that the way it sees the world is so obviously the correct perception that everyone else must view life through the same lens.

To impose this requirement of context is to enfranchise one approach to family therapy over another. In the business world this would be called a monopolistic practice, in the realm of religion it would be called inquisitional, and in politics, totalitarian.

I am willing to attend a meeting of the SC to help clarify where Bowen theory diverges from the philosophy behind its decision on context. Though I must say that for the adherent of one well known, well respected approach to family therapy to have to do this smacks of an auto-da-fe.

If the SC continues in this direction, I believe, it will be treading on very dangerous ground morally, professionally, and legally. I have never seen anything like it in my 25 years as a member and more than 15 years as a supervisor.

References

Friedman, E. (1982).The myth of the shiksa. In M. McGoldrick & B. Carter (Eds.) *Ethnicity and family therapy,* pp. 499-526. New York: Guilford Press.

Friedman, E. (1985). *Generation to generation: Family process in church* and s*ynagogue.* New York: Guilford Press.

Friedman, E. (1991). Bowen theory and therapy. In A. Gurman & D. Kniskern. *Handbook of family therapy,* (vol. 2, pp. 134-170). New York: Brunner Mazel.

Mixed Views on Continuing Contextual Sensitivity: The Supervision Community Responds

Published in the AAMFT Supervision Bulletin, Vol. VII, No. 3, Fall 1994.

Editor's Note: The previous AAMFT Supervision Bulletin carried a piece by Edwin Friedman protesting the AAMFT Supervision Committee's (SC) learning objective that all supervisors must demonstrate a sensitivity to contextual variables. Below is a sampling of the many responses.

Support for Rethinking the Learning Objective

I think Friedman is making a point of enormous value, and one which needs to be carefully heard for what it is and what it is not. My two and a half decades of AAMFT involvement has left me expecting the AAMFT to behave often like a new religious or revolutionary movement: to be highly concerned about orthodoxy, quite intolerant of heretics, yet simultaneously quite unpredictable about what orthodoxy is going to be. Hence it becomes dangerous to disagree and difficult to predict how to agree—so respondents often find themselves being very cautious, spending more energy trying to predict the AAMFT's response than in furthering the elaboration of either thinking or honest dialogue.

It is intriguing that this strong challenge to the contextual demand comes from a theoretical position usually not criticized for indifference to context, despite Friedman's assertion that he is indifferent to what you consider to be context. The work of McGoldrick et al. has been strongly influenced by the Bowenians and sets the norm for much contextual attentiveness within psychotherapy. Certainly many Bowenians have observed that certain kinds of family process are much more normative and widespread within given cultures than others, and the combined attention to contextual and family process variables has been highly fruitful for many therapists. Hence I don't think Friedman can be read as objecting to attention to the ways in which different settings are different, since that's precisely what he is very good at; but I think he is quite appropriately objecting to the orthodox demand that the central focus be on the accidents of historical difference rather than on what he considers the universals of family process.

As a more psychoanalytically oriented family therapist, I'd be inclined to make the same argument from my differing theoretical perspective, also believing that the very real and powerful cultural and gender variables are expressible and discussible within my own theoretical language. In either his case or mine, insisting that candidates couch their self expression in language that pays political homage to a given perspective, encourages more the falsehood of signing a dogmatic creed than the curiosity and creativity of keeping all elements of a conversation alive.
Brian Grant, Ph.D.

I agree emphatically.... Contextual factors need to be included, but with a broad stroke of the pen that includes, rather than excludes, the perspectives provided by Friedman and others. I, too, am greatly alarmed by the push for political correctness emerging in many of the governing bodies of numerous professional organizations. Let us be different, not the same, as those groups who confuse politics and social issues beliefs with systemitherapy and the encouragement of people.
Stephen S. Elliott, Ph.D.

It seems to me that what is happening is becoming more and more narrow and insistent on one point of view and, whether I share a certain view or not, it appears to me that significant dysfunction in the system might be emerging. I question how a group who teaches about process could get so focused on content and insistent that content be the basis of ethics. Is the SC really saying that if I do not agree with their opinion and am not getting myself "educated" to do so, that I am engaging in unethical practice? Can they legislate opinion? Is that either ethical or legal? Under the title of "diversity" or "political correctness" could they kid themselves that they are being more ethical than those who disagree with their opinion? Again I reiterate that I am neither agreeing with an opinion nor disagreeing with it. That is not the point. It just seems to me that we cannot base ethics on content rather than process.

I am always eager to have my consciousness raised and brought to better awareness where it seems sleepy or uninformed. However, I reserve the right to consider all opinions and sides to anything and them take responsibility for what opinion I form. This then remains firm but not fixed. I hope to always be available to new information; new ways of being and thinking of a thing. In either a counseling session or a supervisory session, if my view seems to be getting in the way, I first take it to my consultant. If the countertransference is still in the way, then I let the person working with me know and we see what would be best to do. Actually this is an ongoing part of our mutual dialogue together and is rarely a situation that demands formal confronting. Yet that is available if it should be necessary. I was taught in an AAMFT accredited program as well as in my general counseling studies before that, this is ethical process. Further, my training was centered around knowing myself, my own issues and possible countertransferences and how to work with those.

I am obviously not a big fish. But now that one such has written perhaps it would be alright for a small fish to respond in support of what Friedman has said. I like AAMFT. I am delighted to be a member of the family and growing into greater responsibility within it. It would be a considerable sadness and loss to me if the organization moved in such a way that I could no longer subscribe to what I see as a content-based code of thinking and practice. Even if the people so-moving hold opinions that are congruent with those I hold, or if they are not, my hope would be that the leaders of the system would embrace (not just allow) differences as part of a healthy process. Unlike Friedman I don't suppose I am particularly Bowenian although I do enjoy and practice according to many of his theories and suppositions. Perhaps like Friedman, I am glad that I am free to do so.

Joan Eddy Waldo, M.S.

What characterizes differentiation for me, is that it is a process in nature and evolution where the en-

tity that survives is the one that responds to the world it lives in by having a large enough repertoire of different responses to deal with constantly changing conditions.

Consistent with Bowen's broad-based Natural Systems theory, the perspective for this set of responses can be that of one member of a species on a daily basis, or that of the species as a whole for many generations, or both.

To limit the scope of awareness of the range of differences, critically limits the range of possible responses, which then compromises development and survival. For the human, a useful variable to monitor in this regard is the extent of self focus. The more dealing with anxiety provoked by differences, is other-focused, the narrower is the overall perspective, the more limited the options and the lower the probability of survival. With self as primary reference for orientation to the other, the higher is the probability of adaptive response in the face of differences, precisely because the perspective is large enough to include self.

The learning objective of the SC requiring a focus on contextual variables, is such an other-based orientation. A focus on differences of race, gender and ethnicity as manifestations of the dynamics of family systems is certainly useful; the problem is with the requirement of a focus on the other in terms of these specified differences. Well-intentioned compliance with the requirement can lead to a pseudo cultural sensitivity, with distortions of seeing people of different races and gender from self, either as all the same in their difference among themselves, or as too sharply different from self. What is missing from these polarized distortions, is a self focus from which one can organize a perception of similarities and differences based on a much more comprehensive perspective A position on cultural differences consistent with a specific concept in Bowen theory, might be one that includes the self as part of the larger societal emotional process.

My intention here is the same as Friedman's, namely, to present another valid viewpoint. In addition, I would like to point out that this is not the first time I have taken a position with AAMFT around differences in supervision. While that was in reference to live supervision, the issue of differences and of consistency with Bowen theory is the very same.

It seems to me the challenge in this conflict about

the learning objective, is for each supervisor and for the SC as a whole, to deal with such differences of position within a framework of learning as collegial supervisors.

Thomas Schur, M.S.W.

Endorsing the Current Contextual Emphasis

I believe Friedman has gone a bit overboard in his interpretation of the intent of the committee. It sounds as if you merely added a learning objective to the already rich supervision curriculum.

Friedman implies that you are imposing a contextual and only a contextual training to the curriculum. To deny contextual variables, to me, seems to be short-sighted and somewhat monolithic in approach. Mr. Friedman states that culture is "the medium through which family process works its art." It is clear that he believes that therapy emanates from "what all emotional systems have in common with all proto-plasms since creation." I wish that therapy or the meaning of human feelings and behaviors were so simple as protoplasm.

I work in an inner-city community mental health center; contextual variables are a constant part of our work here. It is an important part to the clinical practice with clients as well as with supervisees. What one person accepts as a strength, another may see as a weakness. I am also profoundly awakened to the differences in meaning that people of other genders and races give to the emotional issues that Friedman seems to think to be common in all protoplasm. They do not seem to be common in all human beings. I agree with White that much of what distresses us in therapy is the meaning "that we give to the stories of our lives." These meanings are often contextual. To avoid this as part of the curriculum would be to avoid richness in supervisees' training. I encourage you to keep this in the curriculum.

Carol R. Zimmerman, M.S.

Friedman's views raise some important questions regarding the nature and purpose of clinical supervision. In challenging one learning objective, he has called the entire enterprise of regulating supervision into question. Unfortunately, his reactivity has the potential to bring any discussion down to the level of emotional responses and defensiveness rather than raise the discussion to a dialogue about the purposes

and goals that govern the supervisory enterprise within AAMFT.

Friedman's arguments about context as he derives them from Bowenian theory had best be challenged from within that intellectual framework by a fellow "believer". What is challengeable from within the community of supervisors is the assumption that raising issues of context is representative of a political agenda being imposed upon supervisors by the SC. If anything is being imposed, it is an understanding of the Approved Supervisor's (AS) responsibility to those aspiring to clinical membership (CM) in AAMFT and the ethos of that organization.

The AS designation is not a mark of superior clinical status. Unfortunately, it is seen that way by many for whom there is no other recognition of advanced clinical competence in AAMFT. It has been my understanding that the AS is someone who has acquired knowledge and skill in the area of clinical pedagogy in order to provide the required mentoring necessary for CM. In most states, supervision leading to certification or licensure need only be done by someone so certified or licensed. However, AAMFT has gone beyond this in order to insure that its CMs receive a broad base of understanding and practice of MFT.

The first learning objective for supervisors-in-training states that they will be familiar with the major models of MFT. From this supervisees articulate their own model. This implies that supervision in a particular model does not preclude understanding and use of other models. This is not to propose an eclecticism, but rather gives supervisees the opportunity to own and articulate their own positions. The espousal of or exclusive use of one model in the training of therapists is not being challenged by these learning objectives. However, it can be expected that supervisors be knowledgeable about theoretical systems other than their own. The entire set of learning objectives for the preparation of supervisors appear to be directed toward developing critical thinking and clarity about issues encountered in therapy and supervision. A clear argument about the irrelevance of context in treatment is not the same as failing to address issues around differences between persons. The SC appears to have said that it expects contextual variables to be addressed, not that a politically correct position be adopted.

Rather than eliminate the goal of sensitivity to contextual variables in supervision, it would seem advantageous to stress the need for greater sensitivity. Certainly such sensitivity is necessary to understand the dogmatism and proof-texting exhibited by Friedman in his letter to the SC. Perhaps, the SC might add to learning goal #7 an additional variable so that it reads, "Approved Supervisors are sensitive to contextual variables such as culture, gender, ethnicity, economics, and systems theory."

Ronald J. Cebik, Ed.D.

I have just read Friedman's protestation of the SC's recent decision to make contextual issues a necessary part of supervision. I strongly agree with his argument that conducting "all supervisory practice under one perspective runs the risk of turning the AAMFT into exactly the kind of poorly differentiated family we are always trying to help," and I appreciate his valuing of difference and personal responsibility in approaching the practice of family therapy and supervision. But just as strongly I believe that a supervisor of systems therapists should be accountable to his or her own ethnocentric purview and encourage the same accountability in supervisees, irrespective of model or theoretical orientation. Therefore, I agree with the SC's mandate to integrate social categories into models of supervision.

I have been guided in my own formation as a therapist and supervisor by Bowen theory but I have found it increasingly unsatisfactory to dismiss the importance of the social categories that Bowen's theory purports to transcend. The artistry of family life is a complex mixture of culture and reactivity that is fueled by emotional forces within and between individuals. Take, for example, a Puerto Rican family in which all members of the family talk simultaneously with rising volume, each trying to make his or her point with great gusto. Is this social pattern more culture or more reactivity? Or is it both? Can these be separated? Should they be? Keeping these questions in mind guards against the tendency to pathologize that which is unfamiliar or to privilege our own particular brand of cultural knowledge above others.... I am involved with students and clients as they construct their genograms and develop an understanding of the intergenerational transmission processes in their families. Hundreds of genograms representing multiple cultures have provided me a level of certainty that the profound workings of the emotional system are sufficient to explain human functioning; but I be-

lieve that the ability to appreciate the complexity of functioning and the different forms the same process can take requires pursuing the particulars of difference.

Responsible family systems training and supervision depends on staying in touch with this tension between sameness and difference, in developing a curiosity for what is common to us all, and for what is unique and different in the ways we experience our commonalities. The heart of my disagreement with Friedman is as follows: reactivity is shaped both by a lack of differentiation and by culture. To believe otherwise is to become trapped in our own particular set of biases. Therefore, in supervision we have a better chance of understanding our reactivity by considering some of the gender, ethnic, racial or other cultural dynamics at play.

Let me give an example which illustrates my understanding. A few days ago I watched a videotaped session with my supervisee. She battled with her client, encouraging him to express his feelings of hurt and pain while he sat in closed-off silence. After several pained minutes of struggle she gave up in exasperation. Her client then proceeded to express anger, berating her for pushing him so hard. She sat paralyzed, and then the session was over. The fusion between them in this societally sanctioned gendered "dance" was all too familiar to me and to my supervisee. It was helpful and (I believe) necessary for us to talk about the anxiety-driven process between herself and her client and to understand this process in the context of the gendered scripts they were enacting-all this towards understanding her own reactivity, increasing her neutrality, and defining her self more responsibly as a therapist.

This brings me to Friedman's own choice phrase that "culture [is] the medium through which family process works its art." Culture gives us our basic sense of belonging, an understanding of the ways we fit into the smaller and bigger pictures of the world. I am not an artist but as one who appreciates art I acknowledge its power to challenge and shape my perspectives. As therapists we must have an appreciation for the importance of culturally defined perspectives as we perceive the brush strokes on the canvas of the lives of the families with whom we work. I believe that the training and practice of family therapy must emphasize both the art and the science of human functioning. Through insisting on the integration of contextual variables into all of the models of family therapy, the Committee is supporting the integration of these aspects of responsible clinical work.

Michelle Naden, Ph.D.

Casting a Larger Net

I would like to cast a larger net in relation to my perspective. It is my experience in reading and utilizing literature from psychology and psychiatry that practice and theoretical development occurs through a democratic and scholarly process from research and theory building to a consensus within the field. ...MFT seems to use personal, executive or committee fiat. I am not aware of sufficient research or a tenable professional consensus process in our field. This leads to alienation within our ranks and lessens our credibility to other professions. However your recent interest in asking fellow supervisors their views may be signaling a change.

So my larger net wonders how is it that contextual variables are a requirement? Also how it is that a "systems" perspective is required? I realize I could be seen as questioning God, country, motherhood and the like, but how do these "requirements" come about? By research? Professional consensus formation? I think not. There has been a political professional boundary marking quality to all of this. I believe (Is this the realm of belief or thinking?) any respectable clinician needs to value and appreciate interactional and contextual variables. I have come to this on the basis of my values more than anything scientific. So what is the process by which we come to these decisions?

From where I sit, if the decision-makers are elected they need to do a better job representing the membership of the supervision community. If the decision-makers are appointed more of a democratic and professional development atmosphere needs to guide your work. As we are all supervisors our views are equal and nonhierarchical. We should expect that from those who value feminist, gender sensitive human interactions. May we continue to be asked, invited to vote and together arrive at what good therapy and supervision looks like.

Richard Wendel, D.Min.

More on the Contextual Learning Objective Debate: Objective Supports Our Democratic Ideals

Monica McGoldrick, Ph.D.

Published in the AAMFT Supervision Bulletin, Vol. VIII, No. 1, Spring 1995.

I was extremely distressed by Edwin Friedman's letter *(see "Dear Supervision Committee" article earlier in this chapter)* challenging the organization's commitment to equal rights. Friedman seems to be confusing a theoretical issue for an ethical one. He claims that the theory of Murray Bowen justifies ignoring inequalities related to gender, race, class, and sexual orientation in his work and in his supervision. This shows a basic confusion of levels of discourse. The issue here is equal rights not a monopoly on theoretical approaches. The Supervision Committee (SC) has been evaluating prospective supervisors to be sure their work reflects nondiscrimination regarding race and culture. This subject is the very first issue mentioned in the AAMFT Code of Ethics: *1.1 Marriage and family therapists do not discriminate against or refuse professional service to anyone on the basis of race, gender, religion, national origin, or sexual orientation.*

This issue is, of course, fundamental to our nation's democratic principles. In 1954 in the Brown v. Board of Education decision the Supreme Court reminded us that there could be no such thing as equality if our schools were segregated. Only integration would provide true equal opportunity to all citizens.

Segregation has been a fact of the family therapy field as it has been of the other institutions of our nation. The leaders, the thinkers, and the students have been primarily white. In our literature, except when specific families of color were referred to, the experience of families discussed was the experience of white families. Human development was white human development, couples were white couples, genograms were genograms of white families and so forth. The norm unless otherwise indicated was white, making people of color invisible. And so it is extremely important that the AAMFT, like other educational and professional institutions of our society, has developed ethical standards to remind us all of the importance of values of nondiscrimination for the survival of a democracy. This issue is so fundamental that it is hard to fathom Friedman's comparing the AAMFT's upholding this anti-discriminatory policy to monopolistic totalitarianism or the Inquisition. By describing efforts to counter gender, racial or class bias as promoting only one perspective, Friedman is not defending Bowen theory, but rather opposing the democratic ideals of our society.

He is confusing different theories of systems change with ethics and guarantees of equality and respect for others of our professional associates. Bowen theory does indeed address societal issues. In fact, Bowen waxed eloquent on the subject of societal regression and even spoke frequently about the applicability of his theory to international politics. His theory focuses on issues of differentiation as applied to the processes of all living systems, which includes societal systems as well as families and includes gender, race, and all other issues. Patterns of bias such as racism, sexism, or classism can be well understood using Bowen theory. There is no contradiction between the ideas of Bowen and the AAMFT ensuring that its prospective supervisors or members, for that matter, follow the organization's ethical standards regarding anti-discrimination. Thus, the assertion that Bowen theory does not address the social context is no excuse for a therapist within our organization not to be held accountable for practicing nondiscriminatory behavior. But, in any case, even if Bowen did say, "We just don't see racism as relevant to our clinical work," the ethical standards of the AAMFT to counter discrimination in clinical practice would require them to hold Bowen therapists to the ethics of the profession. Silence about segregation that exists in our field is discriminatory and it behooves the AAMFT to hold us all accountable for striving toward nondiscrimination and to justify how we are trying to do this.

Friedman says if the AAMFT espouses this value it is subservient to specific political interests. Of course its values reflect specific political interests, namely the democratic values of our society. If prospective supervisors do not have to demonstrate that they are not discriminatory, the AAMFF would be ignoring issues of discrimination. There is no neutral ground. There is no such thing as not espousing any values. As Bowen himself has taught us, silence does not fool an emotional system. Silence supports the status quo.

The only way to know that AAMFT members are not practicing in discriminatory ways is to educate them to be aware of the subtle ways discrimination is perpetuated in our society and encourage them to be attentive to nondiscriminatory values in their practice. This is how we convey all our professional standards: we teach supervisees the values, just as we teach our children the values of democracy, justice, and respect for the rights of others.

"Are We Color Blind?": Contextual Variables Influence Supervision

Cheryl L. Storm, Ph.D.

Published in the AAMFT Supervision Bulletin, Vol. V, No. 3, November 1992.

Recently, I asked my supervisees to bring to group supervision a videotaped therapy excerpt in which their clients were of a different race, ethnic, cultural or socioeconomic background than themselves. After watching five minutes of one of the supervisees' tapes, I asked: What do you notice? One by one the supervisees described the interaction in terms of ways the therapist joined with the client by such actions as smiling, leaning forward to listen, etc. Frankly, I was shocked. The first thing I noticed was that I was watching a female white therapist working with a white mother and her two children of color.

At first, I questioned my own attitudes and values. Was I racist? Were my supervisees truly "color-blind"? When it came to my turn, I shared what I first noted. There was momentary silence and then several supervisees admitted they too had noticed the differences in race between therapist and clients. I learned that my supervisees were, like me, unsure about wether to directly address the differences or to ignore them. I learned that my supervisees were comfortable talking about contextual variables such as race when their clients brought it up, but did not feel comfortable introducing them as significant influences. As a supervisor, I wondered how to address our collective confusion.

Ironically, when we turned our attention back to the case we discovered the presenting problem was that the mother felt her children were being treated unfairly by the school because they were of mixed race! In this case, the mother made the "difference" central.

Response

Michele Weiner-Davis, M.S.W.

Published in the AAMFT Supervision Bulletin, Vol. VI, No. 1, Winter 1993.

I felt inspired to write to you regarding your lead article, "Are we color-blind?" To me there was an obvious reason your supervisees didn't mention the racial differences between client and therapist. You asked your supervisees to show a tape of clients who were of a different race-that was already a given.

Try it again with different supervisees. Show them a tape of a client and therapist with different racial backgrounds without introducing it and then see if more supervisees "notice" and comment on the differences.

Chapter 9

Supervision-of-Supervision

Increased Responsibility for Preparing Supervisors: Preventing Supervisees from Experiencing the Kiss of Death

Cheryl Storm, Ph.D.

Published in the AAMFT Supervision Bulletin, Vol. 9, No. 1, Summer 1996.

In my opinion, gone are the days when supervisors could, for the most part, target supervisees' clinical work as the focus of supervision, leaving the remainder of supervisees' professional responsibilities out of their supervision equation. Instead, I believe our changing professional world has significantly increased supervisors' responsibility for proactively preparing their supervisees for the professional context. For example, because I live in a state where managed care drives public as well as a large part of private funding of mental health, therapists who do not have the competency to work within the larger context of managed care will not survive. In fact, I personally know of two therapists who have outstanding clinical skills (in large part due to the excellent supervision they received), but have been fired from local agencies because they could not manage the documentation required by their work context and became an expensive cog in the organizational wheel. Out of work and seen as the kiss of death for any public agency, but with similar business oriented skills required of them in the private practice world, these clinicians are in danger of remaining permanently unemployed. During their supervision experience these therapists did not learn to effectively balance the documentation responsibilities of their work settings with their love for clinical work. As one of several supervisors of such a therapist, I am painfully aware of my part in not providing appropriate preparation for the current professional world and the need for my supervision to change at all levels—with my supervisees and with my supervisors-in-training— to expand my equation of what constitutes supervision.

Supervisors of supervisors-in-training have long recognized that there are several distinctive aspects of supervising supervisors versus therapists, creating collaborative supervisory relationships, managing multiple levels, highlighting gatekeeping responsibilities and developing supervisors' philosophies of supervision (Storm, Todd, McDowell, & Sutherland, in press). The latter seems to me to be enlarged by our increasing responsibility to prepare supervisees for the evolving professional context. Currently, when I supervise supervisors-in-training, I find myself spending increasing amounts of time focusing on how their supervisees are being prepared for the therapy world of the '90s by considering the wider professional context, expanding their gatekeeping role and developing theories of supervision that encompass the whole professional context.

Adding a Level of Consideration

Managing the levels of the client whether individual, couple or family; the therapist; the supervisor-in-training; and the supervisor of supervision has long been recognized as an integral aspect of the complexity of supervision of supervision (Storm et al., in press; Wright & Coppersmith, 1982). Recently, considering so many levels has become even more complex because supervisors of supervision have to further expand their views of the supervision system by including the larger professional context more carefully and intentionally in their supervision. When one of my supervisors-in-training describes her supervision of one of her supervisee's cases, we both have to consider the context in which supervision and therapy occurs. Is the supervisee able to develop a treatment plan that reflects clear family therapy goals *and* fulfills the organization's requirements for funding? Will their files pass quality control reviews? If the supervisee is struggling in this arena, how can my supervisor-in-training help him/her obtain competency in this crucial area? Supervisors who understand their supervisees' work settings, which are increasingly becoming organizationally based, while keeping in mind the wider professional context may prevent the creation of a generation of unemployed clinicians like those cited earlier.

Expansion of the Gatekeeper's Role

Supervisors-in-training, who are often initially uncomfortable with their evaluative role, but who expand their gatekeeping function beyond the idea of evaluating their supervisees' clinical competency (and only cursory evaluation of their case management abilities) to include evaluation of their supervisees' overall professional competency, engage more frequently in important discussions with their supervisees about what it means to be a marriage and family therapist in today's professional climate. This requires that supervisors-in-training expand their data points regarding their supervisees' work performance beyond what they see clinically to how their supervisees interface their clinical work with their other responsibilities. Relevant issues include assessing how supervisees relate to representatives of outside organizations such as managed care companies who control the treatment dollar, how they cope with the increased emphasis on time limited therapy and whether they are developing skills to create specific treatment plans with clear understandable objectives that non-therapists can comprehend.

In addition, the American Association for Marriage and Family Therapy's (AAMFT) new procedures for processing Approved Supervisors' applications, also increases the supervisors role as gatekeeper for the profession. If the supervisor approaches the task of reviewing articulation by supervisors-in-training of their supervision philosophies and case illustrations with "a nod and a wink" rather than taking the responsibility to keep the gate seriously, the supervisor is helping to prepare supervisors-in-training who may not be ready to mentor the next generation of professionals. Such behavior does a real disservice to their supervisees.

Developing Theories of Supervision Which Encompass the Whole Profession

Supervisors of supervision who encourage their supervisors-in-training to develop supervision philosophies that encompass the whole profession will be more helpful in assisting supervisors-in-training to pre-

pare supervisees for their professional context than those whose theories of supervision are more limited. In my experience, it is not uncommon for supervisors-in-training to address in their philosophy statements how a particular preferred therapy theory is used to guide their supervision and to train their supervisees to practice from that same approach in therapy. The issue, in my opinion, is not what is there, but what is not. Expanding our theories of supervision to include ideas about assisting supervisees in the other areas of their professional development (e.g., emphasizing the inter-connection of clinical work and case management) is important to insure that the clients whom they serve and the organizations in which they work get what they need for a job well done. Examples of areas that could be included in expanded philosophies include: The assumptions that supervisors-in-training have about what types of competency novice therapists need to have to survive in today's professional world; ways they help their supervisees gain this competency; ways we help supervisees deal both clinically and with therapeutic integrity with limitations on resources.

A Challenge Mandate for Supervisors of Supervision

Many of us have fewer discretionary hours in our work lives and fewer dollars to devote to spending on our own professional development. Thus, singly and collectively figuring out how to be innovative in our work as supervisors of supervision in meeting these increasing supervisory responsibilities of preparing supervisees for the professional world of the '90s is truly a challenging mandate. A further issue concerns the question of how we take on the responsibility when our own professional world is also changing rapidly in similar ways.

References

Storm, C., Todd, T., & Sutherland, T. (in press). Supervising supervisors. In T. Todd & C. Storm (Eds.), *The complete systemic supervisor: Context, philosophy, and pragmatics.* Needham Heights: Allyn & Bacon.

Wright, L., & Coppersmith, E. (1982). Supervision of supervision: How to be "meta" to a metaposition. *Journal of Strategic and Systemic Therapies, 2,* 40-50.

Developing the Person of the Supervisor: An Approach to Training

Pieter le Roux, D. Litt. et Phil.

Published in the AAMFT Supervision Bulletin, Vol. 10, No. 1, Summer 1997.

The transition to becoming a family therapy supervisor is a profound learning experience: it extends clinical responsibility to a broader educational responsibility. Supervisors-in-Training should develop a view of this responsibility that goes beyond their clinical training and theoretical preferences.

An important educational challenge, therefore, is to help Supervisors-in-Training develop a new level of integration that will encompass this broader view of their clinical and educational task. Increasingly supervisors need skills to function in multiple clinical settings. This includes the ability to work collaboratively with different professionals within the health and community care system (Liddle & Breunlin, 1988; Seabum, Lorenz, Gunn & Gawlnski, 1996). Enhancing and maintaining professional standards, while also crystallizing an individualized professional self, may be the ultimate goal for supervision training. Many factors can contribute to the achievement of this goal, such as the acquisition of a well-developed theoretical frame, the influence of lived experiences (White & Epston, 1990), trends within the health care system, ethical considerations, and professional knowledge and skills training.

The person of the supervisor seems to be a key variable for maintaining successful long term, as well as flexible supervision and training. Awareness of the role of one's personal narrative and the place of family of origin issues (McDaniel & Landau-Stanton, 1992a) in constructing such a narrative is central in the process of continuing self research and education about the person of the supervisor. Understanding the relevance of a life review (Cohler, 1991) improves the ability to view one's self in the context of both life cycle and professional developments.

In addition, Supervisors-in-Training usually have well-developed notions about their theoretical preferences. Conceptual frames (McDaniel, Weber & McKeever; 1983) guide the way in which practitioners approach clinical situations. Understanding the specific development (Stanton, 1992) of their preferred conceptual view is an important educational task in supervision training. Even integrated approaches are the products of selectivity. Understanding the selective process helps Supervisors-in-Training to form a broader viewpoint of how conceptual frames develop. This is similar to understanding the development and evolution of beliefs in one's family of origin. The history of one's preferred conceptual frame is the result of many educational and personal influences. Supervisors-in-Training usually benefit from exploring the nature of the developments that lead to their preferred conceptual frame. It helps to appreciate and respect diversity in clinical practice, and it helps trainees to develop skills to articulate a preferred model of supervision and therapy.

Supervisors often work at the confluence of clinical complexity and the organizational structure of different work-place settings. Providing a structure in which themes such as the context of the supervisor, supervisee, agency, and family (Liddle & Breunlin, 1988) can be understood as well as themes such as gender, culture, ethnicity and economics are an integral part of developing the person of the supervisor.

The person of the supervisor is also closely related to his or her ethical stance. Ethics are imbedded in constructive interpersonal relationships are central to the development of each profession and professional. Supervisors-in-Training have experienced a range of ethical and probably unethical behaviors during their own personal and professional development. Developing an awareness of how these experiences shaped their behavior can form a critical part of personal development.

This approach to supervision training, which helps Supervisors-in-Training to systematically review key factors related to the person of the supervisor, was developed at the University of Rochester Family Therapy Training Program (McDaniel & Landau-Stanton, 1992b). It emphasizes a long term perspective towards human systems development (le Roux,

1992), the relevance of intergenerational patterns across systems (McDaniel & Landau-Stanton, 1992a) and the nature of organizational growth (Greiner, 1972) as related to the person of the supervisor.

References

Cohler, B. J. (1991). The life story and the study of resilience and response to diversity. *New England Symposium: Narrative studies in the social sciences, 1(2-3),* 169–200.

Greiner, L.E. (1972). Evolution and revolution as organizations grow. *Harvard Business Review,* July/August, pp. 37–46.

Liddle, H. A., Breunlin, D. C., & Schwartz, R. C. (Eds.). (1988). *Handbook of family therapy training and supervision.* New York: Guilford Press.

le Roux, P. (1992). Diversity and dialogue: The healing narrative. In I. Mason, J. Rubinstein, & S. Shuda (Eds.), *From diversity to healing.* SAIMEF, Durban, Belmore, p. 36-48.

McDaniel, S. H., & Landau-Stanton, J. (1992). Family therapy skills training and family of origin work: Both-and. *Family Process, 30, 459–471.*

McDaniel, S.H., & Landau-Stanton, J.(1992b). The University of Rochester family therapy training program. *American Journal of Family Therapy, 20, 361–365.*

McDaniel, S., Weber, T., & McKeever, J. (1983). Multiple theoretical approaches to supervision: Choices in family therapy training. *Family Process, 22,(4),* 491–499.

Seabum, D.B., Lorenz, A., Gum, W., & Gawiuski, B. A. (1996). *Models of collaboration: A guide for family therapists practicing with health care professionals.* New York: Basic Books.

Stanton, M.D. (1992). The time line and the "Why now?" question: A technique and rationale for therapy, training, organizational consultation and research. *Journal of Marital and Family Therapy,* 18, 331–343.

White, M. & Epston, D. (1990) *Narrative means to therapeutic ends.* New York: W. W. Norton.

Fostering Creativity in the Supervisory Process

D. Ray Bardill, Ph.D.

Published in the AAMFT Supervision Bulletin, Vol. 10, No. 3, Winter 1998.

Applicants for the Approved Supervisor Designation are required to illustrate their philosophy of supervision through written case study material that describes a supervisory experienced with one therapist. An organizing purpose of the written case study material is to demonstrate the correlation between the way the applicant thinks about therapy and the way supervision is actually provided.

The purpose of this article is to aid Approved Supervisors with the process of helping their supervisors-in-training (SITs) prepare the Supervision Case Study part of their applications for the Approved Supervisor designation. This particular presentation will focus on the requirement that applicants describe: *Your supervisory interventions that create a supportive learning environment and foster the development and creativity of the therapist rather than fostering imitation of the supervisor. (AAMFT, 1997, p.16).*

The article will therefore suggest three themes, or ideas, that may be considered and integrated into the written Supervision Case Study material. First, what are some of the essential qualities of the above creativity/imitation objective; second, what organizing purpose does the creativity/imitation objective support; and third, what are some enabling objectives the Approved Supervisor may use in helping the SIT prepare the case study material?

The creativity/imitation objective addresses two of the most fundamental dynamics in the supervisory process. The first dynamic speaks to the creation of a supportive learning atmosphere. How does one create a supportive learning atmosphere? What are the considerations vital to the creation of such a supervisory context? As SIT, what do I do with the therapist that will have a high probability of opening him/her to the learning process? How does the supervisor invite the creation of a supportive learning atmosphere?

The second dynamic speaks to fostering creative rather than imitative learning. The importance of understanding the second dynamic for the Approved Supervisor/SIT/therapist/client set of relationships is matched only by the dynamic's immense complexity. For instance, it is said that imitation is the highest form of flattery one person can give to another. Are not supervisors pleased when they see a supervisee emulate one of the supervisor's favorite ideas, approaches or tactics? Indeed, all of us know that the gurus of family therapy have a long list of followers who emulate them in one way or the other. The supervisor's tendency to want supervisees to imitate him or her represents an important consideration.

It may be useful to note that in the early stages of an average supervisory situation the therapist will tend to emulate the work of the supervisor. As supervision progresses the strengths of the therapist will emerge into his/her own creative thinking and doing. For example, it may be recalled that Freud's students Alfred Adler and Carl Jung moved from emulating Freud into their own creative ideas and practices. As we know and teach, isomorphism is at play in the entire supervisory process. Much of what the supervisor says and does as part of supervision likely will be reflected in the work of the SIT. In a wonderful way, the creativity/imitation objective engages a fundamental paradox in the therapeutic process. The enabling objective here is the supportive supervisory atmosphere that openly invites the emergence of creativity on the part of the supervisee.

In the treatment context the therapist cannot avoid using his/her worldview, whatever it may be, in assisting the client to address his/her purpose for seeking therapeutic interventions. To put it another way, we cannot not have a way of thinking about the therapy process. We will use our way of thinking and doing even if our way of thinking and doing is to carefully avoid imposing our way of thinking on the client's problem-solving process. As therapy progresses the client uses his/her own creativity to try out the therapist's thinking and doing model as problems are addressed and hopefully resolved.

In what is a paradox, the therapist (insert Approved Supervisor, or SIT here, if appropriate) will use a specific worldview to seek clarification about the client's (SIT's or therapist's) thinking, feelings and actions. Ideally, there is no attempt to impose a world view on the creativity of the client. The client simply uses the therapist's worldview as a screen to discover his/her inner strengths and creativity. The dynamics of the creativity/imitation paradox of a close examination of the client's worldview from the therapist's worldview provides an essential change element in both therapy and supervision. Alternative ways of thinking and doing are encouraged. A broader perceptual view is opened which may suggest new ways to give meaning to old patterns.

The enabling objectives are energized when the Approved Supervisor has encouraged many straightforward discussions about the creativity/imitation paradox in the process of therapy. Additionally the Approved Supervisor will have enabled the SIT to engage this same issue in the Case Study material.

Finally, it is important to identify an implicit assumption in the creativity/imitation objective. Given the organizing thinking/doing purpose, the objective assumes that the SIT thinks that therapy takes place in a supportive environment that fosters unique and creative problem-solving by the client rather than one that fosters directives, intellectual explanations and subtle here-is-how-I-would-do-it pronouncements by the therapist. At least two actions flow from this assumption. First, the SIT will invite discussions about therapist interventions which were directives and hierarchical. Second, the SIT will openly engage the difficult task of promoting creativity within the bounds of the supervisory process. Again, inviting open and frank discussions about the paradox inherent in the creativity/imitation dynamic provides an opportunity to address a powerful issue in both the supervisory and treatment domains.

How does one create a supportive learning context? There are a number of considerations that are likely to contribute to the creation of a supportive learning atmosphere. One that is essential is the supervisor's conscious intention to establish a learning process that fosters development of the unique strengths of everyone involved. Translated into action, the intention becomes one that uses the supervisory process to discover, examine, and support human strengths, a nonjudgemental stance and accountability. The supervisor's commitment to a supportive process is critical to the learning process. The Approved Supervisor who has invited frank and open discussions about the elements involved in supportive learning environments will have provided the enabling dynamic for similar discussions between the SIT and the therapist.

Much like the treatment process, supervision can go only as far as the emotional maturity level of the Approved Supervisor and the SIT allows. The supportive learning atmosphere is greatly enhanced when all of the participants in the supervisory process personally engage the task of self-differentiation. Essentially, this means attention to the difference between emotional and thinking processes, maintaining a balance between our strong need to be a separate unique individual and our equally strong need to join with other human beings, and distinguishing between our self as the creator and the things we have created such as our values, priorities, beliefs, life stories, etc. The very process of our personal journey to higher levels of emotional maturity will be reflected in our ability to create supportive contexts.

The language of distinctions also seems valuable as an enabling theme for an examination of the creativity/imitation objective. Three items of distinction already have been mentioned including, the difference between purpose and objectives, the subtle and paradoxical difference between creativity and emulation, and the vital distinctions that are fundamental to the self-differentiation process. When SITs are invited to engage in distinction language, a wide range of creative possibilities for treatment, supervision and the preparation of case study material are brought forth—exactly what the SIT may find most useful.

At this point, it is useful to examine the creativity limitation objective within the overall purpose of the case study material. Objectives, by their very nature, must support a larger purpose. The purpose which guides the creativity/imitation objective is the effective use of case study material to show the correlation between the SIT's thinking about supervision and the way the supervision is actually provided (AAMFT, 1997, p. 15). This means that the creativity/imitation objective is to be framed in a context that demonstrates the congruence between the SIT's theoretical perspective and his/her professional actions. In other words, the organizing context is a thinking/doing purpose. The purpose invites frequent in-depth SIT-therapist discussions about the connection between what the therapist thinks and what he/she does in therapy. Direct and specific attention to the thinking that supports a therapist's clinical interventions enable the therapist not only to reflect on the connection between theory and practice but also to support a pattern of thinking about thinking and doing.

The case study material relevant to the creativity/imitation objective must be examined within the context of demonstrating congruency between SIT thinking and doing. In a real sense, the opportunity to distinguish between an organizing purpose and the objectives that support the purpose is consistent with systemically oriented thinking and doing. During the course of supervision the Approved Supervisor will have had many opportunities to give attention to SIT-therapist examinations of each client's purpose for seeking therapy and the treatment goals and objectives which support the client's purpose for treatment.

A supervisory context which has given strong attention to the distinction between an organizing purpose and supporting objectives in the treatment arena will assist the SIT to more powerfully address the creativity/imitation objective as part of the organizing thinking/doing purpose. Again, given the isomorphic nature of our work, the way the Approved Supervisor has approached issues relating to why a client has sought therapy and the way specific goals and objec-

tives are engaged in support of the purpose of therapy will likely be reflected in the SIT's supervision with the therapist.

In conclusion, given the isomorphic nature of the Approved Supervisor/SIT/therapist/client set of relationships it is axiomatic that the most powerful way the Approved Supervisor may help his/her SIT prepare the specific case study material is to personally model a supportive supervisory process that (1) fosters creativity and does not foster imitation and (2) consistently demonstrates congruence between his/her theory and practice. Processes which enable the Approved Supervisor to model such a supervisory process include in-depth discussions with the SIT about the paradoxical nature of the creativity/imitation objective, giving attention to the language of distinctions, attending to the dynamic of purpose in every case situation and frank and open attention to a commitment to creating a supportive learning atmosphere. Finally, it is useful to allow therapists to emulate the SIT at a beginning stage in the process of evolving his/her own unique thinking and doing strengths. The process of creativity is developmental and takes time to mature.

References

AAMFT (1997). Approved Supervisor designation standards and responsibilities handbook. Washington, D.C.: AAMFT.

Methods for Helping the Therapist Recognize His or Her Areas of Inexperience or Discomfort So That He or She Will Make Use of Supervision and Referral When Appropriate

Marcia D. Brown-Standridge, Ph.D.

Published in the AAMFT Supervision Bulletin, Vol. 10, No. 2, Fall 1997.

Four aspects of preparing the Supervisor-in-Training (SIT) may be considered salient for this guideline. First, methods for enhancing **supervisory relationships** will be examined. Second, techniques within common **supervisory modalities** will be discussed. Third, comparisons will be made between various **supervisory conceptualizations** in opening up new vistas for intervention. Finally, **supervisory parameters** will be explored for understanding the limitations of marriage and family therapy (MFT) expertise.

Explications of these four categories will feature conceptual and practical integrations consistent with the Philosophy of Supervision and Case Study sections of the Approved Supervisor application. The more the SIT can describe how internal struggles have been worked through by way of contacts with other professionals to clients' benefit, the more thoroughly this guideline will have been met.

Supervisory Relationships

Approved Supervisors can set the context for SITs to invite therapists' questions and concerns if conferences about uncertainties, fears, stumbling blocks and downright mistakes are rewarded with praise. Such openness can be understood as a marker of the developmental level of that relationship. Isomorphically, if the Approved Supervisor/SIT relationship is comfortable handling both awkwardness and finesse, confidence-building may be expected to cascade down the hierarchical chain of responsibility to the SIT/therapist relationship and the therapist/client system alliance.

The Approved Supervisor can track and highlight SIT progress in bringing about improvement in client functioning to past preparedness for supervisory sessions and the willingness to seek help. Once a single question or vague expression of discomfort becomes the key to unlocking a sound interventive strategy, there will be an incentive for venturing more of the same. Ratifying and utilizing SIT dilemmas begets a similar respect for the therapist which begets redirecting clients' puzzlements toward a case coming to fruition.

The Approved Supervisor can offer ongoing illustrations of how SIT's "stumbles" contribute to a "difference that makes a difference." This modeling should nurture the SIT's ability to notice characteristics of the therapist's participation that advance treatment. The SIT goal of delineating the pathway from ethereal supervisory assessment to interventive mastery should be kept foremost in mind. If languaging about predicaments, successes and their linkages is a regular part of supervisory interchange, writing about them later on in the Approved Supervisor application process will not seem like such a huge leap.

The following are questions and comments an Approved Supervisor can put to the SIT for the purpose of having him or her learn to draw out the therapist:

1. What direction are you planning for the case?

2. What are you thinking and feeling when the therapist ___?

3. This family organizes the direction of therapy by _____ How does that influence choices you see for the therapist intervention?

4. What about this case makes you feel confident? What kind of help would be most useful and at what critical times?

5. What client problems seem to go beyond your level of comfort or training?

6. What you do that really makes a difference is _____ What would happen if you engaged in more _____ and less _____?

Philosophy of Supervision

By applying the concept of isomorphism, the SIT notices that the therapist becomes speechless when confronted by a man whose wife has just announced she wants a divorce. The husband accuses the therapist of being incompetent. The SIT realizes the therapist is looking for help from behind the one-way mirror. Feeling frozen herself, she quickly seeks direction from the Approved Supervisor and calls in to disrupt the course of the session. This buys enough time for a three-way consult, resulting in the therapist joining with the husband over their mutual shock at this turn of events. Attention is then shifted to the wife for further explanation. During the post session, the decision making process is reviewed with special attention to keeping all levels of therapeutic relationship intact.

Case Study Example

During live supervision, a SIT notices that the therapist becomes speechless when confronted by a man whose wife has just announced she wants a divorce. The husband accuses the therapist of being incompetent. The SIT realizes the therapist is looking for help from behind the one way mirror. Feeling frozen herself, she quickly seeks direction from the Approved Supervisor and calls in to disrupt the course of the session. This buys enough time for a three-way consult, resulting in the therapist joining with the husband over their mutual shock at this turn of events Attention is then shifted to the wife for further explanation. During post-session, the decision-making process is reviewed with special attention to keeping all levels of therapeutic relationship intact.

Supervisory Modalities

The most common modalities for therapist/ supervisor training include case conference, audio/ video tape review and live supervision. Each provides variant opportunities for capitalizing upon trainees' inexperience and discomfort to the betterment of the case.

Case conferences lack the distraction of ongoing client interaction and afford an in-depth look at how the context is devised from the outset for therapeutic activity to occur. This modality allows the Approved Supervisor to evaluate the conceptual/practical knowledge base of the SIT, thereby suggesting that he or she behave similarly with the therapist. What can emerge here are roles in the routine planning of the case so as to encourage a more disciplinated tactic up front. Practice can involve eliciting what might be anticipated from reading intake information; what releases, consents, and contacts might be necessary to gather a complete picture of presenting problems; and what key people should ideally be included in conjoint sessions. Case conferences often require "clean up," compensating for what has not yet occurred, and correcting for patterns of relating that are interfering with recovery.

Audio/video tape review offers a post-hoc opportunity for slowing the process down, detecting client system patterns and their organizing influence on therapist decision making. SITs can be trained to observe how the therapist gets reined in to follow the status quo, misses potential turning points and neglects to notice or consolidate more productive client behavior. Similarly, it is a good exercise to accentuate therapist behaviors that positively work toward therapeutic gains. SITs may find role-play useful in rehearsing delivery of constructive critique.

Live supervision can surface unresolved tension in the Approved Supervisor/SIT/therapist relationships in a hurry. More "cooks" can actually "spoil the broth" in the rapid fire decision making that must occur in the therapeutic hour. Clearly defined roles and hierarchical channels along with pre-session planning, mid-session conferences and post session debriefing can ameliorate such problems. In general, SITs are allowed to begin orchestrating the sessions relatively early in their training with increased responsibility over time. Crisis situations that cannot be handled are naturally yielded to more senior supervision. SITs are expected to take a "meta" view of therapist-client communication, perturbing particularly troublesome sequences toward gainful change. The Approved Supervisor can serve to keep track of patterns of import, diminishing session "noise" and isolating questions which must be answered for a fail-safe treatment plan.

Philosophy of Supervision

By demonstrating an appreciation for the kinds of patterns that have materialized during supervision of supervision, the SIT can trace his or her own growth from a preoccupation with self to highlighting relational sequences that eventually alter the course of treatment. The more this growth can be substantiated as "contagious" to the therapist under the SIT's tutelage, the greater he or she can establish that a systems-oriented vision for relieving cases will be carried on to the next generation of practitioners.

Case Study Example

A male therapist is reportedly getting nowhere with a "depressed" wife and her "baffled" husband until the female Approved Supervisor hears the male SIT mention in case references the wife is often criticized by her mother-in-law, resulting in fairly constant arguments. Once the SIT catches on to the pattern of the husband becoming more and more passive rather than allying with his wife, therapeutic focus shifts from scapegoating the wife's "symptom" to what the husband can now do to convince his mother that he is serious about strengthening his marriage—with a full expectation that she will follow suit.

Supervisory Conceptualizations

For any given case, it can be useful for SITs to use complementary theoretical lenses to develop strategy for consideration by the therapist. There is ample precedent for comparing at least two distinct lenses for heuristic purposes. These include the contrasting orientations of stressing historical patterns as having an impact on growth, versus a "here and now" inclination that focuses on interactive sequences in the present. The intent is not to foster procedures with an inconsistent or all too "eclectic" approach but rather to unearth the limitations inherent in each perspective. Such a "bifocal" punctuation may uncover unanswered questions about the connection present behavior has with more longstanding, transgenerational roots and about the nature of what could be preventing change. Also, the SIT may find it easier to articulate what has been missing in his or her "game plan" if these distinctions are delineated.

Therapy training will typically place primary significance on the practitioner getting his or her bearings by exploring clients' notions of either past, present or future. The latter focus is a more recent development and suggests that a "trifocal" view may be derived in supervision. Past-oriented conceptualizations include in-depth, growth bound approaches [e.g. Object Relational, Experiential and Transgenerational (Bowenian and Contextual) rationales], while present-oriented conceptualizations encompass schools of thought that are expected to take effect in a relatively brief period of time (e.g. Ericksonian, Structural and Strategic frames of reference). Future-oriented (e.g. Solution-Focused) conceptualizations concentrate more on meeting goals quickly that on understanding history or comprehending presenting problems as prerequisites to that end.

Some friction is very likely to occur in Approved Supervisor/SIT/therapist relationships when orientations differ by virtue of previous exposure to variant training assumptions. As well, allegiance or identification with particular belief systems can wreak havoc with a unified tactic. It can be advantageous to unfold potentially conflicting postures before they interfere with client care. Opening communication channels to be inclusive of multiple vantage points increases the probability of adopting a common vocabulary, enriches the knowledge base available for designing treatment, and engenders mutual respect.

Philosophy of Supervision

Once SITs can distinguish their own positioning by grounding it in MFT literature and delineating what has been found to work (or fail) across therapist and clinical situations, a more persuasive argument can be made that there has been an adequate identity formation to become an Approved Supervisor. The ability to launch from one's own training into a connection with the therapist's *modus operandi* is crucial to expanding options and broadening viewpoints. Clients can only be helped by this kind of scope.

Case Study Example

Both the therapist and the SIT concede they are stymied in trying to treat a domestic violence case by attending solely to here-and-now patterns of spousal communications. Upon further questioning, it emerges that the husband reportedly has been unemployed for months due to his heavy drinking. Also, his mother-in-law has reportedly thrown him out of her domicile so that his wife and children can live with her in peace. He is said to be living in the woods and is now motivated to seek a sponsor through Alcoholics Anonymous. A critical piece of the puzzle is the wife's clarification that they only have violence problems when he is actually drinking, so if he "really cares" about her he will "just quit."

The Approved Supervisor prompts the SIT to have the therapist ask whether there is a cross-generational aspect to the alcohol abuse and to trace the husband's circumstances when he first began to drink. The man recalls that at age 12 he participated in a "drunken orgy" with all the male adults of the family who danced on his grandfather's grave at the time of burial. This is described as having been a veritable rite of passage for entry into adulthood, one that honored the deceased for his capacity to out-drink them all. Such a first time revelation prods his wife to comment that, between the two of them, they are going to need everything that family therapy, medicine, AA and Al-Anon have to offer combined to bolster his resolve to break free from the pull of that kind of deadly game. The SIT and therapist rework the case around the husband's differentiation from destructive messages rooted in his family of origin and the spouses' mutual coordination with AA.

Supervisory Parameters

From the outset of every case, Approved Supervisors should instill in SITs the discipline of marshaling all relevant professionals to assist in client care. Discussion of what constitutes relevance or sound liability protection should be the common grist of the mill across all supervisory modalities. Ideally, therapists should be directed to discern, during the first session, what systems are impinging on the client family and what subsequent contacts need to be made. Signing papers is routine at that time. Trying later to get releases signed for consults becomes more cumbersome and appears unprofessional

Physicians, nurses, attorneys, teachers, guidance counselors, probation/parole officers, state welfare workers, the clergy, and former therapists are examples of outsiders whose knowledge base and assessment may be brought to bear in case planning. It is not unusual to find out that multiple therapists may be attempting to meet the needs of different family members. Specialized testing may be called for in determining drug/alcohol use or the presence of learning disabilities Depending on state legalities, MFTs may be restricted from offering diagnostics or assessment tools that are in their realm of expertise. Ultimately, the Approved Supervisor is responsible for clarifying the boundaries of the MFT profession in a particular locale.

SITs and therapists alike can benefit from simple exercises in which they are urged to think like an efficient detective, figuring out from isolated clues which high-priority contacts must minimally be secured to gain "big picture" information. Strategies brainstormed are then chosen for their MFT advantage and rejected when violating other professionals authority.

Philosophy of Supervision

The more the SIT can verify increased maneuverability in treatment as a result of referral and coordination with other professionals' skills, the greater his or her competence will be perceived in case planning and direction.

Case Study Example

A wife continues in individual treatment after her husband has dropped out of marital treatment for "constant" arguments. The therapist steers her toward more assertive behavior with her husband and toward seeking a job so that she will be less financially dependent on him. During videotape review, the SIT focuses on the wife's passing comment that she is often out of breath. The therapist is advised to have her see an internist. The physician concludes that the client's rheumatic fever as a child has irreparably damaged her heart and recommends that she avoid employment of any kind. He offers to help her seek disability income but expresses doubt that she will meet new, more stringent eligibility criteria. The SIT and therapist confer about their constrained options but settle on refraining from constant conflict as no good for the wife's heart. This frame takes hold for both partners and the couple purportedly begin to choose their battles more sparingly.

Complexities in Supervision

Nancy Ratliff, Ph.D.

Published in the AAMFT Supervision Bulletin, Vol. 11, No. 2, Winter 1998.

Among several other dimensions, when writing the Supervision Case Study, the SIT is asked to describe: "Your recognition of the complexity of the Approved Supervisor/supervisor-in- training/therapist/client relationship" (AAMFT, 1997, p.16). In the MFT supervision literature, the multifaceted nature of supervision relationships has been called isomorphism. This concept can refer to five different aspects of the supervision relationship (White & Russell, 1997):

1. patterns that occur in the therapy session repeated in supervision, or vice versa (parallel process);

2. theoretical concepts of therapy translated into supervision (conceptual similarities);

3. similarities identified between the therapeutic process and supervision (process similarities);

4. interventions used in the supervisor-supervisee's relationship which have the potential of altering the supervisee's in session behavior (intervention);

5. similarities of the person when doing therapy and supervision (role consistency).

My emphasis is on being a therapeutic person in each context, the fifth aspect of isomorphism.

Indeed, when I think of the complexities of relationships in supervision of supervision, I think of how important my own supervision relationship was. Being a supervisee involved an incredible degree of trust and vulnerability. I remember how lost, overwhelmed, and unsure I felt as I began dealing with real people with real problems. Although I had many supervisors in my professional development, I think of only one or two persons who were "my supervisors." Supervision with those individuals helped me not only to learn techniques and theory, but also to become comfortable with the main tool of therapy: me. One supervisor in particular was a mentor; teacher; advisor; and then eventually colleague and friend.

I recognize how much my own supervision influenced me when I see what I experienced as a supervisee mirrored in what I do as a supervisor. Although trainees must learn necessary technical skills, the main tool for therapy is the person of the therapist. As a supervisor, I am available to discuss emotional reactions to client distress. I help trainees to deal with their own emotions and personal responses as they arise in therapy. When a severely abused child shares her story, when a battered wife returns to the abuser; when a highly distressed marital couple has a major setback, I ask the therapist, "how do you make sense of this?" Our discussions may venture into the supervisee's personal history, theology, spirituality, or culture as we clarify what the therapist brings into therapy and learns from each therapeutic encounter.

While I encourage personal growth and personal awareness in supervision, this is not what I do as a marriage and family therapist; the goals are different. However, at all levels—in therapy, supervision, and supervision of supervision—my behavior is guided by the goal at hand. In therapy, the goal is dictated by the client's concerns, which may or may not include aspects of personal growth. In supervision, the goal is to help supervisees use themselves to facilitate client goals; how the self of the therapist comes into the therapy room is a necessary part of supervision. In supervision of supervision, the goal is for the SIT to learn how to train therapists in conceptual, clinical, and personal dimensions.

Personal therapy and growth are a necessary part of training for most mental health professions. In my current training setting, I use self-reflection during the fundamental skills course. Patterson's book, *In Search of the Wounded Healer* (1990), provides thought-provoking journal exercises to aid professional self-reflection. I find this to be a helpful resource to assign to SITs as well, only now they answer the questions thinking of themselves as supervisors, rather than as therapists. These completed exercises then become the basis of ongoing discussions about roles, power, influence, choices, direction, motivation, openness to learning and the way the process affects each and are mutually influenced by each other: supervisor, SIT, therapist, and client/family.

Although I discuss personal aspects of the therapist along with technical aspects of therapy, I maintain a fine line between doing therapy and doing supervision. In supervision of supervision we discuss how SITs may find that boundary for themselves. I refer them to examples in the literature of incorporating the personal in supervision (Aponte, 1994; Kaiser; 1992; Reid, McDaniel, Donaldson, & Tollers, 1987). In emphasizing the personal aspects of supervision, I must sensitize my SIT to the issues of dual relationships in supervision (Storm, Peterson, & Tomm, 1997). Unlike therapy, supervision is a process of gradually moving from a "one-down" position as a novice trainee to a position of collegiality and professional competence, possibly even to a position of friend or employee (Ryder & Hepworth, 1990).

If I see a therapist's reactivity in a clinical situation, I'll mention it. If he or she responds in a highly emotional way, then we discuss it more. Some of my questions to lead toward some personal reflection are, "How big a deal do you think this is?" "What do you see happening with yourself in there?" "I notice you keep doing.... Do you have any ideas about that?" If I continue to identify personal aspects that are problematic, I make a referral for personal therapy. This same process is true for working with SITs. Supervisors are in danger of getting into trouble when they adopt a "Savior complex," when they think they are the only ones who can help a supervisee with personal difficulties (Ratliff, 1992).

As a supervisor of supervision, how can I help my SITs learn how to teach another not just how to "do therapy," but to "become a therapeutic person?" Just as in live supervision, when I try not to intrude into a delicate moment between therapist and client, in supervision of supervision I observe and make note of the occasions in which the personal becomes part of supervision. More often than not, I end up asking the SIT why she focused on the technical aspects over the personal. I help my SIT find her own balance between the personal and technical aspects of therapy. I find that the SITs who have been my supervisees can address the personal aspects in their supervision more appropriately, an example of modeling in the supervision of supervision relationship.

An additional complexity of the supervision relationship is the legal and ethical responsibilities that I bear for my SITs' judgments in supervision. I am responsible for all clinical decisions by the SIT or the therapist. I want to be part of any decision about a

therapist's duty to protect, to report child abuse, to intervene with suicidal clients, or to refer for medical consultation. For example, one SIT was listening empathically to a trainee's emotional response about an abused child, but never asking if the abuse had been reported. My response was to ask the supervisor what some of the ethical and legal implications of this session might be. This was enough of a prompt to help the SIT recognize that there were other issues to address in this session today. Her assumption, from the way the family in the session had revealed the information, was that the abuse had already been reported. The SIT then discussed this issue with the therapist during the consultation break. The therapist went back into the session and clarified that, indeed, the abuse had never been reported to anyone outside of the family until this session. From this point, both the SIT and therapist handled the situation appropriately.

What I am suggesting is that our SIT's ability to address the complexities involved in the supervisor relationship is directly related to our ability to initiate conversations about this topic throughout the supervision of supervision process. Initiation may involve assigned readings, such as those referenced at the end of this article, self exploration exercises such as those suggested by Patterson (1990), additional journal and process notes assigned to the SIT to complete following each supervision experience, and multiple discussions around this topic as the opportunities arise. In addition, any of the journal work, process notes, or readings completed along this topic will be available for the SITs to use as notes and prompts when writing up their case studies.

References

Aponte, H. (1994). How personal can training get? *Journal of Marital and Family Therapy, 20, 3-15.*

Kaiser, T. (1992). The supervisory relationship: An identification of the primary elements in the relationship and an application of two theories of ethical relationships. *Journal of Marital and Family Therapy,* 18, 283-296.

Patterson, R. (1990) *In search of the wounded healer.* Denville, NJ: Dimension Books, Inc.

Ratliff, N. (1992). Ethical issues for supervision. In G. Brock (Ed.), *The AAMFT ethics casebook.* American Association for Marriage and Family Therapy: Washington, DC.

Reid, E., McDaniel, S., Donaldson, C, & Tollers, M. (1987). Taking it personally: Issues of personal authority and competence for the female in family therapy training. *Journal of Marital and Family Therapy, 13, 157-165.*

Ryder & Hepworth. (1990). AAMFT ethical code: "Dual relationships." *Journal of Marital and Family Therapy, 16(2),* 127-132.

Storm, C., Peterson, M., & Totrun, K. (1997). Multiple relationships in supervision: Stepping up to complexity. In T. C. Todd & C. L. Storm (Eds.), *The complete systemic supervisor: Context, philosophy, and prag-* *matics* (pp. 253-271). Boston: Allyn & Bacon.

White, M., & Russell, C. (1997). Examining the multifaceted notion of isomorphism in marriage and family therapy supervision: A quest for conceptual clarity. *Journal of Marital and Family Therapy,* 23, 315-333.

Evaluation Procedures in Supervision of Supervision

Marshall Fine, Ed.D. & Geraldine Grossman, M.Ed.

Published in the AAMFT Supervision Bulletin, Vol. III, No. 2, June 1990.

The section of *The AAMFT Approved Supervisor Designation: Standards and Responsibilities* titled "Responsibilities and Guidelines for AAMFT Approved Supervisors: Supervising for the AAMFT Approved Supervisor Designation" includes the statements that the Approved Supervisor must evaluate and provide regular feedback regarding areas of the supervisor-in-training's strengths, need for growth, and general professional development as a supervisor. This includes the ability to conceptualize and develop supervisory skills. The Approved Supervisor must have a clear understanding with the supervisor-in-training about responsibility for evaluation of professional performance and competence as well as specific details of ways that evaluation will be shared. We would support these statements and add the following points in order to be more specific about the evaluation process.

We recognize that it can be difficult to develop an informed opinion about the competence of a supervisor-in-training within a brief period of time. However, we would hope that by the midpoint (with respect to hours), the Approved Supervisor would have enough information to offer the supervisor-in-training a relatively thorough mid-term evaluation of his or her progress, strengths and areas of needed improvement. It would be particularly important for the Approved Supervisor to share any major concerns which could affect the final status of the supervisor-in-training. Any major concerns should be documented for the benefit of the supervisor-in-training and the Approved Supervisor, along with a proposed plan for dealing with those concerns. We would suggest that Approved Supervisors follow these guidelines in the mid-term evaluation:

Comment on the supervisor-in-training's:

- State of systemic conceptualization.
- Knowledge of, and competence with, supervision concepts.
- Awareness of the supervision literature.
- Awareness and demonstration of his or her ethical, legal, and contextual responsibilities.
- Ability to foster the professional growth of those he or she supervises.

Comments should also include specific strengths and areas of needed growth for the supervisor-in-training.

If, at any point in the supervision process, the Approved Supervisor or the supervisor-in-training becomes concerned about the relationship with, or the competence and/or behavior of the other, this should be immediately noted and discussed between the two persons. If the discussion is mutually satisfactory, a clear plan should he drawn for resolution of the difficulty. The plan and specific goals to accomplish problem resolution should be mutually agreed upon. The process should be carefully documented by both the Approved Supervisor and the supervisor-in-training.

In the event that the discussion of the difficulty does not lead to an agreed-upon plan for resolution, both the Approved Supervisor and the supervisor-in-training should consult with the Commission on Supervision prior to continuing with further supervision sessions. The Commission on Supervision may:

- Follow suggestions offered by the Approved Supervisor or super-visor-in-training regarding the matter.
- Require another Approved Supervisor for the supervisor-in-training.
- Take any action it deems appropriate under the circumstances. If it is decided that another Approved Supervisor should supervise the supervisor-in-training, some or all of the hours accumulated by the supervisor-in-training with the first Approved Supervisor may be retained by the supervisor-in-training.

We would note that in our opinion it is highly un-desirable (unless late and new information leads the Approved Supervisor to believe that s/he could not approve the supervisor-in-training for ethical reasons) for the Approved Supervisor to reject the supervisor-in-training in the eleventh hour, without having duly informed the supervisor-in-training of this possibility according to the points discussed above.

In the Cauldron: A Case Study of Training for Clinical Supervision

Karen Caldwell, Ph.D. and Doris Diamond, M.S.W.

Published in the AAMFT Supervision Bulletin, Vol. 9, No. 1, Summer 1996.

Few researchers have investigated how supervisors change with experience, and there is currently little indication that supervisors improve with experience. With this in mind, a qualitative study of family therapy supervisors who were participating in a 16-week course in clinical supervision at a mental health agency was conducted. The guiding question was "What is changing about supervisors as they engage in a course of training in clinical supervision?"

We acknowledge two assumptions we held about the process of learning to supervise. First, the process is circular and self-recursive in a myriad of relationships. In addition, adult learners actively construct their experiences and take in information presented in formal learning settings in ways that reflect their previous experiences.

A qualitative case study method was chosen because qualitative approaches are well suited to problems in which there is a need to explore and describe phenomena and develop theory. The qualitative approach also fits well with the language-based approach that characterized the course in supervision. There were seven course participants, two females and five males, all post-graduates actively engaged in supervising therapists and counselors at three different organizations. Notes on class observations were kept along with documents such as the course syllabus, course readings and organizational literature from the three practice sites of the course participants. Participants were interviewed at the beginning of the course and after the course was over regarding 1) their experiences of receiving and giving supervision; 2) their current work settings; 3) their ideas on the important parts of supervision; 4) critical incidents that may have happened in the last six months that changed the way they supervise or think about supervision; and 5) anything from the course that made a difference in how they supervise now.

Data analysis involved using the constant comparison approach to identify themes common to the experiences of the participants. Hypotheses generated in the class observations were either confirmed or refuted in the individual interviews. In addition, a professor who teaches qualitative research methods provided an audit trail of the key decisions made during the research process. Course participants also read the thematic narrative and modifications were made in response to their feedback.

Four Themes from the Class

Coping with Complexity. Various metaphors were used by participants to describe the complexity of the supervisory process. One of the more dramatic metaphors referred to the "cauldron" of supervision. One participant said the process of learning supervision was "a get yourself thrown into it and see what happens; it was trial by fire initially with very little guidance from anybody else in how you do it." Another commented, "living comfortably with complexity appears to me to be a comfortableness with flexibility and ambiguity."

Integrating Theory into Practice. The theme of practice was closely connected to the theme of complexity and incorporated four sub-themes. The *tension between the use of a family systems or individual, psychodynamic theory* was evident on a number of instances. Differences in theoretical leanings emerged in the types of questions and comments made by participants during the weekly case presentations of "supervisory dilemmas." The task of the instructors was a challenging one because of the necessity of negotiating a shared language (when possible) and negotiating "agreements to disagree." The theoretical diversity of the participants made clear the importance of the supervisor making his/her theoretical orientation explicit in the contracting phase of supervision.

Participants' experiences of the *limits of theory* were repeatedly evident. One supervisor talked about this limitation as the "reality factor of real people with real problems in relationships that require compassion, facilitation, trust and confrontation." Another supervisor put it this way, "It's hard to relate to people. It's much easier if you deal with abstraction." While acknowledging the limits of theory, all the course participants mentioned the usefulness of class discussion on *isomorphism/parallel process.*

Another important aspect of the integration of theory into practice was the conflict between making clinical decisions based on theoretical considerations and making clinical decision based on *the constraints of the context or administrative considerations.* Some of the participants struggled with the increasing influence of managed care. The most knotty supervisory dilemmas came about from the interplay of the restrictions of a setting's administrative organization, the complexity of client's problems and the supervisors' theoretical perspectives.

Taking on the Evaluative Role. Taking on the evaluative role was mentioned by four participants as part of their struggle with the supervisory role. One experienced supervisor referred to this aspect of supervision under the rubric of loyalty saying, "I think it would be rather disloyal for a supervisor to be aware that their supervisee has blundered and make the decision not to address it." Another supervisor reflected on having had a bad experience with a supervisee during the course by saying "As a newer supervisor there was always the tendency to say to the supervisee 'Oh you're doing just great'... Now, I'm more apt to give more accurate feedback more frequently. Not really to be any less supportive, but to be more accurate."

Issues of Ethics and Legal Liability. A heightened sense of ethical and legal concerns came about in part from the participants' sharing of experiences of the legal system and ethical dilemmas they had faced. One participant talked about a situation with a supervisee that came up during the course saying, "I've always been aware of liability but it (the situation with the supervisee) really, just really, heightened my awareness of liability issues almost to the point where the considerations became omnipresent."

Differences in Learning

In addition to the previous four themes, differences also were noted between the novice and experienced supervisors. In the initial interviews, the two participants who were "novice" supervisors had very brief; hesitant responses to the questions about what they felt were important parts of supervision. This seemed to indicate that they had little abstract or generalized experience as supervisors. At the end of the course, one of these novice supervisors attributed a growing sense of confidence to having attended the course saying, "It's OK to just be me" and acknowledge "This is my limitation, this is why I do this, I don't have to know it all." The other novice therapist ended the course with the feeling of having a better orientation to the whole process of supervision. On the other hand, the supervisors who entered the course with experience talked at length about the important parts of supervision during their initial interviews. The experienced supervisors ended the course feeling the course had "validated" or "fine tuned" what they had been doing as supervisors.

Conclusions

For agency administrators, the heightened sense of these participants to ethical and legal issues may be an appealing outcome and strong incentive to insist on training for clinical supervisors. In addition, the role of training for supervisors may vary depending upon the level of experience supervisors bring to the training context. The process of becoming more knowledgeable as a supervisor involves both the enrichment of existing knowledge structures, and particularly for novices, the creation of altogether new structures.

A number of contextual issues shaped the particularities of the participants' experience of this course. The setting, a community mental health center, surely impacted the conversations of the course. The differences in theoretical orientations among participants may not be as obvious in a supervision course in an academic setting where one may expect more uniformity in theoretical orientation. In addition, participants were not just reading about supervision and theories of supervision, they were actively engaged in supervision. Source material in the course was thus not only theoretical but also anecdotal. We were unable to have input from therapists being supervised by the course participants. The availability of this perspective would have strengthened the study. There were also no direct observations/videotaping of the supervisors with their supervisees. The length of the course (16 weeks) allowed for ongoing support to the participants and encouraged integration of the material, something that would not be a component of briefer workshops in supervision. By using a methodology that elicited the point of view of supervisors engaged in training, we hopefully have expanded our understanding of the process of developing the capacity to enter into beneficial supervisory relationships.

Considering the "Customer" in Supervision

Arnold Woodruff, M.S.

Published in the AAMFT Supervision Bulletin, Vol. VI, No. 3, Fall 1993.

The idea of "customership" has been explored in recent discussions of therapy. However, this idea has not been extended, to my knowledge, to the provision of supervision or supervision-of-supervision. While the format of this newsletter does not allow a thorough exploration of this idea and how it might impact supervision and supervision-of-supervision, I offer thoughts on this subject in the hopes of generating more complete discussions in other settings.

Briefly, the idea of customership has been presented by de Shazer and others as a means of avoiding unnecessary conflict with clients and, by avoiding such conflict, avoiding the creation of "resistance." For purposes of this article, the customer is described as the individual or group who most wants to see change in a problematic situation. This is very often *not* the individual or family who comes in to "benefit" from the therapist's services. Common examples of customers are judges, probation officers, lawyers, workers in other agencies (social services if you work in mental health and mental health if you work in social services), spouses, parents and grandparents. Most of us have devised strategies for dealing with this common therapy problem, but what impact does customership have on the clinical supervisor?

I think that customership is more likely a problem in agency settings than in training programs or universities. Presumably, the training context where services are given is known to the trainee and to the referral source. It should be clear to all involved that, while a primary obligation for supervision is to the client, there is also a strong obligation to the trainee's leaning by the organization. "Swooping in" to rescue a confused novice therapist is reasonable supervisor behavior in this setting, however embarrassing to the initiate (at least at the beginning). (Note: I frequently pray for someone to swoop in and rescue me now, although I have usually found the client to be an excellent source of relief.)

In an agency, however, such supervisory behavior may lead to a very different outcome. First of all, therapists may not understand that receiving clinical supervision is a requirement of their position. Many still see being supervised as a sign of internship or traineehood. Family therapy is nearly unique among the professions in the strong advocacy for clinical supervision throughout one's career. Secondly, families may not understand the value of clinical supervision, whether live or videotaped, and may also assume that this marks some defect in their therapist. Third, agency administrators may not understand the cost effectiveness of clinical supervision, particularly the live variety, and may feel they are paying for two hours of professional time that can only be billed once. Finally, if the family sitting in the consulting room is "involuntary," then not only is the therapist likewise being compelled but so too is the supervisor of therapy.

Each of these "customers" can and must be dealt with by the therapist and the supervisor (or possibly the supervisor of supervision, particularly when the agency administration is the true customer) if a successful outcome is to be achieved. Neglecting to include them in formulating an approach to the family may create significant difficulties. The systemic understanding we, as family therapists, bring to the work must always be extended to these significant others in the lives of the families we treat and to the supervision we provide.

Author Index